The Leicestershire Law Society 1860 to 2017 – A Local Portrait

Professor David Hughes

 The Leicestershire Law Society

First Printed 2010

Second Printed Edition 2017

Copyright © Hughes 2010

Printed and Published by
Anchorprint Group Ltd, Leicester.

British Library Cataloguing in Publication Data

Data Available

Frst edition ISBN 978-1-907540-23-3

Second edition ISBN 978-1-910181-38-6

Contents

Foreword

I am delighted that Professor David Hughes has written this book to celebrate 150 years of the Leicestershire Law Society. It gives me an even greater pleasure that the 150th anniversary coincides with my own tenure as the President of the Law Society.

Although born in Yorkshire I have made the East Midlands my home. I worked in the region before becoming a Council Member for Leicestershire, Northamptonshire and Rutland in 2003.

As a Council Member I have had the pleasure of meeting and working with many of the hard working, dedicated and skilled individuals who make up the Leicestershire Law Society. Professor Hughes's account brings to life a similar picture of our predecessors; dedicated professionals whose commitment to the practice and the rule of law was absolute. His book is an informative and detailed account of the Leicestershire Law Society's 150 year history of good practice. And it will continue to remind me what a privilege it is to represent the hardworking legal professionals of this constituency.

Professor Hughes skilfully traces the changes that the Leicestershire Law Society has had to undergo to continue to meet the needs of the legal profession in Leicester, Leicestershire and Rutland. That continual process of development is the one thing that hasn't changed throughout 150 years, here, or across the country.

What is new, however, is the rate of change that we face. As a profession, we have all had to adapt to rapid changes in practices brought about by the increasing demands from consumer pressure and the rate of change of technology. We are under increasing pressure to find instant solutions to complex legal problems; sometimes with little understanding from the wider public.

As this book shows, throughout the last 150 years we have always managed to respond positively to the challenges that we face, bound by our commitment to common ethical standards and motivated by our common desire to see the rule of law upheld.

I have promised to dedicate my Presidential year to promoting the excellence of the profession, the importance of our values and ethical standards. It is my personal belief that the legal profession plays a vital role at the very heart of society and commerce. I congratulate Professor Hughes on writing a book which illustrates so clearly that this has always been the case.

Linda Lee
President of The Law Society

Introduction

The celebration of the 150th anniversary of the Leicestershire Law Society is an exciting event for the legal profession in Leicester and Leicestershire and I am very privileged to be the President of the Society in this important year.

The role and the working environment for solicitors have changed out of all recognition from the conditions which prevailed in 1860. The size of legal practices, IT, the rules and regulations which govern the way in which we work, the detail of law and particularly European law, timescales and client expectations are all the product of an increasingly complex world which were not even capable of being contemplated in 1860.

However, perhaps the most marked change of all is in the profile of the profession. In 1860 all members of the Society were white and male. Now we have a profession which is diverse and multi-cultural. Significant change and very much for the better.

But some elements of legal practice have not changed. As lawyers we still have a fundamental belief in justice, access to justice and the rule of law which are concepts which have not changed over that 150 years and nor should they change.

Our 150th anniversary gives us an opportunity both to look back at the past and to look forward. Looking back is usually more comfortable – we have all the answers and a lot of familiar names to stir memories. But we should also be very proud of the achievements of our predecessors. They worked hard and enjoyed an excellent reputation. They gave excellent service to the businesses and private clients of Leicester and Leicestershire.

Still we also need to seize the opportunity to look forward, to set the standards to which we wish our profession to aspire. And we live in a world where significant changes are taking place in the way in which lawyers work and in the funding of legal practices. Our independence is under threat and we face challenges which appear more substantial than any faced by our predecessors.

Doubtless in 50 or 100 years' time our successors will look back at this book and ask what was the profession worried about. The lawyers about whom David Hughes writes in this book had a mutual belief in integrity and independence. The set the highest standards and lived by them. They made a huge contribution to life in our City and County and the lawyers of today and tomorrow need to act similarly.

I congratulate David Hughes on this excellent book. His attention to detail has been immense but through it all we see the lives of ordinary lawyers, dedicated to their profession, to the service of their clients and to the wider community.

Stephen Woolfe
President of the Leicestershire Law Society 2010-11

....

I am so excited and grateful to Professor David Hughes for updating this fascinating book. I really wanted all my guests at the Civic Dinner in January 2017 to receive an up to date copy as a gift from Leicestershire Law Society.

As a Leicester girl, born, bred and educated, I wanted my year as President to celebrate my home city of Leicester. My event venues include the restaurants The Case and 1573 and that iconic Leicester building, The Grand Hotel. Athena, (the former Odeon Cinema) will be the venue of my Awards Dinner and Leicester Town Hall was the amazing setting for my definitive Trial of Richard III which was held there in November 2016.

In his introduction from 2010, our then President Stephen Woolfe talks about the solicitors' profession as becoming more diverse and multicultural in 2010 and I am proud that in the 7 years since then our Presidents have illustrated this diversity with our fifth, sixth and now myself, the seventh, female President in 157 years. Our sixth female President Mehmooda Duke was also the first female ethnic minority President following Ranjit Thaliwal, the first British born President of Asian ethnic descent.

My thanks too to the Society's patrons who have made such a difference to us. The support of AON, Burcher Jennings, De Montfort University, Finance Lab, Finch Consulting, Jonstar, Severn Trent and University of Leicester has been most welcome and we look forward to developing those relationships in the coming years. Thank you also to our sponsors who have helped support me over my year so far. All of your support has helped me raise money for my chosen charity this year which is LOROS.

Imogen Cox
President of the Leicestershire Law Society 2016-2017

Acknowledgements

This work would not have been possible without the help and support of many people. My grateful thanks are due to:

The members and officers of the Leicestershire Law Society for entrusting me with this task, and for allowing me absolute access to their extensive records;

Stephen Woolfe, President of The Society in this "one and a half" centennial year for his Preface, and to Linda Lee, President of The Law Society for her Introduction;

Chris Smith the Committee member who has acted as a link between me and The Society during the writing period for his ever courteous and ready assistance;

Mrs Barbara Goodman, whom those members of The Society who are Leicester University graduates will remember as the ever resourceful Law Departmental Secretary, and who in earlier life trained as a legal secretary at Messrs Ironsides, for typing out my writing with such accuracy and speed;

The production team at Anchorprint Group Limited who have undertaken the printing of this work and made what seemed to me to be insuperable printing and reproduction problems mere happenings;

Jeremy Barlow, Peter Duffin and John Tillotson for sharing with me their memories of practice in the City and County;

Adrian Watson and Robert Hakewell for their assistance with historical material;

Andrew Harper for allowing me access to his work on the development of Clarendon Park, and the involvement of solicitors in that undertaking;

Richard Bloor for allowing me access to the work of the late Donald Hunt on the life and career of H A Owston;

The partners and staff of the erstwhile Freer Bouskell and Co for allowing me access to their premises to photograph and record early presidents of The Society, and for sharing with me the tale of the ghostly apparition of William Napier Reeve;

Staff at the County Record Office in Wigston for facilitating my research;

Professor Aubrey Newman for casting his experienced historian`s eye over my work and helping with proof reading;

The Leicester Mercury for allowing reproduction of the picture of Vera Stamenkovich during her year as first woman president of The Society;

Last but very far from least, my wife, Past President Christl Hughes who promoted the notion of a History of The Society during her term of office, and who has supported me throughout what has been a somewhat lengthy but always enjoyable task.

Chapter 1

Before the Leicestershire Law Society

'[S]olicitors defy easy definition'.[1] While since 1873 a solicitor is a person authorized to practise by The Law Society, before then definition was much harder because of the lack of a single route of qualification. Indeed the word 'solicitor' was only coming into currency in the mid 16th Century and had a most imprecise meaning. 'To solicit' simply meant handling another person's legal affairs and anyone could undertake this work without having to prove any form of qualification. Indeed it is clear that many 'solicitors' had no connection with either the formal court structure nor with the Inns of Court or their long lost lesser counterparts, the Inns of Chancery. However, the modern solicitor can claim a respectable pedigree originating with the 'attornati' who were medieval court officers who assisted parties in the initial stages of a law suit.[2] In due course the attornati became known as attorneys, and over a period of hundreds of years attorneys became associated with the Common Law Courts while solicitors were associated with the Courts of Chancery where they were largely concerned with matters of Land Law. However, the distinction was never as hard and fast as might be supposed. The attorneys themselves did not constitute a single unified branch of the legal profession: King's Bench Attorneys, for example, did not practise before The Court of Common Pleas. On the other hand a man might 'solicit' a cause in a court with which he had no formal connection.

If there is a lack of clarity about the origins of 'solicitors' then there is equal mystery surrounding their early geographical incidence. Of course many were based full time in London, and certainly so during the Law Terms, ie the times of Court Sittings. But it appears that among the attorneys there were many based in the provinces, and some who regularly travelled between the Shires and London in the discharge of business. Professor Brooks in "Pettyfoggers and Vipers of the Commonwealth" estimated that in 1560 the legal profession in London numbered between 350 and 400, some 200 of whom were 'Common Law Attorneys' who linked the provinces

---

[1] Brooks, "Pettyfoggers and Vipers of the Commonwealth", CUP, Cambridge, 1986, p 27
[2] Slapper & Kelly "English Law" 2nd Edition, Routledge-Cavendish, London, 2006, p 912

with the Courts in London, and most of whom had country residences. It is, however, clear that no county had very many attorneys, and Leicestershire and Rutland could have been no exception to this. However, as Professor Brooks further argues, the considerable increase in the amount of litigation between 1550 and 1640 led to a considerable increase in the numbers of practitioners. A right to practise was tied to a link with a particular court, and thus the Common Law Bar reached a size of some 400 by 1640, while the number of 'underclerks' connected with the Chancery Court increased to about 200. A similar increase can be seen in the number of attorneys. In 1480 they had numbered no more than 180, by 1580 that figure was 415 and by 1640 it was 1750.[3] In Warwickshire, according to Brooks, the numbers of attorneys grew from 2 in 1560 to 30 in 1625/40, and there may have been a similar increase in Leicestershire and Rutland.

Professor Brooks argues that the increase in the number of attorneys led to a decline in the 'semi-professional and amateur lawyers' who had previously had an informal relationship with the court system. However, it would be wrong to see this as an automatic or clear process. It was not always easy to distinguish the roles of attorneys and court officials. The latter tended to be remunerated by fees for law suits, while the former earned a living by representing the client who paid the court fees. Thus while there were economic forces which began to divide the two groups, their initial recruitment was not so different. In the 15th Century a statute of Henry IV (repealed by one of James I) had laid down that the judges should exercise control over legal practitioners in general by requiring them to be 'good' and learned in their profession, but there were no specific tests laid down as to either morality or education. The principal court officials in the Common Law Courts were the prothonotaries who both oversaw the administration of the courts and, to an extent, enrolled attorneys as competent to practise. However, as Brooks points out, the various prothonotaries were in competition with one another to get work into court, and so increase their fees, and thus they might not have been as vigilant from time to time as might have been desirable with regard to the qualifications of those they enrolled.

In 1632/33, however, the judges laid down in Court Orders that no one was to be admitted as an attorney unless he had served as a clerk to an attorney for a period of six years in an approved fashion, though there was, yet again, no specific form of approved training laid down. The two principal means of training were either by serving a period as a clerk to an

---

[3] Baker, 'The Attorneys and Officers of the Common Law in 1480' (1980)1, Journal of Legal History (185), and Brooks, op cit p 113

established man or by undertaking a course of study at an Inn of Chancery, but the former, according to Brooks, was the more commonly used mode of training. This would certainly be the case with country attorneys, though there were still other routes of entrance such as being a clerk to a judge or a serjeant at law (the ancestors of our modern 'silks') or a town clerk, or by being a writing clerk in the offices of the prothonotaries or other court officers. Serving as a clerk might involve beginning work at about 14, and then serving 6 or 7, but maybe for up to 10, years before admission; in other words a form of apprenticeship obtained. The clerk would live with his principal and be part of his family, discharging legal and domestic duties, and, of course, the principal would demand a premium for taking on his trainee. But, again as Brooks points out, there were differences between legal training and many craft apprenticeships. In the middle ages Guilds had grown up to supervise the training of craftsmen, but there was no Guild or Mystery or Company or Livery of Attorneys, instead supervision was exercised, as we have seen, via the various courts before which a man wished to practise, sometimes on a less than rigorous basis. It was not until 1728 that statute laid down that only those attorneys who had been bound apprentices by contracts *in writing* should be sworn in as practitioners. A further statute of 1749 then required that these written contracts should be filed with the Courts at Westminster.

Thus by the late 17th Century it is arguable that most practitioners in what is now called the lower branch of the legal profession were trained by clerkship, and while some were members of an Inn of Chancery, this was not the principal means of training. In 1675 George Townsend, a prothonotary and former attorney, in "A Preparative to Pleading … A Work Intended for the Instruction and Help of Young Clerks of the Common Pleas" argued that a clerk should have a good knowledge of Latin, and maybe some Greek, and be able bodied and healthy and able to endure the cold when sitting at writing! A clerkship should ideally be for six years, five as an absolute minimum, and during that time the clerk should first master a 'clerk-like' hand and thus make up his 'precedent books' on the major forms of action, eg trespass, slander, breach of promise, nuisance etc. A clerk should also study the major legal treatises including Coke's Institutes, though there were also students' texts such as "The Attourney's Academy" originally published in 1623.[4]

In so far as attorneys could be members of an Inn of Chancery they might originally receive part of their education alongside the student

---

[4] See for more detail, Brooks, op cit p 173-174. The author wishes to acknowledge his considerable indebtedness to Professor Brooks

Barristers in the Inns of Court. However, as Slapper and Kelly point out in "English Law", between 1550 and 1730 the two branches of the legal profession increasingly diverged until Barristers were finally forbidden to act in the capacity of Attorney and Solicitor, while Professor David Sugarman in his "Brief History of the Law Society",[5] argues that the division of the profession into its two current branches was largely complete by 1680. Interestingly attorneys seem to have adopted the practice of describing themselves as both *Attorneys and Solicitors* from the 1620s.[6]

Attempts to Regulate Practitioners

The attempts to regulate the training and admission, and also the numbers, of attorneys which marked the 17th Century continued into the 18th. In 1701 and 1706 moves were made in Parliament to both regulate and limit the numbers of attorneys, but these failed to reach the statute book. However, in 1729 a group of Yorkshire magistrates successfully promoted an Act 'for the better regulation of Attorneys and Solicitors'. This put into statutory form the requirement that there should be a five year apprenticeship and a judicial examination of the character of would be practitioners. The Act worked imperfectly, however, and some attorneys were found to be practising even when in prison. Nevertheless the terms of the Act and a decline during the 18th Century in the amount of work led to some falling off in the numbers of those in the lower branch of the profession.

Where statute failed to operate perfectly, however, voluntary self regulation began to emerge. Practitioners, especially those in London, started to band together as 'law clubs' who promoted professional values and independent self regulation. In 1739 elite attorneys and solicitors in London formed The Society of Gentlemen Practisers, and this led to the emergence of autonomous Law Societies in the provinces: Bristol (1770); Yorkshire (1786); Somerset (1796); Sunderland (1800); Leeds (1805); Devon and Exeter (1808); Manchester (1809); Plymouth (1815); Gloucester (1817); Birmingham, Hull and Kent (1818). At the same time an independent national society open to all practitioners was advocated from 1795, and in 1823 the London Law Institution was formulated by a number of prominent London attorneys with a building near the Inns of Court; this was the ancestor of the modern Law Society. This aimed, inter alia, to

---

[5] London, Law Society 1994. See also Kirk, Harry, 'Portrait of a Profession: a history of the solicitors' profession 1100 to the present day', London, Oyez, 1976. For more recent developments see also Sugarman, David, 'Bourgeois collectivism, professional power and the boundaries of the state: the private and public life of the Law Society 1825-1914' in International Journal of the Legal Profession 1996(3) pp 81-135.

[6] Brooks, Op Cit p 143

set practice standards and to ensure good compliance with them. In 1825 (on 2nd June) this body, with a membership of 292, was renamed The Law Institution as an indication of its national importance and standing, and even a century later we find examples of letters written by The Leicester Law Society's secretary to 'The Law Institution' so well established had the name become. The Institution acquired a Royal Charter in 1831/32, at the same time acquiring premises in Chancery Lane, and a further Royal Charter of 1845 defined it as an independent private body serving the needs of the lower branch of the legal profession. The body was originally known as the 'Society of Attorneys, Solicitors, Proctors and others not being Barristers, practising in the Courts of Law and Equity in the United Kingdom'. Colloquially this became 'The Law Society' and that name was officially adopted in 1903.

The Law Society soon acquired disciplinary, regulatory and educational functions. In 1834 it initiated proceedings against a dishonest practitioner, and from 1835 it began to codify practice with regard to conveyancing and costs. In 1843 The Solicitors Act gave The Law Society power to register solicitors and in 1888 it gained power to hear complaints against members. As from 1907 there was a statutory disciplinary committee and powers to investigate solicitors' accounts and to issue annual practising certificates. Educationally The Law Society began series of lectures in its Hall in 1835, while The Solicitors Act of 1860 enabled the creation of a three stage examination system leading to qualification as a Solicitor. The Law Society established a registry for articled clerks in 1832 and commenced publication of its own Gazette in 1907.

The erosion of the distinctions between Courts of Common Law and Courts of Equity following the Common Law Procedure Acts, 1852 to 1860, and The Chancery Amendments Acts, 1852 to 1858, which culminated in the Judicature Act of 1873, led to the gradual abandonment of the title 'Attorney' and its replacement by 'Solicitor', which was itself put on a statutory basis in 1873. This was reflected in popular culture. In 'Trial by Jury' (1875) and 'HMS Pinafore' (1878) W.S. Gilbert has his characters, who are looking back to the start of their careers, refer to 'Attorneys'. However, in 'Patience' (1881), 'The Mikado' (1885) and 'The Grand Duke' (1896) he uses the term 'Solicitor'.

In his "Brief History of the Law Society" Professor Sugarman sums up these developments: 'Historically, England's singular state has permitted a wide delegation of power beyond central government. Guilds, local government, chartered bodies, the Established Church, and the Inns of Court, for example, were largely free from interference from the executive elements of the state ... The Glorious Revolution of 1688 ... affirmed the autonomy of professional and other chartered bodies as part of England's balanced and unwritten constitution. One consequence of this was that the state was often reluctant to interfere in what was perceived as the province of the profession ... These developments opened the way for professions ... to enjoy a degree of self-government through the acquisition of royal charters.'

The situation in Leicester

It has been necessary to sketch in the history and development of the profession of solicitors down to the middle of the 19th Century to provide a background to the emergence of Leicester's own Law Society. It will be clear that other towns and cities had Law Societies before Leicester, but, as will become clear in the following chapter the Leicester Law Society not only shared in the established desire of groups of local practitioners nationwide to create and maintain high professional standards, but also had the very specific aim of creating a Law Library for the benefit of its members.

No doubt there were 'attorneys' in Leicester and Leicestershire well before the end of the 18th Century. Oddly enough it is via local government that we may catch a glimpse of these early practitioners. The Hall Book Papers of the Borough of Leicester, which were reproduced in book form under various editors, but particularly Alan Chinnery, down to the mid 1960s, indicate the existence of an office known as the Town Solicitor. This functionary existed separately from the Town Clerk, and while we do not know where the various holders of the office lived, or what their qualifications were, it appears they were legal officers of some importance who were most likely to be local men. They were particularly concerned with upholding the rights of the Borough of Leicester, particularly with regard to trade and markets. On 1st July 1757, for example, the Town Solicitor was instructed to sue two men who were not Freemen of the Borough for trading in Leicester.

The first recorded name is that of John Flampson who was mentioned on 25th January 1611 as 'Under Bayllies (Bailiff), Seriant (Serjeant) at Mace and Attorney in the Court of Records of the Borough of Leicester'. John Maior (Major) is mentioned as Town Solicitor in 1650, 1655, 1658 and 1659. William Browne is recorded in 1673, 1684 and 1685. By 1703 the office holder was Mr Noble, and in 1736 it was Mr Farmer. In 1761 the Town Solicitor was a Mr Halford, while Caleb Lowdham (admitted in 1767) was 'Solicitor of the Corporation' in May 1772.

Lowdham is of interest as he appears to be the first Leicester practitioner for whom a biography can be assembled, and for this I must acknowledge indebtedness to Adrian Watson. Lowdham was the son of the Reverend Caleb Lowdham of Diseworth and was born in 1745. In 1761 he was articled to Thomas Pares of Leicester who, with Joseph Bunney, set up Leicester's first bank, which reflected the growing importance of the town whose population had grown to 9000 from 4500 in 1700. Following admission as an attorney Lowdham set up practice in Fryers (Friar) Lane. Lowdham took on Jesse Berridge as an office boy or clerk and his name occurs in a deed of 1786. Berridge was later to qualify. Meanwhile Lowdham continued as Town Solicitor until 1791 when it appears the office did not continue but was merged with that of the Town Clerk, with William Heyrick in that post. Lowdham apparently continued to act for the Corporation in a few cases left over from his time in office. He is next encountered as a gentleman volunteer in the Local Volunteer Corps in 1797: this body was created following fears of the spread of republicanism from France. By 1801 Lowdham was in partnership with Joseph Spencer Cardale, who may have been a partner previously in Carter and Cardale from whom it may be possible to trace a link back to Thomas Carter of Leicester who was admitted in 1730. This partnership lasted until 1812, while in 1814 Lowdham entered into partnership with John Liptrott Greaves, to whom Jesse Berridge was articled in 1819: he had previously been paid £150 a year as an assistant clerk. Lowdham died at the age of 80 in 1825 and was buried at Diseworth. Jesse Berridge then became a partner in the firm which later became known as Berridges and, in due course, merged with that of Thomas Ingram to become Ingram Berridge Flude and Frearson – an ancestor of Harvey Ingram which can thus demonstrate a link with 18th Century Leicester.

Lowdham, however, certainly did well out of his work for the Corporation. His bill for legal services on 11th March 1777 was £189.8s.5d. (approximately £189.42p), which bore interest at 4%p.a. He was also involved in the promotion of the Bill for Enclosing the Southfields in 1777, and in division of that land for 'improvement' in 1785, while he tendered another bill to the Corporation of 14th July 1798 for £456.14s.3d (approximately £456.71p) for an action against a Mr Ruding. Lowdham was thanked for the 'zeal, ability and assiduity with which he conducted the suit against Mr Ruding', and the Corporation's gratitude was further marked by the presentation to him of a piece of plate of 'the value of 50 guineas'.

The Borough records also record a payment of 10 guineas (£10.50) to Mr Ellis Shipley Pestel, Attorney at Law, on 9th March 1779 in respect of his bill respecting an indictment of the horsepit at the top of Gallowtree Gate.

Speaking to the Leicester Law Students' Society on 12th November 1953 Mr C.E.J. Freer outlined the history of some of Leicester's oldest firms. Messrs Freer & Co, he stated, were founded by Thomas Freer, an attorney, in 1786, (though the official bi-centenary was celebrated in July 1988. Certainly that date represented the 200th anniversary of the firm at its New Street premises.) Over the years this firm drew in: Messrs Harris, Watts and Bouskell; Haxby Partridge and Talbot; Fowler, Fowler and Skillington. Indeed the firm grew largely by amalgamations, for between 1880 and 1953 the firm took only six clerks who completed their articles, and three of those were the relatives of partners. Messrs Stevenson & Co were founded in 1800 by Mr John Stevenson who lived above his offices in Cank Street while his successor, Mr George Stevenson, moved to New Street in 1830 where the firm stayed for well over a hundred years until it was merged with Messrs Owston & Co.[7] In 1827 Richard Toller set up his practice which became in course of time Toller, Pochin and Wright. Joseph Harvey set up his practice in 1848 and his office stood where the Leicester Permanent Building Society was later built in Pocklingtons Walk: this is now the City of Leicester Rent Service Building. Harvey's practice ultimately grew into Harvey, Clarke and Adams whose merger with Ingram & Co created what was reported in Kelly's Classified Directory of Leicester in 1971 as a firm of 8 partners, which was sizeable in Leicester at that time. Harvey Ingram has, of course, also taken in many other well known Leicester firms - Stone & Simpson, itself the result of a merger between Stone & Co and Herbert Simpson, Son and Bennett, and Owston & Co, all of whom had their foundation in the 19th Century.

Through Ingram, this firm can also trace a further link in its ancestry; back into the 18th Century as Thomas Ingram, of whom more in Chapter 2, was the son of a Market Harborough Solicitor who was in partnership as Shuttleworth, Ingram and Wartnaby and some of their records dating from 1825-27 are to be found in the County Record Office. These records take the form of note books (a firm's diary or day book) recording attendances by members of the firm, and also actions in which they represented one of the parties. Much of the work appears to have been connected with the administration of the poor law in the parishes around Market Harborough and extending into Northamptonshire. Poor Relief was then a parochial responsibility, but the firm acted in addition for clients wishing to challenge the Poor Law Rate, such as Mr Burdett of Great Easton in March 1826. The note books indicate that the practice

---

[7] Stevensons' building survives roughly opposite Messrs Freer Bouskell as a set of flats.

was open on Saturdays and also record details of clients' probates. There are other documents in the County Record Office indicating that a George Wartnaby was in practice in 1799 and he features in a conveyance (deed of feoffment) of 25th March 1799, while he appears to have been flourishing in 1821 when he rendered an account in respect of the Will and Probate of Mr Edward Barraud of £13.9s.2d. (approximately £13.46p). Nathaniel Shuttleworth is mentioned as an executor in documents of 25th September 1810 and 5th December 1810. Shuttleworth had married Elizabeth Wartnaby in 1792 and by her had a son,Henry, who in 1835 was in partnership with William Wartnaby, George's nephew.

Messrs Wartnabys of Market Harborough are certainly one of the oldest county firms. The brief history of the firm written by its then senior partner, John Tillotson, indicates that Wartnabys commenced practice around 1740 and practised from the family home (where both George and William Wartnaby lived) in Market Harborough Manor House, before moving to 43, High Street, Market Harborough, which stands on land owned in 1839 by Henry Shuttleworth, though no Shuttleworth owned land in Market Harborough in 1850.[8]

From these early beginnings the lower branch of the profession grew as Leicester itself expanded and prospered. It is not always easy to determine exact numbers a this time as some directories list firms, while others list individuals and some list both. Confusion is worse compounded as some names are listed by both place of work and residence: the two did not always coincide. Sometimes the name of a former partner was retained, as is still the case today, even though he had long since ceased to practice, and this makes 'head counting' more difficult. Thus in 1784 Batty's "British Directory" lists as Attorneys in Leicester Isaac Carter, Jonathan Foster, John Heyrick, John King, Henry King, Thomas Pares and William Tilley, but seemingly makes no reference to Caleb Lowdham, and it may be that only those actually resident in the Borough of Leicester were listed[9]. We know from White's "Leicestershire" of 1846 that the following 'attorneys' were in practice in Leicester[10]: Adcock and Dalton (Dalton continued alone in 1854), Berridge and Macaulay*, Briggs and Sculthorpe (Briggs continued alone in 1854), Brown & Palmer, Burbidge*, Burnaby, Cape*, Dibbin & Dibbin, Dudley*, Fowkes, Freer*, Gregory*, Hardy, Harris and Luck*, Hole, Lawton, Loseby*,

---

[8] I must acknowledge also Mr W Robert H Hakewill whose researches into the Wartnaby, Shuttleworth and Ingram families have assisted me greatly.

[9] I must here once again express my gratitude to Adrian Watson for sharing with me the fruits of his research into the history of Messrs Harvey Ingram and for alerting me to this information.

[10] Where there is an * by the name of a firm or individual this indicates he/they still practised in 1854 according to Melville & Co's Directory and Gazetteer of Leicestershire.

Maddock, Miles and Smith (Miles and Gregory in 1854), Peak, Robinson & Ingram (Robinson and Spooner in 1854), Smith*, Stevenson*, Stone & Paget*, Toller and Toller*, Weston*.This list contains 27 practices which then tallies neatly with the 1855 Law List formerly in The Society's Library which indicated that 28 country attorneys were in practice in Leicester. Some of these practices had divided by the time Melville's 1854 Directory appeared, others had ceased and new practices had started. These included Bellairs and Eddowes, Harvey, Hawker, Haxby, Ingram, Moore and Gregory, Morris, Palmer and Billson and Stretton. However, by 1854 these practitioners were termed 'solicitors'.

The greatest part of the work of these practices would have been with concerned with conveyancing and probate. There would be some litigation but in 1882 when addressing the Leicester Law Students' Society William Napier Reeve, of whom more in Chapter 2, indicated that country solicitors (though Reeve still preferred the old name of attorney) avoided chancery litigation because of its excessive delays and costs. He stated: 'country solicitors were literally afraid of a suit in Chancery ... on coming to Leicester ... my late excellent partner ... was ready to give up a client and his business altogether rather than have a chancery suit in his office'. The delay and expense of litigation contributed to the low esteem in which attorneys and solicitors were held when Reeve began his training in the 1820s in London. He points out that in those days there was no qualifying examination, merely the cost of a stamp on a deed at the end of articles, though that was fixed at the frighteningly high price for the time of £120. However, thereafter the holder of the deed was free to practise as an attorney. As Reeve comments it is no wonder the profession was attacked and a well known joke of the day was 'What is the difference between an attorney and a solicitor? The same as between a crocodile and an alligator'. The lower branch of the profession was as a rule despised, and those who were honest were considered exceptional, while the Bar treated all attorneys and solicitors with contempt and did not expect them to have any opinion on the law in a case. Indeed at the time Reeve started his career the sort of advice given to articled clerks was that contained in Phillips' "Letters to Articled Clerks" which counselled buying 'half a dozen pairs of good washing gloves and put on a clean pair whenever needed'.

That was the background out of which Leicester's Law Society emerged. Lack of esteem fostered by poor professional standards on the part of too many practitioners and the lack of a coherent system of training and qualification had to be countered if the profession of solicitor was to become respectable and autonomous. It is, of course, necessary to add that the worst excesses of the lower branch of the legal profession, as described in the works of Dickens, did not affect the majority of attorneys. As Professor Brooks points out in "Pettyfoggers and Vipers of the Commonwealth" by the middle of the 18th Century most attorneys were based not in London but in the provinces and could earn much more from local non-litigious work than from taking cases to court in London, which, of course, echoes the comment of William Napier Reeve considered earlier. However, attorneys and solicitors never enjoyed the prestige and degree of self rule applicable to the Bar. Barristers claimed their work was a liberal and scientific profession, quite distinct from the mechanical labours of attorneys, and that distinction had grown throughout the 16th and 17th centuries and continued into the 18th. This was reinforced by the distinction between the academic education of the Bar and the practical training of attorneys. The Clergy, Medical Men and Barristers were considered 'esquires' but attorneys, though considered to be worthy of 'gentility' were denied that ascription. Furthermore though some attorneys did amass considerable wealth they rarely figure prominently in the higher ranks of county society.

Against this background of a decentralised and not highly esteemed profession the voluntary and independent law societies mentioned above emerged and became, as Brooks argues, 'the principal instruments through which the profession was organized ... but in the nineteenth century ... the Law Society ... negotiated with government for control over the entire lower branch ... Self regulation for the lower branch came ... only after strenuous efforts to improve the public image of the profession.'[11]

One of the most important ways in which both autonomy and respectability were gained came about as a result of the introduction of qualifying examinations under the auspices of The Law Society. William Napier Reeve recounted how these examinations were regarded with dismay at first but argued they had turned around the fortunes of the entire profession. By 1882 to be admitted a man – and the profession remained exclusively male until 1919 – had to have knowledge of Geography, History, two languages other than English, and be acquainted with Classics. In this way solicitors could claim they had the benefit of a liberal education equivalent to that of barristers. Professor Brooks further comments on this phenomenon: 'Amongst social theorists and modern historians, it is a commonplace that, since the Industrial Revolution, the professions have come to play a uniquely important place in the social and

---

[11] Brooks, op cit pp 265-268.

political life of modern capitalist society .. few would question that the emphasis on specialized training, self regulation and sense of vocation which are characteristic of professional men have greatly influenced modern attitudes towards work and social structure.'[12]

However, if the vast change in the status and standing of solicitors in the 19th Century is largely the result of the imposition of nationally coordinated educational qualification standards, the existence of local organisations committed to the maintenance of good practice standards in their areas cannot be dismissed as unimportant.

Leicester may have been quite late in the foundation of its Law Society in 1860 compared to the other towns and areas mentioned earlier, but the formation of the Leicester Law Society was undoubtedly an event of considerable significance, and one in which neighbouring Nottingham was beaten. Its Law Society did not begin until 1875. Furthermore, as will become clear in Chapter 2, the infant society soon became a vigorous and highly respected participant in the organization and development of the Solicitors' Profession. Some of that success must be attributed to the character and quality of early members, some of whose lives and careers will be touched on in the following chapter.

The late 1850s must have been a period of considerable interest and prosperity for local practitioners in Leicester. The town was growing. Indeed it increased from some 17,000 inhabitants to about 60,000 in 1851. Such an increase of population must have meant an increase in legal work, even if only for conveyancers selling land for house building. But Leicester's principal industry, hosiery, grew also, and while it was still primarily a 'cottage industry' with people working their 'frames' at home, it appears the number of stocking frames increased tenfold between 1801 and 1850. This did not mean prosperity for workers as wages actually declined between 1815 and 1845, and they were kept low by a constant influx of incomers from surrounding areas, though after 1848 a buoyant domestic market improved local fortunes, aided by the growth of the railway system enabling goods to be sold nationwide. The 'hosiers' who owned the knitting frames did, however, make a constant and reliable income from frame rent. Leicester also witnessed the opening of the first mechanically operated public railway in the Midlands with the building of the Leicester & Swannington Railway in 1832/3. This brought cheap coal into the borough and helped revive the fortunes of the Leicestershire Coalfield. Indeed the extractive industries in the County, coal, granite

---

[12] Brooks, op cit p 263.

and lime, which had begun in the 18th Century, were much stimulated by the railways so that by 1849 some 200 men were employed in the Mountsorrel quarry alone. During 1850s the railway system continued to grow, stretching to Burton, Peterborough, Rugby, and in 1857 a more direct route to London was opened via Bedford and Hitchin. The boot and shoe trade also increased greatly after 1850 when Thomas Crick and his son John set up at 34 High Cross Street, employing initially 22 men and 21 women, and began to eclipse that of Northampton. Henry Norman and David Hollins, both of Belgrave Gate, employed 27 and 30 workers respectively. In 1853 a machine for riveting uppers to soles of shoes was introduced and Stead & Simpson took up the use of Blake's sole-sewing machine in 1858. Similarly elastic web manufacture increased rapidly after 1850.

By the 1850s Leicester was three times the size of Coventry and was considerably larger than Northampton and Derby, and, for a while, Nottingham. The borough also acquired the function of a local board of health in 1849 and set about dealing with pig sties, heaps of manure and ordure, bad drainage and cesspits. In 1859 the Corporation took powers to control private building and also regulated effluvia and smoke from factories. Leicester established a waterworks company in 1851 and piped water reached the town in 1853, while a system of main sewers was begun, with a sewage works in operation by 1855. These improvements were the result of private/municipal enterprise partnerships, while Thomas Cook had begun an enterprise that was to change the face of the world – the holiday and tourism industry.[13]

The Borough Council had been radically reformed some years earlier (1835) and there must still have been a very conscious air of pride in the achievements of the last quarter century which included the provision of the first municipal recreation ground (now Nelson Mandela Park) in 1835, the laying out of Welford Road Cemetery in 1849, the closing of the old town churchyards in the 1850s, and the building of what was, for its time, a very progressive lunatic asylum in 1835. Participation in local affairs had been broadened out from the Anglican few to include leading members of the Non Conformist and Unitarian communities – indeed they took over local government. The Leicester Literary and Philosophical Society had also established a fine reputation for the quality of its debates and deliberations.

---

[13] See further R H Evans, Chapters 7 and 8 in A E Brown (Ed) The Growth of Leicester, Leicester, Leicester University Press, (1970) to which indebtedness is acknowledged, and also, passim, Leicester and its Region, Ed N Pye, Leicester, Leicester University Press, 1972.

This increase in economic, industrial and municipal activity must have led to an increased flow of work for lawyers. In addition attorneys and solicitors who had funds to invest on behalf of clients and their dependants were, in those days before the emergence of our modern financial system of Banks, Insurance Companies and Building Societies, an important source of finance for the development of land and house and factory building. Not only, however, did builders and entrepreneurs need advice and finance, but every office and function in local government had to have its clerk, and those positions were held by attorneys and solicitors. William Napier Reeve, for example, of Messrs Freer & Co, was Clerk of the Peace, Clerk to the Lieutenancy, and Clerk to the Visitors of the Leicester and Rutland Lunatic Asylum. Though such offices were not mere sinecures, they nevertheless represented steady, regular and guaranteed income. Leicester's attorneys and solicitors must have shared in the general prosperity of the local middle class. What more natural then for these practitioners, concentrated as they were in a closely knit geographical area and sufficiently small in number for all to be well acquainted, to consider whether the formation of a local Law Society could advance their professional interests.

It is not known who sent round the circular letter which brought together a group of influential Leicester practitioners at The Bell Hotel on 27th November 1860, or exactly why they did so. The economic cause, however, was almost certainly the growing prosperity of the borough, and the social cause a desire to enhance professional status and to set members apart from those 'in trade'. It is surely no coincidence that 1860 was also the year of foundation of the Leicester Chamber of Commerce, and that may have prompted local practitioners to 'consider the propriety', as the Book of Proceedings informs us, of forming a Law Society locally. Was it Richard Toller, who chaired the meeting who took the initiative, or Richard Luck who moved the motion proposing The Society's formation, or Thomas Ingram who seconded it? There must have been considerable informal discussions before this meeting took place for there to have been so much unanimity on the day, and indeed for the first 'Book of Proceedings' to be available on the day for the record of the meeting to be made. It has been claimed[14] that it was James Bouskell who promoted the initial meeting, but he may not have been alone in this idea. Furthermore, there must have been for some time a perceived need for a Law Library. But certainly that day saw the inception of an important and honourable professional institution.

---

[14] Leicestershire Law Society Newsletter No 86, October 1998.

Chapter 2

Formation and Early Years

The records of The Society exist from 1860[15]. These are supplemented by an early copy of the original constitution and cognate documents in the County Record Office at Wigston, the late Donald Hunt's privately published biography of H. A. Owston, "The Master Builder" (1991) and a volume entitled "Edwardian Biography: Leicestershire" originally published by W. T. Pike of Brighton in 1902.

The Society was formed in 1860 as The Leicester Law Society, with its inaugural meeting at 'The Bell' Hotel – that now long lost and much lamented coaching inn in Humberstone Gate where the Primark store now stands. Or was it? There is a long standing tradition within The Society (which has been repeated on Annual Dinner Menus) that its first meeting was at The Guildhall, which was then Leicester's Town Hall, on 13th December 1860. On the other hand, Donald Hunt in "The Master Builder" maintains the first meeting was at The Bell. The Bell was Leicester's premier commercial hotel. On the other hand given the prestigious initial membership which included both Samuel Stone, the Town Clerk of Leicester, William Napier Reeve, the Clerk to the Lieutenancy, and Clement Stretton, a member of the Borough Council, the Guildhall would have been a natural choice for a first meeting. The Book of Proceedings No. 1 clarifies the issue. A meeting to convene 'Attorneys and Solicitors' was summoned by circular and met at The Bell on 27th November 1860. There were present Messrs Arnall, Billings, Bouskell, Gregory, Harris, Hawker, Ingram, Luck, Macaulay, Nevinson, Owston, Paget, Reeve, Spooner, Stevenson, Stretton, R. Toller (in the Chair) and G. Toller. That was when the proposal to found The Society was moved and passed. A Rules Committee was set up under Thomas Ingram to draft a constitution and then the meeting was adjourned until 13th December 1860 at 4.00 pm to meet in the Town Hall Library. Nearly all the solicitors in Leicester joined, and on 13th December the Rules were formally adopted and it was proposed that Joseph Harris be the first President. It appears, however, that he did not attend after the inaugural meeting.

---

[15] This is in fulfilment of a requirement in the 1860 Constitution that *all* Society and Committee transactions were to be recorded in a 'Book of Proceedings'.

The original constitution makes it clear that the prime object of The Society was the formation and maintenance of a Law Library (and a resolution of 10th January 1861 refers to taking premises), followed by the protection of the character, status and interests of solicitors and attorneys practising in the town and county of Leicester, the promotion of honourable practice and the consideration of all general questions affecting the profession or the alteration or administration of the law. The rules provided for a President, Vice President, Secretary, Treasurer, and a committee of management of ten, the officers being ex-officio members, with a quorum being fixed at four. The committee and the officers were to be elected annually at a general meeting and they were to have the powers to dispose of The Society's funds and to select and maintain the Library, to manage The Society's affairs, call meetings, regulate proceedings, fill casual vacancies and to make interim provision for any contingency not contemplated by the rules until action could be taken by a general meeting.

Committee members were clearly expected to be assiduous in attendance on The Society's business for absence from four consecutive meetings, save for illness or absence from Leicester, was deemed to amount to resignation, though that rule did not apply to the President or Vice President!

Membership was open to any solicitor practising or residing in the town or county of Leicester, though membership could only be conferred at a general meeting of which five clear days' notice had to be given by the Secretary to all members. Five votes against were required to exclude a candidate. This somewhat cumbersome procedure was amended early on for by 1861 the Committee was given power to elect members. It is, however, interesting to note that no member of a firm was to be elected to membership of the Society unless his partners also became members. This was clearly intended to prevent firms from using the Library without paying subscriptions in full. The election fee for a member in Leicester was 5 guineas (£5.25) and the annual subscription was 2 guineas (£2.10), though there was a reduced rate for partnerships, of 3 guineas for firms with two partners, 4 guineas for those with three and 5 guineas with four. That may well indicate that in 1860 no firm had more than four partners. 'Clerks' (ie what are now termed 'trainee solicitors') were required to pay an election fee of 2 guineas and an annual subscription of 1 guinea, while county members who might be expected to make less use of the Library, were also to pay an annual subscription of 1 guinea, with, once more, reduced rates for firms of two or three partners. These subscriptions were quite expensive, for, as the Office for National Statistics 2004 table shows, £1 in 1860 would be the equivalent of £43.42, while £1 was also the average weekly wage of a general labourer. The 1860 entry fee for a Leicester practitioner was thus the equivalent in modern terms of over £200. Subscriptions were payable in advance on 1st January, and if arrears of one month accrued the defaulters were to be 'reminded' of their obligation by the Secretary and if the default continued the privileges of membership were to be suspended. Continuing non-payment down to 1st April would result in defaulters losing their membership unless some excuse acceptable to The Committee was offered.

The Committee had power to borrow up to £200 from members who were entitled to deduct interest at 5% from their annual subscriptions. Any such loan was only repayable on the death of the lender or at the discretion of the Committee.

The Society's Annual General Meeting was to be held in January each year and was to receive the Committee's reports and accounts, the latter having been audited by the Secretary and Vice President. Such a meeting had the power to amend the constitution, though such changes had to be signed by the proposer and conspicuously posted in the Reading Room for at least 4 weeks before the meeting, and were subject to a requirement of a 75% majority of those present and voting at the meeting to come into effect – a simple majority was to suffice for all other matters with the chairman of the meeting having a casting vote in the event of a tie. Special general meetings could be convened on the initiative of the President or of five members, but five days' written notice had to be given to each member, though that period was reduced to two days in 1862, with the President, Vice President or Committee having power to reduce the period still further in the case of an emergency.

Particular provision was made for the Library by the Constitution. Single day borrowing only was the rule, with all volumes having to be returned before 11 am on the day following their being borrowed. All borrowings had to be recorded on pain of a fine of 2/6d (12½ pence), and no member was to borrow more than two volumes at any time, with a daily fine of 1/- (5 pence) being the consequence of failure to comply. Members who lost or defaced volumes were either to replace the book, or pay for its replacement or to make such other compensation as The Committee should direct. Clerks in articles could, on the nomination of their principals, provided the latter were also members of the Society, be allowed to read in the Library, while Barristers were given reading and borrowing rights in return for either a 5 guinea payment or an annual subscription of 1 guinea, these rates were halved in 1862, maybe following representation by impecunious members of the Bar!

Members could be expelled from The Society for failure to observe its rules, or proof of dishonest, dishonourable or unprofessional conduct. Such an expulsion could only take place at a special general meeting of which the accused had to have five clear days' notice, and a 75% majority of members present and voting was required for a proposed expulsion to become effective.

A list of Society members from 1871 survives in the County Record Office. Many names still current in local legal circles can be found there:

Joseph Arnall (Leicester); Thomas Baxter (Lutterworth); G C Bellairs; R Berridge; Thomas Berridge; William Billings; William Billson; A H Burgess; J B Bouskell (all of Leicester); E Clarke (Melton Mowbray); William Cowdell (Hinckley); H Deane (Loughborough); J B Fowler (Leicester); J B C Fox and B H C Fox (Lutterworth); William Freer (Leicester); C H Gate (Lutterworth); W M Goode (Loughborough); J Gregory; William Gregory; Joseph Harris; Samuel Harris; William Harris; Joseph Harvey; J. Barber Haxby; C J Hunter; Thomas Ingram, F J Kirby (all of Leicester); W Latham (Melton Mowbray); W H Macaulay; Thomas Miles; William Moore; Charles Morris; George Nevinson; Thomas Nevinson; H A Owston (all of Leicester); - Paddison (Melton Mowbray); Alfred Paget (Leicester); Stephen Pilgrim and C Sansome Preston (both of Hinckley); William Napier Reeve; C Smith; George Stevenson; Samuel Stone; S Francis Stone; Clement Stretton; Albert Stretton; Richard Toller; George Toller (all of Leicester); T Herbert Watson (Lutterworth) and C C Woodcock (Leicester). (52 names)

A further list from 1886 also survives in the County Records. Many of the foregoing were still members, but we must now add A D Bartlett and W F Beardsley (Loughborough); R R Blackwell, G H Blunt (Leicester); H W Bosworth (Loughborough); C S Burnaby; A H Burgess; L P Chamberlain (Leicester); J S Channer (Lutterworth); R S Clifford; J D G Cradock (Loughborough); W J Curtis; E Dutton; A C Faire; W J Freer (all of Leicester): T Jesson (Ashby); J Kidney (Leicester); A J Loseby (Market Bosworth); E Miles; T B Neale (both of Leicester); W J New (Melton); S B Noon; S S Partridge; W G Place; G Rowlatt; W J Salusbury; B A Shire; W Simpson; G F Stevenson; S F M Stone; J Storey (all of Leicester); W H Toone (Loughborough); J B Waring; H S Warwick; T Watts (Leicester); T J Webb (Loughborough); W Whetstone (Leicester); W Wilkins (Ashby); W Willcox; E K Williams; W M Williams (Leicester); W J Woolley, C D Woolley (Loughborough); and T Wright (Leicester). There were thus 79 members in 1886, a considerable increase from 1871, but the membership was still overwhelmingly concentrated in Leicester.

It is clear that the creation and functioning of the Law Library was central to the existence of The Society. The first reading room (of 1861) was in the Church of England Institute in Loseby Lane. The Church was clearly a lessee as the building was owned by Mrs Payne Johnson. The initial yearly rent was £10.00. However, in 1866 the landlord proposed an increase in the rent of the premises from £30 to £45 together with parochial rates. At that point the firm of Davis and Owston (subsequently Owston and Co) who had purchased premises at 23, Friar Lane, on 4th May 1866, offered the use of the stables of these premises to The Society. The offer was gratefully accepted on 16th November 1866 and a rent of £10 pa was fixed. The Library was to remain in the ground floor of the former stables until 1960[16].

The earliest acquisition included volumes of 'named' Law Reports, with a strong bias towards Chancery subjects. Thereafter textbooks were ordered, the first list including Smith's "Mercantile Law", Chitty on "Bills of Exchange", Lindley on "Partnerships", Selwyn's "Nisi Prius", Miller and Collier on "Bills of Sale", Hayes and Jarman on "Wills", Chitty's "Equity Index" and Smith's "Compendium on Real and Personal Property". The initial cost of acquisition was quite high. Law Reports prior to 1861 cost £173 while a yearly subscription to various series cost £17.2s.0d (£17.10), and books cost £54.10s.0d (£54.50). There were, however, a number of donations, including one to the value of £10 from the first President, Joseph Harris.

While spending much time in acquiring books for the Library, the Committee, with considerable self confidence for a new organisation, approved Bills to consolidate the Common Law Courts, and declared itself generally satisfied with the various examinations set for The Law Society's preliminary and intermediate examinations. The 'Inner Man' was also considered, for The Committee resolved that the annual dinner after the 1863 AGM should be held at 5.30 pm for 6.00 pm at the Stag and Pheasant Hotel at a cost of 6s (30p) for 'Dinner, Dessert and Attendance'.

It is clear that from an early stage The Society was much concerned with enhancing the professional standing of solicitors. Thus in 1864 The Committee took exception to clauses in the Attorneys and Solicitors Remuneration Bill dealing with the enforceability of contracts between solicitors and clients as this could lead to bargaining and place solicitors on a level with builders, architects and other contractors! In 1865 the annual report stressed the 'constant communication' had with The Law Society in London and other provincial Law Societies in defence of members' interests, while in January 1865 The Society petitioned the House of

---

[16] See further D. S. Hunt "The Master Builder" p52.

Commons to reform the system of Courts as the existing concentration of Courts in London was 'inconvenient and insufficient'. A further petition followed in April 1865 on the issue of Stamp Duty. The 1866 annual report records that these petitions had resulted in some legislative changes.

Standards of Entry

The 1866 Annual Report is noteworthy in that it concludes that the introduction of more stringent examination standards would 'effect a great improvement in the status of the profession, and that, in course of time, the ranks of members will be comprised entirely and solely of gentlemen by habit and education'. There may, as we have seen in Chapter 1, have been opposition in some quarters to the introduction of examinations for solicitors, but in Leicester it was clearly felt that stringent entry standards were the only way to rid the profession of Dickens's condemnations in "Bleak House" and "David Copperfield". In seeking to promote the standing of the profession, The Society cooperated regularly with other provincial Societies and with what were then the two Law Societies in London [The Incorporated Law Society and The Metropolitan and Provincial Law Association]. It is interesting to note, as the 1867 annual report records, the considerable extent to which in the seven years since its foundation The Society had played an active role in consultation exercises with regard to proposed legislation before Parliament and had campaigned for law reform measures. At the same time membership had increased to 44, comprising virtually all Leicester solicitors and a high proportion of those in the County. These trends continued for the rest of the 1860s, while at the same time the Library continued a process of expansion. This did not, however, mean that the Library was free of problems. On 15th October 1870 the Hon. Secretary, Mr Owston, reported that a number of volumes were missing from the Library and it was accepted by The Committee that in future one of Mr Owston's clerks should accompany members seeking to borrow books and record the borrower's name in a book to be kept for that purpose. In due course a sum of £15 per annum was paid to Mr Owston in respect of his clerk's services, a system which continued until 1876.

Legal Education and Other Matters

The 1871 annual report contained notice of the formation of a Legal Education Association which was to press for the creation of a Law

University for the education of students intended for the profession. Mr William Napier Reeve was an active member of this body and The Committee supported its endeavours in this year and again in 1872. It must be remembered that for hundreds of years the Inns of Court had been 'the University' for the Bar, indeed 'Barrister-at-Law' is a degree, and while the Legal Education Association did not achieve its object, its existence is further proof of the desire of solicitors to raise standards within their profession. A similar development can be seen in the legislation relating to the remuneration of attorneys and solicitors which legalised agreements between solicitors and clients but only on the basis that payments in respect of actions at law or suits in equity had been allowed by a taxing officer. In this way the integrity of those seeking remuneration could be made clear. At the same time solicitors were prevented from contracting out of liability for negligence, though it was to be many years before general liability in the Tort of Negligence was to be established.

In 1871, at the request of a deputation of clerks, The Committee resolved that members should grant to their clerks the following holidays: Easter Monday, Whit Monday, the two Leicester Race days from 12 noon, and the 26th of December, if a weekday. This is an early example of The Society acting in a quasi-regulatory capacity with regard to its members. In 1879 Good Friday and Christmas Day were formally added to this list. While in 1880 the principle of a weekly half holiday was adopted, though this led to a diversity of practice, some offices closing at 2.00 pm on Thursday, some on Friday, and some on Saturday – then, of course, a full working day. Articled Clerks also made requests. In 1872 the Leicester Articled Clerks Society made a request to be allowed to use the Library and this was granted.

1872 also saw moves towards a local scale of conveyancing charges. It is interesting to note that this issue was in one form or another to dominate much of the work of The Committee for the next hundred years until scale charges were abolished in the early 1970s.

The 1873 annual report drew particular attention to a defect in the drafting of the Bastardy Laws Amendment Act 1872 and commented: 'Errors of this kind form a strong condemnation of the practise [sic] of passing a number of Acts involving legal changes at the fag end of a session devoted to the consideration of important national or social subjects, when no sufficient consideration can be given to their debate.' It is a comfort of some sort to know that the deficiencies of the enactment process under which all lawyers labour are no new thing!

The report for 1874 contained a memorandum of some length on the Supreme Court of Judicature Act 1874 which created the basis for the modern High Court and Court of Appeal structure. Those changes likely to affect local practitioners most were detailed, viz the naming of all litigation matters as 'actions', and their commencement by writ, abolition of rules relating to nonjoinder and misjoinder, the ability for partners to sue in the name of a firm and that of married women to defend actions without joining their husbands, reform of pleadings, institution of powers to settle issues and counterclaims. Many issues now taken for granted were thus established. That report also noted the first deaths to be recorded amongst Society members, including that of Mr William Freer, the third president.

While the 1874 Act became a cornerstone of our legal system, the 1875 report dealt with the failure of a proposal that was not to become law for many years, namely registration of title. The Society was in favour of registration on a County basis under the Land Transfer Bill but it was not proceeded with after its second reading in The Commons. Many other Acts dealing with the reform of Land Law and Conveyancing were, however, passed in this year and the concentration of the annual report on them is an indication that the overwhelming majority of the work of members of The Society lay in these areas. This is further evidenced by the 1876 report which details the adoption locally of a Common Form of Conditions of Sale and a Purchase Contract.

Between 1876 and 1877 The Society was much concerned with the administration of the Library. The annual rental payment for the Library was fixed at £25 pa, to include coals and gas lighting, and an arrangement was made with a Mr Clarke, a Law Stationer, for him to have a room over the Library and to provide a clerk to act as a Librarian. In 1878 the Annual Report contained news of the continued expansion of the Library consequent on the gift of a series of Law Reports by members of The Society. Bills presented to Parliament were also being obtained for the Library. 1878/79 on the other hand was much taken up with agreeing the holiday times previously alluded to and the revision of the General Conditions of Sale adopted in 1876.

The beginning of the 1880s saw the practice adopted of printing the Annual Report, for which the present author is grateful as the handwritten documents previous encountered – often compiled in different hands – were not always models of conveyancer's copperplate!

Into the 1880s

In 1881/82 and in 1883 much of the work of The Committee was concerned with the Solicitors' Remuneration Act 1881 and the provision it made for making an Order fixing *minimum* scales of fees to be adopted by local Law Societies. The order was made in 1883 and The Society appointed a Sub-Committee to draw up a scale founded not only on local agreement but also on statute, once again reinforcing the professional standing of solicitors. The proposed local scale was the subject of two special general meetings before finally being adopted. The Committee stated: 'they believe that the public will gladly welcome the change to an ad valorem scale of fees, and will soon recognize that authorised by the Order as the guide for Solicitors to follow'. By 1884, however, The Committee had decided against having a particular local scale and stated that the fees authorised by the General Order should be a sufficient guide.

The continued expansion of the Library continued in 1884/1885 with the issue of a new catalogue and the purchase of a number of titles, including, of course, the current edition of Stone's "Justices Manual", by then in its 22nd edition – local pride alone would have been enough to warrant that purchase – and the wonderfully titled Oliphant's "Law of Horses", 4th Edition – in a hunting county the purchase of such a volume can be readily understood. The Society's Conditions of Sale and Purchase agreements, as revised by the well known Conveyancing Counsel, Mr Wolstenholme, were also placed on sale at a price, per dozen, of 1/8d (approximately 9p) for the Conditions and 11d (approximately 5p) for the Agreement. Non members were charged a significantly higher figure!

The Society's 1886 Annual Report, a copy of which also survives in the County Record Office, related to the 25th AGM of The Society held in the Library on 19th January 1886. Some of the names of those present still have a resonance for local firms. The retiring president was C S Burnaby, and there were also present Messrs Arnall, Billings, Blunt, Dickinson, Fowler, Kilby, Macaulay, Neale, Nevinson, Owston, Rowlatt, Salusbury, Stevenson, Stone, Storey, Warwick and Willcox. The officers and committee for the forthcoming year were W Billings (President), J Arnall (Vice President), T Ingram (Treasurer), W Simpson (Secretary), with G H Blunt, C S Burnaby, L P C Chamberlain, J B Fowler, W H Macaulay and S F Stone as The Committee. C J Billson, A C Faire, J F Hodding, S F M Stone and W Whetstone were elected as members and The Society had healthy funds of £289.2s.10d (£289.10½).

Several new volumes had been added to the Library in the preceding year, some of them being titles still current today, viz Buckley on "Companies" (4th Ed), Byles on "Bills" (14th Ed), Prideaux's "Precedents" (13th Ed) and Stephen's "Digest of the Criminal Law" (3rd Ed). Other titles have not fared so well, such as Higginson on the "Pollution and Obstruction of Water Courses" (1877) or Sebastian on "Trademarks" (2nd Edn. 1884). It must also be asked why the Library had purchased the Clergy Directory of 1885 and the Index to the London Gazette of 1830-1883, though, given the continuing importance in those days of landed wealth, a case can still be made for the purchase of Kelly's 1885 "Handbook to the Titled, Landed and Official Classes".

It was reported that The Committee had supported the passage of the Trustee Relief (Investments) Bill whereby Parliament had reversed certain inconvenient restrictions imposed by case law. It was, however, otherwise stated that: 'very few statutes have been passed during the last session of special interest to our profession, the attention of the Legislature having been almost exclusively devoted to Acts extending the franchise and amending the machinery for Registration and Elections'. One is forced to comment – how different from our current times.

On a more local level the 1886 AGM amended The Society's rules to add to its objects 'The encouragement of Legal Education'. Regulations were then also recommended to provide for the giving of prizes to articled clerks who had secured places in either the 1st or 2nd Honours Classes in The Law Society's Final Examinations. The value of prizes was to be £10 for a 1st and £5 for a 2nd, in the form of either a medal or books to be presented at the AGM.

While The Society existed to maintain its Library, promote the interests of solicitors, and to encourage, from 1886, Legal Education, a separate body had existed from 1872 to promote the interests of law students and the younger members of the solicitors' profession. This was the Leicester Law Students Society, a body mirrored today by organisations catering for the needs of trainee and young solicitors, both of which groups are now entitled to representation on The Society's Committee. The 1872 Society was very much in the Victorian tradition of 'mutual improvement'. Its objects were the acquisition of information in connection with the study and practice of the law, cultivation of the art of public speaking and the promotion of the interests of students and younger solicitors. Membership was available to all articled clerks and members of the Law Society of Leicester and 'local gentlemen' reading for the Bar. The entry fee was 5/- (25p) and the annual subscription was the same amount. Election to membership took place at the fortnightly meetings which commenced at 7.00 pm. An extensive table of fines was drawn up, no doubt to encourage both attendance and participation, for example 2/6d (12½p) for failure to speak on an issue for debate when appointed to do so or for failure to appoint a deputy, or 1/6d (7½p) for student members (ie those who were not admitted as solicitors) for being absent from three successive meetings unless away from Leicester on professional business or ill. Failure to pay fines and annual dues could result in expulsion from this society. The 1872 Society's constitution generally followed that of The Leicester Law Society, but provision was made for the post of President, who had to be a qualified Solicitor or Barrister, though the position would appear to have been quite honorary as it was the task of the committee to elect a Chairman to preside over its meetings.

The business of the 1872 Society was very much concerned with debates and lectures. Once a fortnight on alternate Wednesday evenings, with a close season between 1st June and 1st October, a meeting was to commence at 7.00 pm and was to continue until the end of debate or an adjournment was called. The committee was tasked with choosing which topics should be debated, though matters of theological or religious controversy were forbidden. It must be remembered that religious divisions within the Christian faith still ran quite deep in 19th Century Leicester, not just between 'Church' and 'Chapel', but also between the Trinitarian majority and the powerful Unitarian minority, and hence this particular prohibition.

Debates could take place on either 'jurisprudential' or 'legal' issues. For the former speakers addressed the meeting in the order named on the order paper, while for the latter, which *may* have been somewhat in the nature of moots, the order was first and second affirmative speakers then first and second negative speakers. Strict time limits were also laid down with regard to the length of speeches.

Members could offer to deliver lectures or to read papers on legal or jurisprudential issues, though no lecture was to last more than an hour. Any such lecture or paper was open to comment and criticism from the membership. Once again the 1872 Society's committee was empowered to determine which offers of lectures or papers should be taken up. The committee also had power to invite practitioners to deliver lectures to the membership.

One of these lectures has survived in the County Record Office. It was delivered in 1882 by William Napier Reeve, of whom more below. The morally earnest quality of the lecture is evident early on as Reeve speaks on the issue of Law Reform and entitles his address as a 'sermon'. Reviewing the progress of reform during his lifetime, Reeve commences with Brougham's six hour attack on the abuses of the law in 1828 which led to the creation of a Commission to reform the law of real property. In particular Reeve alludes to the extreme expense and complexity of conveyancing: 'Every conveyance required two deeds, the lease and release ... the stamp on the lease was 35/- (£1.75), and *ad valorem* on the principal deed, thrice the present amount, and every follower £1, ... conveyances were then three or four skins long.' It is clear that complaints about the conveyancing process have a long history. Reeve alludes also to the extreme delays in both the Common Law and Chancery Courts, while he is particularly critical of the cruel punishments inflicted by the Criminal Law. At Leicester Assizes in 1817 out of 31 defendants sentenced, 17 were to be hanged, though not all the executions were carried out. It was then believed that such punishments were necessary, but by 1882 Reeve averred: 'Men are kinder to each other than they were'.

Reeve exhorted his audience to diligence and hard work; the object of the successful practitioner was 'spurning delights and living laborious days' coupled with a refusal to accept failure. Patient waiting was the lot of the successful man and there should be no desire to 'get rich quick' as we might say today. Reeve pointed out that some solicitors had misused clients' money in the pursuit of 'trading enterprises'. The successful solicitor was to be a 'counsellor, guide, philosopher, and friend to his client', and was also to be 'industrious, patient [and] frugal'. 'An attorney (I like the old name) ... is responsible for the works that he undertakes, for the clients that he chooses to act for, for the work that he chooses to do. If it becomes his duty to fight, he can, beforehand, examine into and judge of the justice of the quarrel, and he is responsible alike for the work that he does and the manner in which he does it'. In carrying out that work Reeve urges his listeners to use no untrue or unfair means. A solicitor should not encourage litigation, but rather should speak patiently and soothingly to his enraged client, and if he goes to court it should only be to seek justice, not the oppression of the other side. A solicitor should remind his client that honesty is always the best policy and that the client should not indulge in cunning so as to avoid his creditors.

This is a most earnest exhortation, and while much of it is still morally appropriate one must wonder today how far a practitioner could go in pursuing such a 'holier than thou' approach with a client. Indeed we may ask whether it was possible to do so in 1882. Let us, however, note Reeve's final quotation from James Mill, the father of John Stuart Mill:

'He who works more than all the others will in the end excel all others. Difficulties are made to be overcome. Life consists of a succession of them, and he gets best through them who has made up his mind to contend with them.' Stirring stuff for the young lawyer!

It must be remembered that at the time in question the opportunities for debate and instruction offered by the 1872 Society would have been an invaluable addition to the otherwise limited facilities available for the study of the law. There was no University Law School anywhere near Leicester, while the correspondence and tutorial service provided by Gibson and Weldon (the forerunner of the College of Law) did not begin until 1876, and then only in a limited form until 1881. It is therefore quite clear that the educational and library services provided by both the principal society and its 1872 student 'shadow' were essential to the functioning of a well educated and properly informed local legal profession.

By 1886/87 The Society's membership stood at 81, through the deaths of two very senior members, William Latham of Melton Mowbray who was President in 1866 and James Bouskell who was The Society's first Secretary and President in 1884. The original rules had made no provision for members retiring from practice to assume honorary status: that change was now proposed. The Committee also felt constrained to remind members to return borrowed library books promptly as some were being kept out for unreasonably long periods. They also felt it necessary to complain that the new County Court Rules penalised solicitors acting as advocates in the County Court by limiting allowances they could claim thus inducing the employment of counsel. The Committee drew attention to legislation enabling married women deserted by their husbands to obtain orders for maintenance from the Magistrates 'without resorting to the Workhouse' – that was certainly an extension of the rights of women.

Membership continued to increase as the 1880s drew to their close. By 1887/88 it stood at 86. The Committee was saddened, however, to note the demise of the society formerly serving the needs of Articled Clerks as Law Students, and felt that some steps should be taken to provide lectures and classes on the Law in provincial centres. It is clear that a society of Law Students did arise at another time as we shall encounter its activities later on, but it appears that such bodies lead a somewhat precarious existence. The Society was also concerned at the activities of unqualified persons acting as solicitors and *The Leicester Daily Post* of 2nd June 1888 carried a report of an action taken by The Society against Thomas Lewin and John Proctor, Accountants of Bowling Green Street, in which it was alleged the form of letters sent out by the defendants gave the impression that they were solicitors, contrary to the terms of the Solicitors Act 1874. The Magistrates found the case proved but imposed no penalty when the defendants undertook to amend their ways. The Committee also resolved on the 1st November 1888 that no one other than a solicitor or barrister should represent a client in licensing cases. This was in response to appearances by Auctioneers and other persons. The views of The Society were brought to the attention of the licensing justices. The problem of unqualified practitioners did not, however, disappear and The Committee's minutes in subsequent years indicate that from time to time action had to be taken in respect of such incidents. Generally speaking this took the form of a letter of reproof from the Secretary.

Membership in 1888/89 increased to 88, but the death of another founder and past President, William Napier Reeve, had to be noted. The Committee also viewed with approval the invitation from the Incorporated Law Society whereby members of local Law Societies could obtain membership of the principal body at a reduced rate of 10/- (50p). This was seen as fostering links between the central and the provincial bodies without 'interfering in any way with the separate existence and independent action of the [provincial] societies'. As membership increased so did the holdings of the Library and new catalogues were regularly sent to members. Sadly, however, membership decreased slightly in 1889/90 to 83, largely as a consequence of death, including that of Mr William Billings, President in 1886, and a number of resignations upon retirement from practice. Even so the Library had been increased as Messrs Miles and Co, one of the oldest firms in Leicester, had been dissolved and their Library had been acquired at an attractive price.

Fast Trains to London

On 4th December 1890 The Committee urged the Midland Railway Co. to introduce an early morning fast train to London to enable members of the legal profession in Leicester to attend personally upon business in London and thus avoid the need for an overnight stay. Clearly The Society took action on its members' behalf in relation to a wide variety of issues. This assiduity was rewarded by an increase of membership to 90. The Society was also instrumental, along with other provincial societies and The Law Society in mounting a successful campaign to prevent the introduction of a Land Transfer Bill some of whose provisions would have related to the compulsory registration of title to land. The objections of The Society were not founded on an objection to the principle of registration but to the fact that no practicable scheme of registration had been devised.

It had for a number of years been the established practice of The Society to hold its Annual Dinner after the AGM, and in January 1892 this event was held at The Assembly Rooms. This presumably refers to the premises later known as The County Rooms, and now operated as The City Rooms, just off the Market Place. Sadly the 1891/92 Report also recorded the deaths of Mr J B Haxby and Mr Clement Stretton, both founder members, and President in 1872 and 1878 respectively. The Committee also found it necessary to remind members of the need to observe Library Regulations and stated that though the imposition of fines for breaches of the regulations had fallen into disuse, it would be reactivated to ensure the proper functioning of the Library. It is also a mark of how much The Society felt itself to be part of wider civic society in that at the 1892 AGM a resolution was passed: 'That this meeting records its profound sympathy and condolence with Her Majesty The Queen, the Prince and Princess of Wales and Princess Victoria of Teck, and all the Royal Family on the sad calamity which has befallen them and the whole Empire by the death of His Royal Highness the Duke of Clarence and Avondale'. How marked also is the contrast between the formal dignity of this resolution and the effusions of grief we so often encounter today. Is a return to 'the stiff upper lip' called for?

On the other hand The Society was still firmly imbued with laissez-faire economic liberalism, and so in 1892 opposed, along with nearly all the provincial law societies, the creation of the Public Trustee Office: the legislation was not proceeded with for many years. The Society also noted with disquiet the extension of what was called 'officialism' – now bureaucracy – within society, and also protested vigorously against proposals to end the holding of civil assizes in Leicester and sending relevant business to Nottingham. This particular problem became a preoccupation of The Society for many years. Repeated attempts, sadly somewhat unsuccessful, have been made to maintain Leicester's position judicially in the face of competition from the larger, but much younger, urban centre north of the Trent. In 1893, however, the strong line taken by The Society over the civil assizes saved them. A similar strong line had to be taken, this time in conjunction with all other solicitors, in respect of the reintroduction of the Land Transfer Bill of 1893 which if passed, it was confidently predicted, would destroy conveyancing practice. The Society played its part in lobbying local MPs and members of the aristocracy to use their influence in Parliament against the Bill, and it was, once again, dropped by the Government.

Towards the end of the Century

By the mid 1890s membership of The Society stood at over 100, while the accounts disclosed a very healthy balance of income over expenditure with an accumulated fund of over £300. The Society was in a position to consider extending the Library and negotiations were entered into with H A Owston, the landlord. The Society also lost the services through death of its Librarian, Mr Morgan, and undertook to pay the undertaker's bill of £5.2s.0d (£5.10p) in respect of his funeral. This was a magnanimous gesture as funeral expenditure was often cripplingly expensive for families, especially when it is remembered that the Librarian's annual salary was only £20 pa, though this was effectively a part time position. The Committee also agreed that the Librarian and his clerk could have a half holiday each week and sanctioned the closing of the Library each Saturday at 2.00 pm. At the same time the purchase of volumes continued regularly with new acquisitions being recorded at most committee meetings.

1897, however, found The Society once again having to argue against the notion of compulsory registration of title as the Land Transfer Bill had once again been reintroduced in Parliament. There were also strong representations made about proposed changes to the County Court Rules: the proposed changes were withdrawn. However, the Land Transfer Act did reach the statute book, but the solicitors had gained important concessions in that any introduction of compulsory registration was to take place on an experimental basis, and furthermore only with the consent of the County Council in whose shire the affected area lay. How much more deferential to local government and professional opinion was central government in those days.

1898 saw The Society having to condemn the twin practice of touting and undercharging. Again these were to become preoccupations in future years. The Society stated in its Report that such practices were 'absolutely inconsistent with the maintenance of our profession as a learned profession. Much has been done in the present century to raise the status of solicitors, but if such practices as touting and advertising are introduced or tolerated amongst professional men the result must be to degrade an honourable and dignified profession to the level of a petty trade ... Any attempts on the part of clients to induce one professional man to underbid another in reference to charges ought to be firmly resisted as an insult to an honourable profession'. To further The Society's intent, a form was issued on 6th March 1899 to all members asking them to return a signed document to the Hon. Secretary stating: 'I am willing to pledge myself not to charge less than two-thirds of the Scale under the Solicitors Remuneration Act in the case of all purchases on condition that such pledge is practically unanimous from the Solicitors practising in Leicester'. This did not receive sufficient support to be proceeded with, but nevertheless The Society continued to be vigilant to deal with individual allegations of touting and undercutting.

Solicitors had indeed come along way during Victoria's reign, and The Society was not prepared to see their enhanced status being eroded, but just over a century later we must look back to those days and acknowledge the revolutionary changes that have since taken place.

As the 19th Century drew to its close The Society noted in 1899 the death of Mr Joseph Arnall, a founder member and President in 1887, and in 1900 of W H Macaulay, President in 1881. There were also the tragic deaths to two young solicitors to report, Mr S R Wykes and Mr A Dexter. They had been drowned and Mr Dexter had lost his life trying to save that of his friend. The Society was also distressed to record that the reputation of solicitors had been injured by a number of recent instances where solicitors had become bankrupt and injured their clients as a result of extravagant spending and speculation on the Stock Exchange. Such failures had occurred in London; as yet Leicester was untainted by any such misconduct.

The Society entered the 20th Century with 119 members and healthy accounts, though in a somewhat backward looking gesture it had determined not to introduce electric lighting into the Library as the capital cost would have been £15.2s.9d. (approximately £15.15p) while gas light was costing only 13/- (65p) a year.

Some notable early members

One name which still lives on amongst practitioners' books is that of Samuel Stone who was President of the Society in 1862. He was the first author of Stone's "Justices Manual", and has a strong claim to be considered as one of the founding fathers of the local solicitors' profession. He is listed in White's 1846 "Leicestershire", a directory, as being in partnership as Stone and Paget with an office in Welford Place. He was still in practice there in 1854 when listed in Melville and Co's "Directory and Gazetteer of Leicestershire", though his private residence was stated to be in Stoneygate. By 1885/86, after Samuel Stone's death, Wright's "Directory of Leicester" states that the firm, still in practice in Welford Place, was now Stone, Billson, Willcox and Dalton.

Samuel Stone is arguably the most famous of all The Society's Presidents. He was a Unitarian in religion and a Liberal in politics and a most prominent member of Leicester's elite society. Malcolm Elliott in "Victorian Leicester"[17] and A Temple Patterson in "Radical Leicester"[18], record that Stone was prominent in the movement to reform municipal corporations – Leicester's Council being clearly unreformed with most of the offices of profit being in the hands of Thomas Burbidge, the Town Clerk. Stone joined the Leicester and Leicestershire Political Union, the committee of which formed a 'shadow town council' for the Borough in the years preceding the Municipal Reform Act of 1835. Following that legislation Stone became Town Clerk in 1836, a post he held for 36 years. Astoundingly Stone continued his private practice as well and discharged his municipal duties with the aid of only two assistants. He was cautiously in favour of central oversight of local government, especially with regard to public health, though his criticism of the 1847 Health of Towns Bill led to its modification before it reached the statute book in 1848. He was also much concerned with the deficiencies of Acts which enabled house builders to evade controls on the size and ventilation of rooms. He was further influential in forcing the move of Leicester's cattle market from Horsefair Street to Welford Road in the 1870s, the former market site now being occupied by the Town Hall. Stone was not, however, omniscient and his deficient drafting of local legislation made the municipalisation of local water works and undertakings in the 1870s a difficult issue.

In wider local society Stone became one of the original 12 trustees of the Leicester Museum in 1846 and was a regular attender at meetings of the Leicester Literary and Philosophical Society, where he was recorded as an 'acute' critic of papers delivered.[19]

Stone became increasingly infirm with age and felt obliged to resign as Town Clerk in 1872, dying in 1874. His successor, George Toller, resigned within six months of being appointed, not having appreciated how onerous the office of Town Clerk was! The Reverend C C Coe of the Unitarian Great Meeting summed Stone up as follows:

'essentially a moderate man holding his own convictions faithfully and conscientiously and defending them vigorously if need be, but never in the spirit of blind or angry partisanship ... He served this town as towns are seldom served; he organised the institutions in the midst of which we

---

[17] Phillimore, 1979.
[18] Leicester University Press 1975.
[19] F.B. Lott "Centenary Book of the Leicester Literary and Philosophical Society" (1935).

live; he advised the magistrates upon the bench, and the councillor in the council chamber and in the committee room.'[20]

Samuel Stone's son, Samuel Francis, (Society President in 1888) was much involved in the development of Clarendon Park along with local developers, Charles Smith and Alfred Russell Donisthorpe. They purchased land formerly belonging to the Cradock-Hartopp family in the late 1870s for just over £60,000, and added this to land they already owned in the area which they had purchased from William Freer's estate in 1875. The 135 acres they thus owned became the basis of operations for the Clarendon Park Company which then sold off plots of land for individual development. A number of other local solicitors also became involved in this process including Pares, Miles & Co., and their successors Miles, Gregory and Bouskell.. The former firm was operating as early as 1802; Thomas Miles flourished c 1791-1873 while his son, Roger Dutton Miles, lived from 1817 to 1880.[21]

We have already encountered William Napier Reeve in his capacity as President of the Leicester Law Students Society. Reeve served his articles in London with Messrs Taylor and Roscoe in The Temple. That firm at the time had thirteen members, two principals, a chancery clerk and two assistants, other clerks and writers and 'young gentlemen from the country' such as Reeve. In the 1820s Taylor and Roscoe opened for business at 9.00 am and remained open until between 6.00 pm and 8.00 p.m. Work was apportioned out in the morning and it was expected it would be finished by the end of business – long working days of thirteen hours were then, as now, not unusual for young practitioners. Taylor and Roscoe was a prosperous practice for it briefed in Reeve's time two future Lord Chancellors, Lord St Leonards and Lord Cottenham, as well as the future Chief Baron Pollock and Mr Justice Maule. It also produced Roscoe on "Evidence" on which Reeve worked. Leaving London Reeve came to Leicester where he became a partner in what became Messrs Freer Bouskell and held various other offices such as Clerk to the Lieutenancy, Clerk of the Peace, and Clerk to the Visitors of the Leicestershire and Rutland Lunatic Asylum. He must have remained fond of his former principal in articles for he adopted the name Eliot Roscoe as a *Nom de Plume* under which he published, inter alia, "Letters to the Young men of Leicester", which ran through at least two editions being republished in 1875. Reeve was also a Justice of the Peace, a Fellow of the Society of Antiquaries, a numismatist and historian.

---

[20] Eliott, Op. Cit. p142.

[21] Readers interested in this history are referred to an article by Dr Steve Gurman and Mr Andrew Harper in The Leicestershire Law Society Newsletter No 129, December 2005 to which the present author wishes to express his indebtedness.

On retirement Reeve left Leicester for Essex where he died aged 77 in 1888 and was buried at Bocking. However, his ghost was reputed still to appear at the New Street offices of Messrs Freer Bouskell. Oddly enough the description of the apparition does not coincide with the engraved portrait of Reeve owned by his former firm. It does, however, correspond very closely to the bust of Napier Reeve which is to be found in the County Record Office at Wigston – a case of stranger than fiction?

Hiram Abiff Owston, son of John H A W Owston of Snarestone, was born in 1830 and was educated at Appleby Magna. He qualified as a solicitor in 1852 and worked for a while in Bristol before returning as an admitted man for Richard Toller in Leicester. In 1862 he became a partner in Davis and Owston, Harry Davis having been in practice for some years in Leicester and having acquired the practice of Stephen Mash in Lutterworth. Davis persuaded Owston to join the Leicester Amateur Dramatic Society to improve his public speaking, and 'H A' became also Secretary and Treasurer of LADS! By 1865 Owston had become a very well established advocate, and shortly thereafter Davis and Owston had their premises in Friar Lane where Owston's role in fostering the infant Leicester Law Society and its Library has already been recorded. Harry Davis died at the early age of 33 in 1866, but H A Owston continued the firm and prospered,[22] and he became prominent in both local and national commercial and industrial circles. He was a director of the Leicestershire Banking Company and a member of the advisory board of its successor, The London, City and Midland Bank. He was also a member of the local board of the Commercial Union Insurance Company, solicitor to the Leicestershire and Northamptonshire Union Canal and the Grand Union Canal Company, negotiating the merger of those concerns with the Grand Junction Canal Company. H A Owston also developed an extensive practice in company formation, one of the first being the Leicestershire Butchers Hide Skin and Fat Co. Ltd. He was most influential in securing the creation of Wigston Urban District Council and was Chairman of that authority for many years. His home, Bushloe House, which he purchased in 1866 and extended in 1880, is now the headquarters of Oadby and Wigston Borough Council.

Unlike Samuel Stone, Owston was active in Conservative politics and was Hon. Secretary of the Central Conservative Association of the Harborough Division and was successful in securing the return of a Conservative member for Leicester in 1861, the first since the Reform

---

[22] See generally Donald Hunt: "The Master Builder".

Act of 1832. Owston was a JP for both the Borough and County, and, like Stone and Napier Reeve, he published: "Law Relating to Highways" and "The Duties of Overseers".

H A Owston was prominent in the affairs of the Church of England locally, purchasing the advowson, or right to present a priest to the living, of Bruntingthorpe in 1880, and also supporting the work of All Saints, Wigston, and its daughter church, St. Thomas, South Wigston. The Chancel Screen in All Saints, where 'H A' was a sidesman, was his gift. He acted as Under Sheriff of Leicestershire in 1885 and 1886 and was President of the Leicester Law Society in 1883, taking on that office despite having been widowed recently following the death of his wife from exhaustion consequent on childbirth. Owston's son, however, survived his mother and went on to be a professional soldier. But, as Donald Hunt points out in "The Master Builder", no other Owston became a member of 'H A's' firm, and indeed, no son of any partner in Owstons ever succeeded his father into the partnership.

H A Owston retired from practice in 1898 and died peacefully at home following a heart attack on 18th October 1905. Despite their political differences the firms established by Samuel Stone and H A Owston are now both merged in Messrs Harvey Ingram.

The name of Billson has figured in Leicester's legal history for many years. Frederick William Billson was born in Leicester in 1864, educated at Wyggeston School, the ancestor of the current Wyggeston and Queen Elizabeth Sixth Form College, and then read Law in London where he graduated in 1884. He was articled to George Stevenson, who was President of the Society in 1873, and admitted as a solicitor in 1886 when he moved to Stratford-on-Avon to join Messrs Slatter, Sons and Gibbs and there married his employer's daughter. F W Billson returned to Leicester in 1889 and commenced his own practice where he soon built up a commercial practice acting as solicitor to a number of Leicester companies. He was a very keen yachtsman and was a member of the Trent Valley Sailing Club.

Charles James Billson was the son of William Billson, who was President of the Society in 1880. He was born in Leicester in 1857 and educated at Winchester and Corpus Christi College, Oxford, where he graduated BA in 1881, proceeding to the MA in 1883. Though he became a partner in Stone, Billson, Willcox and Dutton, his interests were mainly concerned with literature and folklore. He was President of the Leicester Literary and Philosophical Society in 1893-94, and published works including "The Archarnians of Aristophones" (1882), "County Folklore of Leicestershire and Rutland" (1895), "The Popular Poetry of the Finns" (1900), and contributed to "Winchester College 1393-1893" (1893) and "Noctes Shakesperiane" (1897). He also found time to be President of the Leicestershire Golf Club 1897-1899. He died in 1932.

William Freer was The Society's third President in 1863, and one of his articled clerks was George Henry Blunt born in Wigston Magna in 1843. Blunt was privately educated and articled to William Freer, being admitted as a solicitor in 1866. He joined what became Freer, Reeve and Blunt in 1870; the firm subsequently becoming Freer, Blunt, Rowlatt and Winterton. Blunt was also a director of the Stamford, Spalding and Boston Banking Company and was Hon. Secretary of the Leicester Infant Orphan Asylum. He was President of The Society in 1898.

Before considering another famous member of what became Messrs Freer Bouskell, it is interesting to note that the practice in 19th Century Leicester seems to have been for the majority of firms to change their names to reflect the identities of the partners.

William Jesse Freer who was President of The Society in 1901 was the eldest son of the Reverend Thomas Freer, Rector of Houghton on the Hill. Born in 1853, he was the grandson of William Freer to whom earlier allusion has been made, and was articled to his Grandfather, who was also Clerk of the Peace for Leicestershire from 1841 to 1873. W J Freer was admitted in 1875, became Deputy Clerk of Peace in 1880 and Clerk of Peace and to the Lieutenancy in 1888. He then also became Clerk to Leicestershire County Council, in 1889.

Outside the Law W J Freer was active in the local Volunteers, the ancestor of the modern Territorial Army, and held the substantive rank of Captain, and the honorary rank of Major, in the 1st Volunteer Battalion of the Leicestershire Regiment, for which he was awarded the Volunteer Distinction. He was a Fellow of the Society of Antiquaries of London, and its local Hon. Secretary in 1901. He also served as Hon. Secretary of the Leicestershire Architectural and Archeological Society; was President of the Committee for the Archeological Survey of Leicestershire; Hon. Secretary and Acting Treasurer of the Leicestershire, Leicester and Rutland Discharged Prisoners Aid Society from its foundation in 1883. Like H A Owston, W J Freer was a prominent local Anglican, being Hon. Secretary of the Leicester Church Extension Society and Churchwarden of St John the Baptist, Clarendon Park. The last generation of the Freer family to practise law as part of the family firm was Charles Edward Jesse Freer who was admitted in February 1924 and became a member of The Society in 1927. C.E.J served as Society President in 1956/57, a 'hat trick' for the Freer family.

Speaking to the Leicester Law Students Society on 12th November 1953 Mr C E J Freer gave some delightful vignettes into the lives of eminent Victorian members of his firm. Mr J Bouskell was driven to his home, Knighton Grange, every day in a carriage and insisted on sitting on the floor of the cab with his feet out of the window. Mr J.B. Haxby was even more colourful. He resigned as Clerk to the Leicester Justices after a violent dispute with an assize judge, but retained the chair on which he had sat as Clerk, and refused to return it! Mr Haxby's coachman had to be tested daily for alcohol to see whether he was fit to drive his employer home to Blaby as, being drunk once, his erratic driving had resulted in the coach and its occupant being thrown into a ditch.

Harry Bray was the son of Henry Bray and was born at Knighton in 1859. He was articled to Richard Gratton of Chesterfield and was admitted as a solicitor in 1892. He set up his own practice in Leicester in 1893 and took into partnership W E Price in 1900. Bray was a prominent athlete in his younger days and married (before qualifying) in 1884, subsequently having two sons and four daughters. He was the solicitor of the Leicester Ratepayers Association.

Henry Deane, President in 1891, was a Loughborough solicitor. Though born in Berkshire, he was educated at Christs Hospital School, which was still then located in London. He served his articles with the Town Clerk and Registrar of the County Court of Andover and was admitted in 1862. He then set up his practice in Loughborough and continued therein until 1901 when he became Registrar of Leicester County Court and District Registrar of the Supreme Court of Judicature, having previously been Coroner for the County of Leicestershire. He married in 1872 and had twelve children, seven sons and five daughters, all of whom were still living in 1902.

John Bennett Fowler, President in 1892, was born in Leicester in 1841, son of Edward Fowler, a surgeon. He was educated at Leicester Collegiate School and then articled to Thomas Ingram, being admitted as Attorney at Law and Solicitor in Chancery in 1863. He then was employed by Freshfields and Newman of London, working in their railway department and being involved in the legal side of building the London Chatham and Dover Railway and the laying of the first transatlantic cable by the 'Great Eastern'. Overwork for a period of three and a half years brought on illness and Fowler decided, despite lucrative offers from his employers, to return to Leicester where he commenced practice in 1867. He, like H A Owston, was prominent in the Conservative Party locally, acting as Conservative Agent and also serving for nine years between 1877 and 1886 as a Leicester Councillor. He was also Lord of the Manor of Earl Shilton.

Another name still current as a firm in Leicester is that of William Harding who was born in Leicester in 1863 and privately educated. He was articled in Leicester and admitted in 1886, moving to the North of England for a while, before commencing his own practice in Leicester in 1888. He took his articled clerk, H Barnett, into partnership in 1895. Harding was prominent in Liberal Party circles, acting for a while as their Agent for the Rugby Division. He lived at Kirby Muxloe and was Chairman of Kirby Muxloe Parish Council from 1896. He was also Chairman of the Leicester Laundry and Dyeing Company and was a keen golfer, serving as Hon. Secretary of the Kirby Muxloe Golf Club from its foundation in 1893.

Joseph Harvey, founder of a well known local firm, was born at Loughborough in 1825. He was articled to Stone and Paget and commenced his practice in 1847, continuing in it until his retirement in 1895. He was additionally a JP for the Borough of Leicester and was Secretary of the local Liberal Association. His eldest son, Robert, followed him into the profession and served for a time as Coroner of Leicester, becoming President of The Society in 1906.

Edward John Holyoak was born in 1857 and after private education went up to St John's College, Cambridge. He was then articled to William Napier Reeve, see above, and was admitted in 1881. He was a keen sportsman and played tennis, football and cricket and was a founder member of, and solicitor to, the Belgrave Recreation Ground and Eleemosynary Charity. He was President of The Society in 1914.

Thomas Ingram was born in Market Harborough in 1810 and was the son of another Thomas who was a partner there in the firm then known as Shuttleworth, Ingram and Wartnaby, which flourished in Market Harborough in the early 19th Century. The younger Ingram was educated between 1816 and 1821 at a private boarding school kept by James Mitchell who was the grandfather of Sir Frank Lockwood, a Victorian Solicitor General. Between 1822 and 1825 Ingram was educated in London. He was admitted as a solicitor in 1833 and by 1902 he was the oldest solicitor living. According to Mr C E J Freer's speech to the Leicester Law Students Society of 12th November 1953, Mr Ingram always maintained that 'whisky, smoking and the smell of old parchment never killed a lawyer!' He became Clerk of the Billesdon Poor Law Union in April 1836 and resigned only in November 1891 having given 55 years service and being the oldest Clerk in the Kingdom. He also served as Registrar of the Leicester County Court from 1860, as well as being District Registrar of the High Court. The office of the County Court was No. 29 Friar Lane, which is now the New Street Barristers' Chambers.

Like his friend H A Owston, Thomas Ingram was a leading local Anglican. He was prominent in founding in 1895 a parish church for South Wigston. This, not surprisingly, is dedicated to St. Thomas! The fine organ at St. Thomas carries a plate recording its donation by Thomas Ingram in 1895 in memory of his wife Frances Dowley Ingram to whom he was married for 57 years. Ingram's house stood in the area between Albion Street, Glengate and Blaby Road, South Wigston. Unlike H A Owston's former home, this property has not survived and has been replaced by mediocre modern developments.

Thomas Jesson of Hill House, Ashby-de-la-Zouch, was born at Grace Dieu in 1856 and privately educated. He served his articles with Fisher and Cheatle of Ashby and was admitted in 1879, becoming a partner in Fisher and Co. In 1880, that firm subsequently becoming Fisher, Jesson and Wilkins. He too was prominent in local Conservative politics, being President of Ashby Conservative Association, and Chairman of Ashby Urban District Council. In addition he served as Clerk of Coalville Urban District Council from its formation in 1892. This is an interesting early example of an officer of one authority serving as a member of a neighbouring authority. Urban and Rural District Councils, the forerunners of our modern District and Borough Councils, were the creation of that great reform of local government that took place between 1888 and 1893 when the patchwork of sanitary and school board authorities, etc was rationalised. Jesson also served as a governor of the Ashby Grammar School.

We next encounter the Loseby family. John Loseby was the first registrar of the Leicester, Ashby, Market Harborough and Melton Mowbray County Courts. His son, Arthur John, was a member of The Society in 1886 and he in turn was Registrar of Market Bosworth County Court. A J Loseby had a son, Reginald Arthur, born in 1877 and articled to his father, being admitted in 1899. R A Loseby practised in Leicester and was keen on shooting, hunting and field sports generally. He served as President of The Society in 1938.

John Parsons was born in Leicester in 1860 and educated privately. He was articled to Messrs Berridge and Miles and admitted in 1887. In his youth he was a keen sportsman and was an originator of the Leicester Football Club which originally played both Soccer and Rugby. 'The Tigers' now, of course, play only the latter game. Parsons filled every position from time to time on the field and also every office in the club, being President for a number of years. He was also fond of cricket and played for the county side. He was in 1902 Hon. Treasurer of Leicestershire County Cricket Club. He too was prominent in local Conservative politics, being in 1902 Hon. Secretary and Election Agent for the Harborough Division of the Leicestershire Conservative Association and a member of Leicester Town Council. Parsons was President of The Society in 1918.

Frederick Pochin was born at Hemel Hempstead in 1858, but was a lineal descendant of the old established Pochin family of Barkby. It is through Pochin that we also encounter the firm of Toller. Richard Toller, who founded his firm in 1827, was President of The Society in 1865 and served for sixty years as Clerk of the Peace for the Borough of Leicester, another example of astonishingly long service scarcely capable of contemplation today. George Toller, who was President of The Society in 1870, was also a partner in the firm. Richard Toller had a son, Richard Seddon Toller, who for a number of years also served as Registrar of the Leicester County Court and District Registrar of the High Court. The next generation of the Toller family was represented by Thomas Eric Toller who entered the firm as an articled clerk in 1906 and qualified in February 1910. He was elected into membership of The Society in 1913 and was commissioned in the 10th Battalion of the Leicestershire Regiment during the Great War, seeing service in Gallipoli, Suez, Macedonia, Palestine and France. He became Clerk of the Peace to Leicester Quarter Sessions in 1920 and served for 44 years. He was also senior partner of what had by then become Messrs Toller, Pochin and Wright, and was also a director and past chairman of Donisthorpe and Co., the hosiery concern, and a former master of the Worshipful Company of Framework Knitters. T E Toller died in June 1975 thus breaking a family connection with the law in Leicester which had lasted for some 150 years. Frederick Pochin was Tollers' managing clerk for many years and became a partner in 1898, having the sole management responsibility following the death of R S Toller.

George Rowlatt, son of Thomas Rowlatt of Great Bowden, was born at Sutton Bassett in Northamptonshire in 1850. He was educated at Kettering Grammar School and the Leicester Collegiate School. Admitted as a solicitor in 1871 he became a partner in what was then Messrs Freer, Blunt, Rowlatt and Winterton. He served as Deputy Clerk of the Peace and Returning Officer for Leicestershire, and also an Under Sherriff of the County, in which capacity he proclaimed the accession of Edward VII at Leicester Castle in 1901.

The firm of Stevensons was for many years a feature of New Street in Leicester. George Stevenson was President of The Society in 1873 and also served as a JP. His son, George Frederick, was born in Leicester in 1852 and was educated at Cheltenham College and the University of London. He was articled to his father, and also to Field Roscoe and Co of London.

G F Stevenson served as Hon. Secretary to the Leicester Society for Promoting the General Welfare of the Blind and was Hon. Financial Secretary of the Leicester Literary and Philosophical Society. He was President of The Society in 1909, another example, quite common at one time, for sons to serve in the office previously held by their fathers, the most recent examples being members of the Moore (1962/63 and 2001/2002), Foxon (1967/68 and 1979/80) and Crane (1947-1949, 1972/73 and 2000/2001) families.

William Wilkins was not originally a Leicestershire man. He had served his articles with L J Deacon of Peterborough and then entered into partnership with his former principal. In 1882 he became a member of Fisher Jesson and Wilkins of Ashby. He was a member of Leicestershire County Council, and a governor of Ashby Grammar School along with his partner Thomas Jesson. He was Churchwarden of St. Helen's, Ashby-de-la-Zouch and Chairman of the Managers of Ashby Cottage Hospital. He was married twice and had two sons and a daughter by his first marriage and four sons and two daughters by his second. One of the sons of his first marriage, Granville Augustus Wilkins, was a solicitor with his father's firm.

We finally encounter the notable Wright family. If Samuel Stone is the most famous President of The Society, Sir Thomas Wright, the only President of The Society ever to be knighted – at least so far – runs him a close second. Sir Thomas was the son of Joseph Wright of Northampton, being born there in 1838. He was educated privately and first came to prominence in his native Northamptonshire being a member of the Northampton School Board, 1870-76, (Vice-Chairman 1873-1877), and the Corporation of Northampton, 1875-1878. Moving to Leicester he set up in practice and was an Alderman of Leicestershire County Council from 1888-1894, a Councillor for the Borough of Leicester from 1879 to 1888 and an Alderman from 1888 to 1898. 'Alderman' in those days was not an honorific title but betokened a senior working member of an authority. Sir Thomas was instrumental in securing a large extension of Leicester's borough boundaries in 1890-91. Much of the area now known as Clarendon Park, which had previously fallen under the somewhat distant jurisdiction of the Blaby Sanitary Union, was, for example, brought within Leicester at this time. In recognition of his services to the borough, Sir Thomas was made the first Honorary Freeman of Leicester. He was also the founder of the Leicester Children's Hospital and was a major moving force in creating the Leicester Technical and Art Schools, the ancestor of De Montfort University, whose foundation stone he laid. He served as a JP for Leicester and was President of the Leicester Rifle Club and various other sporting and social societies including the Leicestershire Club. Sir Thomas served as President of The Society in 1902. His eldest son, Thomas Harry, was born in Northampton in 1864, but had his education in Leicester at Wyggeston School. He was articled to his father and was admitted in 1885, subsequently becoming a partner in Sir Thomas Wright and Son. T H Wright continued the father/son link by becoming President of The Society in 1920. Sir Thomas's second son was Arthur Ernest Wright, born in Northampton in 1866, but educated at Oakham. He too was articled to his father and was admitted in 1891. He was a keen sportsman and was capped for the North of England at hockey. He played for the Leicestershire County Cricket Club and for the borough at Soccer and Rugby. He was also a Captain in the Volunteer Battalion of the Leicestershire Regiment.

End of an Era

At the end of Victoria's reign The Society served a local legal population that had grown throughout the 19th Century reflecting in particular Leicester's growth as a major manufacturing and commercial centre. White's "Leicestershire" of 1846 (to which allusion was made in Chapter 1) listed some thirty five names of firms. By 1854 Melville's "Directory and Gazetteer of Leicestershire" listed forty two names, but this cannot be taken as an authoritative statement of the number of firms as many practitioners are listed at both their practices and their residences. Rather more reliable is an 1855 Law List formerly in The Society's Library which listed 28 'Country Attorneys' in Leicester. Wright's "Directory of Leicester 1885-86" is more reliable in listing only the names of firms and here we find thirty-nine names, some of whom represent mergers between or expansion of previously well established firms. However, by 1900 Wright's "Directory of Leicestershire and Rutland" lists sixty four firms of solicitors in Leicester, and that was clearly a marked increase on the earlier 1885-86 edition.

Despite the growth in the size of the local profession, however, The Society was still a remarkably homogeneous organisation. It is clear that there were differences between members in respect of religious and political affiliations as well as in leisure, social and philanthropic involvements. Nevertheless the convergences between members were clearly more important than their divergences. First of all the local solicitors' profession was exclusively male. Secondly, it was very largely locally born, bred and educated, even though some of the younger members had gone to University, generally speaking Oxford, Cambridge or London. Thirdly, there was a strong family tradition with sons succeeding fathers, and sometimes grandfathers in their practices. This was particularly true of the Freer and Stone families, but it was also true of, for example, the Tollers, Stevensons and Wrights. Fourthly, The Society served a profession predominantly situated in Leicester, and, even more notably, concentrated in a particular part of the historic borough centre. In 1846 the principal office locations were to be found in Cank Street, Friar Lane and New Street, and, despite some expansions into other streets, these places remained central to the location of solicitors forty years later. It could well be that the existence of The Society's Library in Friar Lane had an influence in congregating members into a small geographical area. Fifthly, though, obviously, county members lived in the area of their practices, the Leicester solicitors, in so far as we know the information, tended to live in the 'desirable' new suburbs opening up along the London Road, ie what is now known as Stoneygate and Knighton. The Leicester Law Society was almost certainly a very cohesive body because it was made up of members who: shared strong professional ethical ties and interests; had a generally common educational background; enjoyed a similar class inheritance, and, perhaps most importantly all knew one another and practised in close proximity.

The Society thus entered the 20th Century with a strong local reputation, founded to a considerable extent on the impeccable reforming credentials of Samuel Stone, and the involvement in local good causes of members such as Thomas Ingram, H A Owston, William Napier Reeve and the Wright and Freer families. It also enjoyed a national reputation and was vigorous and active in promoting its members' interests. It was fully committed to pursuing and preserving the professional status of the local solicitors and with that agenda in place the new century opened.

Chapter 3

The Edwardian Era to the End of the 1ˢᵗ World War

The written records for the new century in the possession of The Society continue with a folio volume entitled *Leicester Law Society No. 3*. This is supplemented by a secretarial correspondence book which consists of a series of numbered sheets of 'bible paper' on which hand written copies of letters sent out by the Hon. Secretary to various people are found. At the front of the volume the recipients of those letters are identified in an alphabetical file. As much of the correspondence is concerned with non or late payment of annual subscriptions, or the improper retention of books borrowed from the Library, this file is an indication of those 'rapped over the knuckles' for their default. At this distance of time it would serve little purpose to list them, but the problems certainly existed and persisted in some cases.

Such domestic concerns, however, were far from The Committee's mind in the 1901 Report when they recorded the 'overwhelming loss' caused to the Nation and the Empire of the death of Queen Victoria. Locally the deaths of, inter alia, Mr William Billson, a founder member and President in 1880, and Mr R S Toller, Treasurer since 1892 and President in 1899 were also recorded. Other notable events in the year so far as Parliament was concerned included the passing of the Youthful Offenders Act which imposed liability on parents and guardians where they had contributed to the commission of an offence by a child or young person by wilful default or habitual neglect to exercise due care of the child: that has an oddly contemporary sound about it. The Intoxicating Liquors (Sale to Children) Act forbade the sale to children under 14 of any intoxicating liquor *except* a pint or upwards in corked and sealed vessels for consumption off the premises. Underage drinking then, as now, was a problem. Locally, The Society had drawn up a minimum scale of conveyancing charges following a special general meeting which had condemned touting, and under cutting. It was not, however, possible to obtain the unanimous support of all members for the new scale. The proposed scale was 50% of that allowed under The Solicitors' Remuneration Act 1881.

When students of the law all solicitors must have received tuition on how the rules relating to frustration of contracts were developed consequent on the postponement of the Coronation of King Edward VII when the monarch had to undergo emergency surgery for an appendectomy. When the ceremony was rearranged in 1902 the Hon. Secretary, W Simpson, wrote on 17th March to E W Williamson at 'The Law Institution', an interesting use of the by then somewhat archaic former name of The Law Society: 'Kindly let me know whether it is proposed to make any arrangements for allowing seats or otherwise to representatives of provincial law societies on the 26th or 27th of June'. Some response must have been received for a further letter of April 12th stated: 'I shall be glad to learn as soon as possible what arrangement (if any) is about to be made for the Procession.' Clearly the Society did not expect to get seats in Westminster Abbey, but was anxious to have some representation along the Coronation processional route.

Correspondence on national affairs such as the Coronation was, however, rare, though there was a regular, if somewhat routine, correspondence between The Society and Chancery Lane. For the most part, however, the majority of the Secretary's work related to the previously alluded to chasing up of late subscriptions and errant volumes, together with Library book orders, printing of various forms and Library catalogues and rates of agency fees between firms. From time to time, however, matters of greater import occurred.

On 10th May 1902 following a committee meeting the previous day, The Society objected to the Office of Works in Westminster about the proposed removal of the High Court Registry and County Court Offices from Friar Lane to Albion Street. Fifty five out of the 105 solicitors in Leicester had their offices within 200 yards of the existing offices and would have been inconvenienced by the move. A 'high powered' delegation consisting of Sir Thomas Wright, Society President, W J Freer, in his capacity as Clerk to the County Council and the Hon. Secretary were deputed to attend the Commissioners 'to emphasise the objections to the proposed removal, in case the proposal is seriously entertained'. The move finally involved a new building in Newarke Street, now The Crown Building of De Montfort University.

Sir Thomas Wright was also informed on 30th June 1902 of various somewhat vague complaints that had been made by a Mr J G Baines against his solicitor, Mr Curtis, of whom more later. Mr Baines had complained to The Society, an interesting example of a local law society assuming a jurisdiction now considered to rest exclusively with national regulatory bodies. The Society requested a full written statement setting out the exact nature of the complaint. Mr Baines submitted two bundles of papers, but on 30th July 1902 these were considered by the Hon. Secretary to disclose no cause of complaint. Mr Baines had in fact already made a complaint to Chancery Lane and had received no redress there. What is of further interest about the 30th July letter is that it is the first typewritten letter in the records; modern 20th Century technology was making its first mark, though it was staunchly resisted for some years thereafter and correspondence continued to be handwritten.

In November 1902 The Society was concerned with the question of whether solicitors should robe when appearing as advocates in the County Court. It was established that this had been the regular practice in Leicester for over 20 years. The question of the appropriateness and style of court dress was clearly an issue then as now. The 1902 Annual Report did, however, record the installation of 'new technology' at Leicester Castle in the form of a telephone for which frequent application had been made by The Society to the County Council.

On 14th July 1903 Thomas Ingram and Henry Deane, the then Registrar of Leicester County Court, were made honorary members of The Society. In Mr Ingram's case this was merited not only in view of his long local service but also his exceptional longevity as a solicitor, see Chapter 2 above. During the same year The Society was much concerned with legislative affairs. The Society wrote to Sir Albert Rollet MP urging him to support the County Courts (Jurisdiction Extension) Bill, and subsequently lobbied a further 6 MPs in the same cause. The Society further argued in support of the Prevention of Corruption Bill, though arguing for the specific exclusion of certain commissions paid to solicitors! This activity in respect of Parliamentary affairs continued into 1904 with multiple letters to MPs supporting the Solicitors' Bill and the reform of the Licensing Acts 1828-1902.

Interest in law reform continued when in 1906 Henry Broadhurst MP was requested to ensure that The Society continued to receive copies of all Bills presented to Parliament. A similar request was made to Franklin Thomasson MP in 1907 and to Williams Eyre MP in 1910. The Society wrote in particular to various MPs in May 1909 expressing apprehension of proposed increases in rates of stamp duty put forward by the Chancellor of the Exchequer, and Messrs Harvey and Burgess were nominated to express The Society's concern, and to make such representations to the government as they though fit. Then as now Stamp Duty was an issue!

More local concerns at this time related to allegations of professional misconduct by a Mr North, a London solicitor, against Mr J L Douglas, a Market Harborough member of The Society. The Society was further involved in allegations of impersonating a solicitor contrary to the Solicitors' Act 1874 by a man simply identified as 'Hodson', while a letter was also sent to a Mr C Newick of Spencer Chambers, Market Street, Leicester, advising him not to style himself as an 'advertising solicitor'. J W Fernyhough, a printer of High Cross Street, was, in 1903, warned against printing forms with 'County Court' headings which could be confused with official forms, while some years later in 1911 a Mr E George Brown, an insurance broker, was warned against acting in debt collection matters as if he was a solicitor, as was William Armston in 1913. These are all interesting examples of The Society using its powers under its constitution to protect the interests of solicitors, but they also represent the assumption of a local private regulatory jurisdiction.

The Society was, however, surely on safer ground when it expressed its concern to the Cornwall Law Society in August 1903 over the latter's Conditions of Sale, which were somewhat ad hoc in nature and handwritten, much in contrast to the prevalent Midlands custom of always using printed forms. The Society further acted in a mediatorial capacity in connection with the disputed costs of a lease between two of its members on 13th July 1904. On 29th November 1904 The Society further acted in defence of its members' interests by undertaking correspondence with Chancery Lane concerning the rights of audience of solicitors in respect of licensing applications in the Borough and County Magistrates' Courts.

Correspondence also occurred from time to time between The Leicester Law Society and The Law Society, and with other local Law Societies over the election of suitable members to the Council of The Law Society. In 1906 a number of sister bodies canvassed for support for their candidates, for example Derby, Worcester, Northampton and Wolverhampton. It is interesting to note that the Hon. Secretary of the Northampton Law Society was the progenitor of a famous firm, namely W B Shoosmith. In 1908 The Leicester Law Society threw its weight behind the Birmingham Law Society's nominee for the Council. The Society lobbied itself in 1909 for the election of Mr J S Dickinson of Messrs Owston, Dickinson, Simpson and Bigg. This correspondence took place with the Berks, Bucks and Oxon Law Society and the Worcester Law Society. J S Dickinson was the son of a Leicester bookkeeper and was born in Northampton Street in the 1850s. He obtained employment with H A Owston at the age of 19 and at 24 years of age he became an articled clerk, being admitted in 1876. He specialised in Company Law and became H A Owston's partner in 1877. In due course Dickinson became Senior Partner and in "The Master Builder" Donald Hunt describes how Dickinson would summon his clerk at 23 Friar Lane, not by telephone but by a speaking tube down which he would send a blast: 'There was a code, for example, one blast "Come to me at once"; two blasts "Come to me sooner than at once"; three blasts "I am choleric".[23] Mr Dickinson was Society President in 1904.

The Annual Report for 1903/04 records the death, inter alia, of Mr Joseph Harvey, a founder member and President in 1877. More happily it also records the revival of The Leicester Law Students Society which had been in suspension for some years and which was now meeting fortnightly at The Library. In 1904/05 the deaths of two further founding members were recorded, Mr Alfred Paget, President in 1867, and Mr George Stevenson, President in 1873.

In 1904 W Simpson stood down as Secretary and Thomas Wright took over the task. He was soon the recipient of a letter from his predecessor requesting enforcement of the rule that smoking was prohibited in the Law Library! Shortly thereafter, on 2nd July 1904, Wright described himself as the holder of the 'unenviable position of Secretary to the Leicester Law Society'.

Earlier allusion has been made to the volume of correspondence concerning the Library, the maintenance of which was clearly an object of prime importance. Inflation not being the problem it has since been on occasion, membership subscriptions and entry fees were still kept at their 19th Century levels of £5.25 election fee for borough members with a yearly subscription of £2.10, while the annual subscription for county members remained £1.5. In return for their payments members clearly expected that the borrowing rules would be enforced, which, it is clear from correspondence of 28th November 1903, 22nd March 1905 and May 19th 1905, they were not: the 1905/06 Annual Report urged members not to borrow more books than they were entitled to, and new borrowing regulations were drawn up and adopted at that time. The Society could, however, be lenient to Library malefactors. Thus in November 1906 a compromise was reached with Messrs Stevenson and Sons who had been fined for the over retention of a book from the Library. The Society refused altogether to excuse the fine, but reduced it to 1/- (5p) in view of, undisclosed, exceptional circumstances. On June 3rd 1907 Mr Cooper and

---

[23] "The Master Builder", p61.

Mr Payne were reminded they had not paid their Library subscriptions, as were Messrs Loseby and Edwards and Watson. Edwards and Loseby were further pursued over the matter of subscriptions on 28th October 1907, and these two again were written to on the same issue in July 1909. There do seem to have been some persistent offenders, but in June 1910 it was Messrs G E and F Bouskell who received a gentle reminder: 'No doubt you have overlooked it but I shall be grateful if you will kindly let Mr Willcox have a cheque.' Such a 'polite request' usually produced a positive response, but even so rather more stern 'second reminders' had to be sent out to certain members in 1911 and 1912. This matter will be further considered below. It certainly appears that it was neither always easy to extract subscriptions from members, nor to get new members to join. Overtures were made to a number of local practitioners in 1910 encouraging them to become members of The Society, while members who had taken on partners were later reminded of the obligation under The Society's Constitution for them to propose the new men as members.

While it was not always easy to levy certain members' subscriptions, there were also difficulties in obtaining volumes desired for the Library, especially where these were sought *gratis*. The lack of Patent Office reports was apparently a cause of concern for members, and, on 2nd July 1904 the Hon. Secretary wrote to a fellow solicitor about how to obtain copies of the Patent and Trade Mark Cases. He further wrote to the Comptroller General of Patents in London on 5th July 1904. His efforts were not to go unrewarded for by 7th July 1904 it had been determined that the Library would henceforth receive free copies of Patent Office reports, in addition to receiving a back run of 23 volumes. 1904 also witnessed discussions of a proposal to move the Law Library to a new location at the rear of the old County Court Office in Friar Lane (now New Street Chambers), but this came to nought. Instead upgrading of the existing Library took place with the installation of electric lighting and new glass in the windows.

The Annual Dinner

At the beginning of the 20th Century, very unlike a century later, The Society's Annual Dinner followed its Annual General Meeting. Copies of correspondence survive from 1904 and 1905 regarding the booking of the Leicester Assembly Rooms for the 1905 and 1906 General Meetings. Invitations to the Annual Dinner were sent not just to members but also to His Honour Judge Wightman Wood of Leicester County Court and to Mr Buzzard KC, the Recorder of Leicester. All this correspondence was undertaken by the Hon. Secretary. There was initially no separate office of Dinner Secretary. This burden of work may well explain why the Secretary's letters throughout the Edwardian period are so terse and to the point: he had no time to write at length! Organising the Annual Dinner could, however, cause problems and in 1905 a Dinner Sub Committee was formed. The 1906 Dinner had to be postponed from mid January until 21st February 1906 because a bye-election had to take place for the Bosworth Division of Leicestershire and the Assembly Rooms were needed for electoral purposes. The 1907 Dinner returned to the traditional mid January date, but by the end of 1907 a decision had been taken to appoint an Annual Dinner Committee. In 1909 the venue for the dinner moved to the Leicestershire Club in Welford Place, but even so the 1910 dinner had to be postponed because of an impending general election. That election, as solicitors will no doubt recall from their study of Parliament as law students, was caused by the decision of H A Asquith's Liberal Government to resign following the rejection of Lloyd George's 'People's Budget' in 1909 by The House of Lords. The Constitutional Crisis thus precipitated by the Upper House continued, of course, until the Peers capitulated in 1911 when the Parliament Act of that year determined that the Upper House of Parliament had no power to veto, inter alia, the Budget accepted by the democratically elected Lower House. Thus did an event of national significance affect the pleasure of members of The Society!

The 1905/06 Annual Report indicates The Society had a membership of 113, a slight decline from 117 the previous year, but there had been a number of deaths including those of Mr H A Owston, President in 1883, Sir Thomas Wright, President in 1902, and Mr J B Fowler, President in 1892.

Education

Mr Robert Harvey was appointed on 15th November 1905 to be The Society's delegate to a meeting in Nottingham on 28th November 1905 to consider the creation of a School of Law at the, then, University College of Nottingham, which was to take place if there was a sufficient degree of support from local Law Societies and Law Students Societies in the area. Harvey himself held the LLB degree and was then the Vice-President of The Society. He was accompanied by Mr A P Moore who held the BA and BCL degrees from Oxford. It must have been considered that these two 'University Men' were the most appropriate delegates to send to the meeting. Following this in February 1906 The Society resolved at its AGM to pay a subscription of £20.00 p.a. towards the funds of the proposed Law School, which The

Committee did in May 1906. The Nottingham University College Legal Education School came into operation in 1909. The University College at Nottingham was then a regional offshoot of the University of London, and, like the sister College that was to be established in Leicester after the end of the Great War, it awarded external London degrees.

On a more social plane the interests of younger members of the local profession were taken into consideration when on 29th October 1907 Mr Josiah Hincks, then care of Messrs Stevenson and Co, was informed that The Committee would allow the use of its rooms at the Library for a preliminary meeting in connection with the formation of the Leicester Law Clerks Football Club.

By 1906/07 membership stood at 114 and The Committee was also pleased to report the much smoother running of the Library following the introduction the previous year of new borrowing rules. The imposition of a few fines had had a salutary effect on members' conduct! The Society was also grouped, along with Stafford, Nottingham, Derby, Northampton, Berks, Bucks and Oxon, and Worcester Law Societies into a Midland District for the purpose of electing Members of the Council of The Law Society. The Society had been successful in obtaining the election of its candidate to The Council in preference to one nominated by Northampton. There was also in 1907 a sub committee appointed to consider how to make the annual dinner more popular. This body proposed to reduce the cost from 1 guinea (£1.5p) to 15/- (75p), to move the venue to the Leicestershire Club in Welford Place where the Billiard Room and Card Room would be available for after dinner pastimes, and that 'a musical entertainment' should accompany the dinner. The Committee was also pleased to record that Mr Huntsman, the Secretary of the Board of Legal Studies in Nottingham, would attend Leicester every Tuesday from 4 to 6 pm to lecture law students for the Intermediate and Final Examinations. It was hoped this would markedly improve the performance of Leicester students in these examinations!

Scandal

On 28th October 1908, following a committee meeting of the same date, the Hon. Secretary wrote as follows to the Secretary at Chancery Lane: 'At a meeting of the Committee of this Society held this afternoon it was desired that I should report to you the fact that Mr William James Curtis, a solicitor of this town and a member of this Society and also a member of The Law Society, has absconded – that a petition in bankruptcy has been presented against him and that he has been adjudicated bankrupt. The failure is a very bad one – you will see by the enclosed newspaper that the creditors are mostly executors whose estates have been squandered and the Committee feel that this is one of those cases in which a certificate to practise should not be further issued to Mr Curtis if it is applied for.'

W J Curtis was in practice at 13 Halford Street, Leicester, in 1891 and 1892 as there is documentary evidence of this in the County Record Office. He also acted as a mortgagee, for a deed of 24th August 1885 survives, witnessed by his clerk, William Herrick, by which he advanced £250 on the security of 9 'messuages' in Edward Road, and 4 in Montague Road – both locations in Clarendon Park. The mortgagors were Mary Ann Pretty and Clement Pretty. In Chapter 2 we encountered firms of solicitors involved in the development of Clarendon Park. Through the kindness of Mr Andrew Harper there is information that W J Curtis was also involved. He lent money to the builder William Holland who went bankrupt on August 20th 1884. Curtis foreclosed the mortgages he had financed thereby acquiring the freehold of some three dozen properties. It was then discovered that Holland had failed to build in accordance with the byelaws in that some houses had single brick walls, and an acrimonious correspondence then ensued between Curtis and the local authority for the area at the time, Blaby Sanitary Union. Once this was settled Curtis lent further money of which he was a trustee to enable mortgagors to purchase the houses which he had come to own, and the transaction with the Prettys appears to fall into that category. Curtis's downfall may have resulted from over speculation in property transactions of this sort. Following bankruptcy he seems to have disappeared without trace.

The unfortunate W J Curtis, (a member of The Society since 1878) was not, however, the W F Curtis who was *elected* into membership of The Society on January 20th 1909 at the Annual General Meeting. However, this later W F Curtis had to be chased for both his entrance fee and annual subscription on July 20th 1909. Poor young Curtis (he was born in 1880 and admitted in 1903) was obviously having difficulty establishing his practice as for a while it appeared he would find it impossible to pay his entrance fee and annual subscription and so might have to be struck from the list of members. Fortunately things did not reach that sorry pass, but Curtis had to be chased again for his subscription in 1910 when he was 'reminded' twice. There was further correspondence in relation to a conveyancing taxation issue with 'Dear Curtis' on 31st October 1910, but he was once again in arrears with his subscription in 1911 when he was reminded of this both half way through and at the end of the year. The same problem recurred in 1912 and 1913 when, once again, two letters were sent. Curtis, however, managed to stabilise his practice and we shall encounter him again in connection with the Poor Mans Lawyer Scheme, though sadly his subscription had to be chased three times again in 1914. Mr W F Curtis practised on his own account in Granby Street. He died on 24th December 1962.

Social Concerns

The first mention of The Society becoming involved in subscriptions to the Solicitors' Benevolent Association occurs in 1908, though only a few individual members volunteered to pay! In 1913, however, The Society as a body donated 10 guineas (£10.50) to The Association. In that year The Society also decided to establish a Poor Mans Lawyer Association for Leicester, though discussion of this proposal appears to have been protracted. Thirteen solicitors initially agreed to attend on one evening each week in the Law Library at Friar Lane from 6 until 7 pm to 'advise any poor person on any legal subject'. The 'poor' in question were those unable to pay for advice and not members of societies or unions who could look after their interests. The scheme was to commence on the first Monday in 1914. The obligation to attend then fell only four times a year. A second rota was established of solicitors willing to carry forward cases initially received and sent to them by solicitors on the first rota. Nineteen members were on the second rota. It was also determined that a second person should also be in attendance on the Monday evening sessions to take notes of cases received and advice given, 'as a precaution lest the Solicitor might hereafter be charged with saying what he in fact did not say'. The constitution of the scheme is preserved in The Society's Annual Report for 1913/14. In addition to the restriction that 'none but the poor shall be advised', the rules further provided that: 'the Solicitor advising must not allow his name to be mentioned to the applicant for advice ... that he must not act professionally in any case upon which he has advised as a Poor Man's Lawyer ... That correspondence must be conducted only on the note paper of the department and signed only with the initial of the Solicitor, unless the correspondence be with a Government Department, when the Solicitor should sign his name ...'

The first solicitors involved were the Brays, father and son, M J Hincks, R A Loseby, S Payne, J J Sharpe (of Coalville even though the scheme operated in Leicester), J Hincks, W F Curtis, S Woodrow, Evan Barlow, A Bertram

Plummer, C S Bigg and K McAlpin. (Mr McAlpin served as President of The Society in 1926, Mr Bigg in 1941 and Mr A B Plummer in 1942.) These solicitors were also asked by the Hon. Secretary to promote the scheme, though direct advertising of its existence in newspapers was discouraged as 'distasteful to solicitors'. Various other organisations were also written to to advise of the scheme's existence, eg the Adult School Union and the Hosiery Manufacturers' Association. The working constitution of the scheme was based on a similar one operating in Manchester and Salford.

Some Edwardian Characters

A vignette of practice at this time has been provided by Mr Jeremy Barlow. Evan Barlow, admitted in 1897, set up his practice at 1 Berridge Street, Leicester, in 1902 and soon made £200.00 p.a. income. He determined to operate a mixed general practice, but was fortunate to act locally for both the Royal Automobile Club and the Automobile Association which in those days met the costs of their members' motoring cases. Evan Barlow also began his firm's long association with licensing practice. He was joined by his son, E Morgan Barlow, in 1927, while Jeremy Barlow completed the third generation in 1957. Evan Barlow, as we shall further find in the next chapter, was quite a character. A severe storm once blew the roof off his premises, yet he wrote a cheerful letter from 'Evan Barlow, Solicitors, ½ Berridge Street!' Mr Barlow was fond of snuff and used two of his senior legal executives, Mr Plumb and Mr Underwood, to fetch his supplies from the tobacconists. They, however, always had to close Mr Barlow's door quietly on delivering the goods as their principal suffered from gout. Even the slightest vibration could cause him agony and rumour had it that a number of office boys had been instantly dismissed for forgetting that!

Another character whose practice set off at this time was Basil Edwards, a member of The Society from 1906, and still active in 1947. He 'enjoyed an occasional glass'. Once before the Justices one of his cases was held over for lunch in order for a witness to arrive. By the time the case came to be heard Basil had consumed more than an occasional glass, and the Chairman of the Bench said the case should be adjourned. Basil was not best pleased and asked for the reason for this decision. The Chairman was forced to state that he did not think Mr Edwards was in sufficient control of his senses. Rising unsteadily to his feet, Basil stated, with the gracious gravity of the inebriated, that this was the first time in his long career that this Bench had come to a correct decision!

Where nowadays could one encounter characters such as Evan Barlow and Basil Edwards!

The last years of peace

The 1909/10 report begins by recording two deaths, Mr N C Daniel who had been a member since 1892, and more notably, Thomas Ingram who died at the age of 98, having been Treasurer of The Society from 1861 to 1892 and President in 1868. The committee reported the membership of The Society at 115 most of whom were still concentrated in Leicester, though there were, leaving aside retired honorary members, 30 who were in the outlying towns of Ashby, Coalville, Loughborough, Lutterworth, Melton Mowbray and Market Harborough. The majority of members had received their education in the 'traditional' fashion, ie via articles. There were, however, a number with degrees:

A H Bennett, LLB London; C S Bigg, BA Oxon; C J Billson, MA Oxon; F W Billson, LLB London; F W Harris, MA Oxon; W C Harris, MA Cantab; R Harvey, LLB London; E J Holyoak, MA Cantab; Sherard Joyce, MA Cantab; A P Moore, BA, BCL Oxon; W J New, BA London; G C Sprigge, BA Cantab, and G F Stevenson, LLB London. Possession of a first degree was still exceptional, the possession of a second virtually unheard of!

The Committee's report otherwise detailed the addition of a number of titles to the Law Library, and mentioned that an attempt should be made to standardise opening hours in Leicester, at least during the summer months, at 9.00 am to 5.30 pm. This was then considered a form of early closing. The Committee had, however, been unable to obtain the agreement of members to this.

The other matters in the report relate to the continuing concerns of The Society with: legislative matters (in particular the Royal Commission on Divorce and the unsuccessful County Courts Bill); the Solicitors' Benevolent Association (3 members had received substantial benefits and the Committee urged members to become individual subscribers to the SBA), and representation on The Law Society Council. In this connection Mr A H Burgess, a member of The Society, had stepped down as a member of the Council and another member had been nominated in his place but had failed to gain the requisite number of votes from 7 provincial Law Societies forming the Midland District. With regard to elections a rule that Committee membership should expire after two years' service appears to have been strongly enforced and new members were duly elected in the place of those stepping down. These requirements did not apply, inter alia, to the Secretary and Treasurer.

The pattern established in the 1909/10 report is continued in 1910/11. There had been one death, Thomas Watts who had been President in 1894, but membership had risen to 116, and further volumes had been added to the Library. The Society had continued to be concerned with legislative matters, in particular certain proposals under the Finance Act to charge Increment Value Duty and the duties of solicitors acting in connection with land sales that could attract such a levy. The Society had also protested to the Lord Chief Justice about a proposal to abolish Leicester Assizes and group Leicester with Nottingham and Derby. The protest was successful, but it is interesting to note that the proposal was another early example of a tendency to make Nottingham the East Midlands 'legal capital' just as today it is a Civil Trial Centre for the High Court, while Leicester has only a Criminal Trial jurisdiction. The Society was clearly here exercising its duty to protect its members' interests.

Two other matters of domestic interest are worthy of note, as they relate to concerns still current a century later. The Committee was concerned that annual expenditure was exceeding normal annual income and that the reserves were being drawn upon. The Committee sought means *not* to increase income but to reduce expenditure, for example by discontinuing the annual payment to the Nottingham University College Law School, but that proposal came to nought at the AGM. There was also concern over the Annual Dinner. Current members, and especially that one charged with the duty of Dinner Secretary, may be interested to learn that out of an average membership of 114 over the previous three years, only 17 had bothered to attend the Dinner. The Committee had tried to make the event more attractive by changes of venue, reduced costs and adding musical entertainment, but all to no avail and they felt inclined to recommend discontinuation of the event. The AGM, however, determined that a dinner should be held, but that tickets should not cost more than 5/- (25p) – still a substantial sum for the time.

The 1911/1912 Report follows the pattern of its predecessors. New titles had been added to the Library and, once again, members were urged to support the SBA, it being noted that of the 170 solicitors in the County, only 30 subscribed to the SBA. Membership of the Society stood at 114, so clearly the majority of Leicestershire's solicitors were members, though an appreciable minority were not, and one suspects they were largely outside Leicester. The lack of support for the SBA was a particular embarrassment as, inter alia, the Report records the death of Samuel Harris, a founder member of The Society and President in 1889. He had also been a Trustee of the SBA and that Association had asked for another nomination from Leicester, but the SBA had additionally pointed out the poor level of local support for its work.

The situation concerning the SBA was also central to the 1912/1913 report and AGM, and yet again the concern of the Committee was expressed at the poor level of local support. Once again in support of its members' interests The Society had protested against a change of practice whereby Probate and Other Duties had to be paid in London instead of via provincial offices of Inland Revenue and Excise. Sir Maurice Levy, Bart., MP, had taken this matter up on The Society's behalf. Also to safeguard members, The Committee drew attention to the House of Lords' decision in 1911 in *Lloyd v Grace Smith & Co* with which solicitor readers will, no doubt, be familiar from their student days in connection with vicarious liability. Solicitors were reminded they would be liable for acts done by a Clerk for his own benefit provided they were in the scope of the authority delegated to him.

In view, however, of the small number of students from Leicester attending lectures at the Nottingham University College Law School it was recommended that the annual subscription of £20.00 should be discontinued. This notion was carried at the AGM. It was clearly felt that the 'core business' of The Society was the maintenance of its Library. The AGM did, however, request the Committee to consider an alteration of that rule of The Society which required that no member of a firm should become a member of The Society unless his partner or partners also took on membership.

The report also noted the death of Stephen Pilgrim who had been a founder member of The Society in 1860 and had been President in 1875. Membership had risen to 118.

The 1913/14 report records the deaths of two other past Presidents, G H Blunt, Hon. Secretary from 1875 to 1884, and President in 1898, and G F Stevenson, President in 1909. These and other deaths, despite new members being elected, reduced membership to 117. There were a number of concerns ongoing from previous years, in particular the issue of the payment of Probate and Other Duties. Despite the best efforts of Sir Maurice Levy, the Treasury had remained adamant on this issue. Similarly the Committee reported that it had continued to press for a Civil Assize jurisdiction to remain in Leicester. The Poor Man's Lawyer

Scheme to which earlier allusion was made had also come under national inspection, and the President, Mr E J Holyoak, had attended meetings in London on the issue. The Society declared its willingness to cooperate in the creation of a Poor Man's Lawyer Scheme for England and Wales provided this would receive the approval of the General Council of the Bar and the Council of The Law Society.

On a more local level The Committee reported that it had reconsidered that rule of the Constitution providing that no member of a firm could be a member of The Society unless his partner or partners also became members, but that it was 'not disposed to recommend that any alteration be made in the rule'.

A name of national note does, however, appear in this report. The Treasurer, Mr T H Wright, moved: 'That the thanks of the Society be given to J Ramsay Macdonald MP, for his kindness in sending the Society prints of the Bills introduced in Parliament'. Ramsay Macdonald was, of course, to go on to become the United Kingdom's first Labour Prime Minister.

The outbreak of war in August 1914 initially made little formal impact on the functioning of The Society. There is one letter from the Hon. Secretary of 21st October 1914 acknowledging that certain articled clerks were 'engaged in this war'. However, the Annual Report for 1914/15 is rather more concerned with recording the deaths of His Honour Judge Wightman Wood, who for some 20 years was Judge of Leicester County Court, and four members of The Society, including W F Beardsley, President in 1910. Even so, with new elections membership continued to stand at 117. The Hon. Secretary's work continued to be much concerned with the perennial problem of chasing membership subscriptions. The Poor Man's Lawyer Scheme, now known as the Leicester Poor Man's Lawyer Association, made its report indicating that in its first year it had dealt with 302 cases: Workmen's Compensation (40); Matrimonial Troubles (54); Landlord and Tenant (29); Master and Servant (37); Debts (36); Wills and Intestacies (24); Miscellaneous (82). Some 64 cases had been referred to solicitors on the Second Rota, though only 34 of the advisees had then attended further. In some of these cases, however, substantial sums had been recovered.

The War, however, soon impinged more directly on the life of The Society. A number of Belgian Refugee Lawyers had fled to the UK in consequence of the occupation of their country. Many had no resources and had been deprived of their livelihood. In December 1914 the Hon. Secretary responded to a letter from E J Cox-Sinclair of 2, Plowden

Buildings, Temple, London, stating that The Society was anxious to help 'those unfortunate Belgian lawyers who are stranded in this country'. Relief work was undertaken by The Law Society and a grant of 20 guineas (£21) was made towards this work. A rather more immediate impact of war was the result of men joining the colours. All the articled clerks in the Borough, save four, had 'joined up', together with 19 solicitors, most of whom had been commissioned. It was determined by the AGM that no annual subscription should be charged to any of those serving with the forces, but no Annual Dinner was held on the basis that, given the circumstances, it would be 'undesirable'. Despite war time restrictions, however, a number of volumes had been added to the Library, including volume runs of Halsbury's Laws, The Revised Reports, Times Law Reports and 400 volumes of Law Reports presented by Mr J T Hincks.

The Society's Committee met on only three recorded occasions in 1916, the first meeting being concerned to deal with letters written by a Mr P C Osborne who had signed them ' M C Turner, Solicitor'. The matter had been dealt with by the County Court Judge who had delivered a 'severe reprimand' and it was thought no further police action should be taken. The Annual Report for 1915/16 reported the death of two members, one being S F Stone, son of Samuel Stone, a joining member in 1860 and President in 1888. Membership stood at 115. One member had been killed on active service, Major H J F Jeffries, while Lieutenant F N Tarr, an articled clerk, had also been killed. Four more solicitors and articled clerks had joined the forces, while 9 solicitors had attested their readiness to serve.

On a happier note the annual report recorded the continued acquisition of volumes for the Library, and the continuing work of the Leicester Poor Man's Law Association which had dealt with 302 cases in 1914 and 180 in 1915. Mr Alfred Halkyard, an articled clerk with Mr K McAlpin, had been placed first in the order of merit in the First Class for Honours of The Law Society's examinations and had been awarded the Daniel Reardon Prize (£22) and the Clements Inn Prize (£9). He had also been awarded the Broderip Gold Medal for his knowledge of Real Property and Conveyancing. Mr Halkyard was also entitled to receive a prize to the value of £10 given by The Society. The prize consisted of "The Cambridge Modern History" and Pollock and Maitland's "History of English Law". Mr Halkyard was unable to accept the prize in person as he was on active service. The Cambridge History set is now in Leicester University Library.

The Society's funds were in good order, with a balance of £862.11s.7d. (£862.55 approximately) and a donation of 15 guineas (£15.75) was given to the Solicitors' Benevolent Association in lieu of the collection normally taken for the SBA at the Annual Dinner as, once more, that was not held. Indeed it was recorded that it was 'undesirable that any Dinner should be held until the War has ceased'.

By 1916 the War was certainly impinging more on the life of The Society. The Society sent its congratulations to David Lloyd George on becoming Prime Minister. Lloyd George was, of course, a solicitor by profession, and The Committee was asked to consider whether £100 of The Society's funds should be invested in the War Loan. On January 18th 1917 Lloyd George's Secretary wrote from 10 Downing Street thanking The Society for 'their kind good wishes'. The Society's funds remained virtually in the same balance as in 1915, but fewer books were purchased for the Library. The Poor Man's Lawyer Scheme had continued, but there was a decrease in the number of cases received to 124. This may have been the consequence of so many men being on active service. The Society also expressed its willingness to attend at the YMCA or any of the field hospitals in its area to assist any soldier needing advice.

34 solicitors were by now on active service, including Alfred Halkyard whom we have already encountered. He had become a 2nd Lieutenant in the 8th Leicestershire Regiment. In addition 17 Articled Clerks were also serving, as were 57 Clerks. The numbers of men on active service must have had a considerable impact on the functioning of the profession locally, and one must ask whether women were recruited to fill the posts of the absent clerks; at that time, of course, women could not become solicitors. However, on 30th April 1918 The Committee considered the proposed Solicitors (Qualification of Women) Bill. The Secretary had received a circular letter from the Associated Provincial Law Societies asking that local MPs should be lobbied to oppose the proposal on the basis that it was 'inopportune' as so many solicitors were on active service.

The 1917/1918 Annual Report once again recorded the continuing work of the Poor Man's Lawyer Scheme. Despite the War and the absence of many on war service, a solicitor had been in attendance every Monday evening, though the number of cases received had once more declined, slightly, to 120. Few books had been added to the Library in 1917. Maybe in consequence of this the balance in hand on the accounts had risen to some £933, and out of this a donation of 15 guineas (£15.75) was given to the SBA. The number of solicitors who were or who had been on active service was now 36, of whom two had been killed, the previously mentioned Major H J F Jeffries and Lieutenant J W Spanton. 16 Articled Clerks had seen service of whom a further one had been killed, Lieutenant J P Hodgkins, while two had been awarded the Military Cross, Captains A H

Joliffe and C F Wright. 61 Clerks had also seen service of whom 3 had been killed, while one, Staff Sergeant N P Laird had received the Distinguished Conduct Medal.

The 1917/1918 report looked forward to the end of the War, though it recorded the names of yet more local solicitors and their clerks who had joined the services. 37 solicitors were recorded as having seen service. Captain A Stone had been killed in action, while Lieutenant Alfred Halkyard had further distinguished himself by being awarded the Military Cross. (Alfred Halkyard was officially admitted in February 1918 and was elected as a member of The Society in 1920. He later became a partner with his former principal in the firm of McAlpin and Halkyard of 34, Friar Lane, and retired in 1958.) 19 Articled Clerks had seen service; Lieutenant T F McCarthy had been awarded the Military Cross but had also been killed in action. Major J S Parsons had been awarded the Distinguished Service Order. 72 Clerks had seen service of whom 3 had been killed, while Sergeant A H Pollard had received the Distinguished Conduct Medal. 3 civilian members of The Society had died during year, including Mr Joseph Hands of Loughborough, President in 1907.

The Poor Man's Lawyer Scheme had continued, despite a dearth of volunteers, and had dealt with 106 cases. The Library had received rather more additions than in the previous year, but The Society's account still had a healthy balance of some £915.

Despite opposing the qualification of women as solicitors, The Society noted the provisions of The Solicitors' (Articled Clerks) Act 1918 which enabled men 'approved' by the Master of the Rolls, to have a period service in the Army to be counted as Service under Articles, and further to exempt any person from the requirements of the intermediate examination – the preliminary to the final examinations for qualification.

The Society returned to more local matters in noting the retirement of Mr Deane as Registrar of the County Court, District Registrar of the High Court and Registrar in Bankruptcy and the appointment of Mr Squire to these offices. It also congratulated Mr A J Loseby on completing 50 years service as Registrar of Market Bosworth County Court. Mr Loseby had also presented a book of his own poems to The Society. One member had been prevented from continuing in practice because of rheumatoid arthritis and Mr Evan Barlow agreed to raise a relief fund for him. Over £500 was collected, sufficient to make a monthly payment of £8.6s.8d. (approximately £8.33) to the member in question. The Society here was clearly acting in the interests of at least one of its members.

The Return of Peace

Despite the Armistice of 11th November 1918, at the first peacetime committee meeting of The Society it was agreed that while the AGM should be held at 3.00 pm on 15th January 1919, ie the traditional period, once again there should be no dinner. Once the new Committee was in place one of its first tasks was consideration of a proposal from The Law Society that legislation should be promoted making it compulsory for would-be entrants to the profession to attend for a minimum period at a Public Law School. The Committee unanimously agreed to support this proposal. However, in July 1919 The Committee argued that the forced attendance of articled clerks from remote country districts might give rise to difficulties and argued that the Council of The Law Society should be given a dispensing power in cases of special hardship, that is those 'living at a distance from any Law School'.

With the return of peace The Society was once more able to concentrate its attentions on its traditional concerns. To protect its members' interests The Committee had written to sister societies in Derbyshire, Lincolnshire, Nottinghamshire, Northamptonshire, and Warwickshire asking that their members should use the Leicester Law Society's Conditions of Sale in all cases involving sales of property in Leicestershire. Nottinghamshire and Warwickshire agreed to promote this practice. The AGM also agreed that the whole issue of conveyancing scale charges be referred to The Committee because some members were opposed to the practice of certain solicitors charging less than the amount permitted under the Solicitors' Remuneration Act: cut price conveyancing had clearly become an issue!

The Poor Man's Lawyer Scheme had continued to operate and in 1918/19 had dealt with 128 cases, an increase on previous years.

A matter of some contention affecting members in their capacity as employers was a communication from the National Federation of Law Clerks which, inter alia, requested the formation of a Joint Council of Solicitors and Clerks to: adjust and settle all questions affecting the conditions of service and interests of Clerks; reinstatement of all ex-soldier Clerks at increased wages to reflect increased costs of living; the establishment of a minimum scale of remuneration for Clerks; equal remuneration for equal service, *irrespective of sex*; the extension of the principle of participation by employees in the profits of their employers' businesses; the institution of tests and the granting of certificates of efficiency to Clerks to test and demonstrate their knowledge of Law and Practice, and Clerks of 10 years standing to be exempt from the preliminary examination, to be exempt from Articles and to have permission to take the Intermediate and Final Examination by stages – the '10 year man' qualification route.

These somewhat wide reaching proposals had been the subject of a meeting at Chancery Lane, but no agreement had been reached by the time of the 1919 report. They do, however, indicate that change would be in the air for the future, and that some changes would be radical.

The Society reported that virtually all the Solicitors, Articled Clerks and Clerks who had seen active service had been demobilized. It recorded a final death tally of 3 Solicitors, 3 Articled Clerks and 3 Clerks. Those killed were: Major H J F Jeffries, 5th Leicestershire Regiment; Second Lieutenant J W Spanton, 6th Rifle Brigade; Captain A Stone, 5th Sherwood Foresters; Lieutenant J P Hodgkins, 4th Leicestershire Regiment; Second Lieutenant T F McCarthy, Loyal North Lancashire Regiment; Lieutenant F H Tarr, 4th Leicestershire Regiment; Sergeant H Aspden, 3rd Leicestershire Regiment; Trooper F P Brown, Leicestershire Yeomanry, and Private C Ward, 4th Leicestershire Regiment. It is interesting to note this comparatively low death rate. Remembering that the average life expectancy of newly arrived young infantry officers on the Western Front could be measured in days, almost minutes, the men from legal practice in Leicestershire might seem to have borne charmed lives.[24] This must have had implications for the future for few gaps in the ranks of the local profession had been caused by death on active service. In addition it would appear that those attributes of The Society identified in the previous chapter, ie its social, geographical and familial cohesiveness had continued to give support throughout the difficult wartime years, but what might the future bring?

---

[24] There is, however, a more mundane explanation. First of all The Society's records note only those killed in action, not those wounded and invalided out of service. Secondly it may be assumed from the spread of units in which the men in question served (which included Infantry Battalions, The Army Service Corps, The Royal Engineers, The Royal Marines, The Royal Artillery [both Garrison and Field], the RAF and the Navy) that not all were in front line service. Indeed in any unit one might expect highly trained legal personnel to be placed in Regimental and Brigade Staff positions away from the field of battle.

Chapter 4

The Inter War Years

The number of firms listed in Kelly's "Directory for Leicestershire and Rutland", (1922 Edition), was 83.[25] Kelly is, of course, not always the most reliable of sources as it is not always made clear whether a Solicitor is in sole practice or in partnership. In addition, as previously stated, double listing can occur as both home and business addresses are sometimes given. In addition a number of firms were multi-locational, and that was particularly true of firms in Loughborough and Melton Mowbray. By 1925 Kelly listed 78 firms, but the apparent decline can be accounted for by the factors outlined above. In 1928 the figure was 79 and in 1938 when the Directory related only to Leicester the number was 55 firms. The problems relating to establishing the number of firms are largely concerned with Leicester as the number of county practices in Loughborough, Hinckley, Melton Mowbray, Market Harborough, Ashby, Lutterworth, Coalville and Market Bosworth remained generally constant. Even so it would appear that the Borough, and subsequently City, of Leicester supported between 50 and 55 firms between the wars. The majority of these remained focussed on the area of Friar Lane, New Street and Millstone Lane, and most remained small family affairs with but few members, though the names of long departed former members were retained. The membership of The Society was generally between 120 and 129 between 1920 and 1930. By 1939 it had risen, slowly, to 142.

It will be remembered that the issue of Scale Charges for Conveyancing had been referred to The Committee in 1919, and in July 1920 The Committee's decision following a Special General Meeting of The Society was that all conveyancing work should henceforth be charged for according to the scale rates fixed by the meeting, save where a departure could be justified on a case by case basis. Most Leicester member firms assented to this proposal, but as late as September 1920 two had yet to assent. The Annual Report for 1920/21 reported the names of those firms

---

[25] This includes 4 firms in Rutland. One should not be too hard on Kelly, even today the telephone book listings are not always reliable.

who had agreed to the Scale Charges. The scheme, however, could not be applied to County members as they had to work with solicitors in adjoining counties 'all of whom had scales of charges which differed from that of the Leicester Society'. The Report continued: 'The Committee feels that it is a subject of congratulation that a minimum scale has at last been agreed on to which every practising Solicitor who is a member of the Society was able to agree.' - remarkable unanimity indeed.

The report otherwise contained the by now usual items of information. The deaths of three former presidents, Alfred Howard Burgess (1897), Henry Deane (1891) and Colonel Robert Harvey (1906) were noted with regret. The Poor Man's Lawyer Scheme had continued and in 1920 had dealt with 117 cases of which 36 were referred onwards for action. There had been a number of additions to the Library. At the AGM The Society's accounts continued to show a healthy balance of approximately £864, and a donation of 10 guineas (£10.50) was made to the Solicitors' Benevolent Association. Leaving aside honorary members the membership was 114, but of those only 66 were also members of The Incorporated Law Society, and the AGM resolved that it was desirable for it to be compulsory for all Solicitors to be members of this body.

Safeguarding the Library continued to be a major function of The Society, for in February 1921 The Committee replied to a letter from the General Secretary of the Leicester, Leicestershire and Rutland College that 'the Society had no books of value which they felt they would be justified in parting with, since editions of legal text books rapidly became out of date and that any surplus books as the Society possessed would be useless to the College'. Many years in the future, however, The Society's Library would find a home, albeit temporary, in what had by then become The University of Leicester.

The refusal to donate old books to the University College did not, however, prevent the College Principal, Dr Rattray, from requesting The Society to assist with the provision of Law Lectures either by providing a lecturer from its membership, or by making a donation towards a lecturer's stipend. This was felt to be an issue that could only be resolved by a Special Meeting of The Society. For the meantime The Society's main educational emphasis remained its Library, even though Messrs Owston and Co had increased the rent on the premises. The outcome was that it was determined to leave the issue of Dr Rattray's request to the next AGM, but that one held on 15th February 1922 failed to deal with the issue.

The 1921/1922 Annual Report as usual recorded deaths, including Mr Benjamin Arthur Shires, President in 1911, and the continuing work of the Poor Man's Lawyer Scheme which had in 1921 dealt with 118 cases of which 35 were referred onwards. This Report also refers to the holding of the Annual Dinner for 1921 on 12th January, so the historic practice of The Society seems to have been restored at this point.

In defence of its members' interests The Society took grave exception to the proposal from the Inland Revenue to remove The Stamp Office from Leicester. In this The Society obtained the support of The Leicester Chamber of Commerce, The Leicester Ratepayers and Property Owners Association, The House Agents' Society, The Bankers' Clearing House and local MPs. Various organisations would be put to expense and inconvenience if documents could no longer be stamped in Leicester. The Inland Revenue argued that the volume of business transacted was insufficient to occupy the time of an expensive legally trained officer and that a number of local stamp offices were to be shut. The campaign to retain stamping facilities in Leicester continued into the next year, but the Report for 1922/23 had to record the failure of the struggle. By then, however, The Society had, once more, to address whether the Assizes, the forerunner in part of The Crown Court System and The High Court on Circuit, should no longer be held in Leicester. However, it was not felt opportune at that point to register a protest.

The Annual Report for 1922/23 recorded a number of deaths, including that of Mr George Rowlatt, President in 1890, the continuation of The Poor Man's Lawyer Scheme which in 1922 had dealt with 139 cases – a steady increase in the volume of its work – and the purchase of further volumes for the Library. The Society also noted the passing of the Solicitors Act 1922 which, inter alia, required the overwhelming majority of articled clerks to attend a course of legal education for a year at an approved Law School. No mention was made then of the removal in 1919 of the bar on women qualifying as Solicitors. The profession in Leicester was male and was to remain so for many years to come.

Education

It will be remembered that The Society had ended its support for the University College of Nottingham Law teaching programme before The Great War, preferring to concentrate its resources on the Library. However, with the 'compulsory year' imposed thinking had to alter. The 1923/24 Report therefore, while referring with the usual routine matters of the number of cases dealt with by The Poor Man's Lawyer (107) and the maintenance of the Library (in which connection it is pleasing to note that Alfred Halkyard was appointed Honorary Librarian – of which more below), was primarily concerned with the need for a Law School. Nottingham Law Society had intimated that a Law School was to be established at Nottingham University College, and asked The Society for its support. Initially The Committee wished to speak to Dr Rattray at Leicestershire and Rutland University College, having, let it be remembered, not been over enthusiastic in its response to his earlier overtures. The Committee felt that if it was not possible to establish a Law School in Leicester that support should be given to Nottingham, but *with and through* the Leicestershire and Rutland University College. In the event The Committee decided to support Nottingham's application for an approved Law School. That School was to be subject to a Committee representing the various law societies together with members from the two University Colleges, with lectures being given, according to need, at each centre.

On a more parochial level, The Committee minutes record, for the first time in years, correspondence in connection with unpaid fines in respect of borrowings from the Library. A number of firms owed quite considerable sums and their names were recorded – maybe an early example of 'naming and shaming'. The Library was clearly in need of supervision and hence the proposal in December 1923 that an Honorary Librarian be appointed. As we have seen this task fell to Alfred Halkyard.

The Law School issue kept The Committee quite busy throughout 1924. In particular it was felt that fees were too high, particularly in respect of the Intermediate Examination. The cost of legal education was clearly an issue then as now. The Society determined that a request should be made for a reduction in fees, but that if this proved unsuccessful principals of Articled Clerks should be asked to make a contribution to their fees. Funding was also clearly an issue.

Domestic Concerns

The 1924/1925 report recorded, inter alia, the deaths of Mr B H C Fox, President in 1925, Mr W L Salusbury-White, President in 1903, and Mr W J New, President in 1913. More happily congratulations were given to Mr Herbert Simpson on his election as Mayor of Leicester. The Society also congratulated its members for keeping honourably to the Conveyancing Scale Charges, which were amended by resolution. Where members charged less they had been conscientious in reporting and explaining their actions, though one case of undercharging had been investigated by The Committee. This activity provides another example of the quasi-regulatory powers of The Society.

The Poor Man's Lawyer Scheme had continued and had dealt with 115 cases, while the Library had been kept up to date by the purchase of new volumes. The membership stood at 120 and, the funds of The Society being in a healthy state, a donation of 10 guineas (£10.50) was made to the Solicitors' Benevolent Association, while a further £250 was invested in 3½% Conversion Stock, this was followed by a further £150 investment in 1926. A proposal that the Society should make a contribution to the Diocesan Fund for the establishment of the Bishopric of Leicester was deferred until the 1926 AGM where it was not, however, considered.

An important change was proposed to the Annual Dinner arrangements at this time. It was argued that the Dinner should be more in the nature of a public event, and that representatives of other professions in Leicester should be invited to attend, with each member being entitled to bring one guest. The AGM on this occasion failed to agree this.

1925 is a date engraven in every Law Student's studies, and The Society was much concerned with the impact the new property legislation would have on practice. The concept of what is now called Continuing Professional Development was raised, seemingly for the first time. A course of six lectures on the new law was given by a visiting speaker from Halifax in November 1925 and these were attended by over 150 members and their clerks. Such was the volume of attendance that surplus income was generated! The 1925 legislation also eroded local autonomy to a degree. A National Form of Conditions of Sale had been drawn up under the terms of the legislation by The Law Society and there was little option but to adopt this in Leicestershire as from 1st January 1926. Solicitors were also entitled to charge higher fees under the Solicitors' Remuneration Act General Order 1925, but The Committee recommended that the existing local scale of conveyancing charges be adhered to. This seemed to be working well and those member firms who felt constrained to depart from it from time to time were generally punctilious in reporting and explaining their actions to The Committee. Two alleged cases of undercharging were investigated in 1925 but in each case it was found that the firm in question had made a genuine mistake. Once again it is interesting to note the existence of the local quasi-regulatory power and that it was relied on in preference to a national, albeit persuasive, legislative scheme. The Society, of course, had a Standing Rule of Practice adopted in 1900 that the practice of offering free conveyances stood condemned 'as being a form of unfair competition, as well as fraught with possible prejudice to purchasers'. The ability of The Society to exercise these powers, founded generally not on statute but on contractual agreement which might nowadays be condemned as an anti-competitive cartel, depended on nearly all Leicester Solicitors being members of The Society. They were bound by ties of contract, shared ethical codes, kinship and friendship, and, of course, self interest. The Society's influence in County areas where there were fewer members would appear to have been less considerable.

The Law and the Poor

Though the Poor Man's Lawyer Scheme had continued, and had dealt with 131 cases, change was in the air following Mr Justice Lawrence's Report on the Poor Persons' Rules. The current national provision for the poor was clearly a failure and an alternative, which would involve more work and responsibility for Solicitors, was clearly needed. The Lawrence Report proposed that each Provincial Law Society should appoint a committee to undertake control of poor persons' cases. This committee, to be elected every three years, was to consist of between 7 and 13 Solicitors who would have power to nominate a panel of 'conducting solicitors' to take on cases for poor persons. The committee would be serviced by a Secretary or Clerk, on an honorary basis!

It has to be remembered that in those long distant days of generally low taxation and low, indeed even negative, inflation, and at a time when state provision of public services was much less developed than it is now, the concept of voluntary work by professional men was quite commonly accepted. It was reinforced by a sense of local pride and moral obligation. Similar voluntary activity was undertaken in hospitals by members of the medical profession. There was also a fear, expressed by The Committee in the Annual Report, that if a voluntary local poor persons' scheme could not be made to work 'failure ... would undoubtedly lead to the formation of a State Department to deal with these cases'. Such a 'National Legal Service' has never, of course, been set up, but it is interesting to reflect that Central Government, despite the proliferation of State Welfare Services since 1945, and the imposition of considerable taxation burdens in various forms, still puts pressure on Solicitors to undertake Pro Bono work.

The necessary resolution to create the Poor Persons' Cases Committee was passed by the 1926 AGM and the initial members were Messrs Evan Barlow, H D M Barnett, C S Bigg, W A Clarke, E G B Fowler, W B Frearson, A A Ironside, K McAlpin, J Parsons, S W Pike and S F M Stone.

It is interesting to note the presence of both Evan Barlow, founder of Evan Barlow, Son & Poyner (now known following various mergers as Barlows) and Alfred Ironside on this committee. According to Mr Jeremy

Barlow 'my grandfather, the founder of our firm, was a bit of a character it seems. He always referred to the founder of Ironsides, Mr Ironside, [who became a member of The Society in 1920], himself no less, as "tin ribs". Mr Ironside – a very serious fellow – was not amused.' Messrs Barlow and Ironside must have left wit outside the door when sitting together in committee!

1925 was clearly a year of considerable import for The Society, and not just with regard to what the older members of the profession may still call 'Lord Birkenhead's Acts'.

The 1926/1927 annual report continues with the issue of the Poor Persons' Rules, which came into effect on 6th April 1926. Though the Poor Man's Lawyer Scheme had continued and had dealt with 123 cases, of which 28 were taken forward for further action. 48 applications had been received under the new rules, all being in connection with Divorce proceedings. It was hoped that a grant would be forthcoming from The Law Society in London to cover the expenses of the scheme.

There was also continuing activity consequent on the 1925 property legislation. The new General Conditions of Sale were found to be too cumbersome for everyday use and so a Form of Special Conditions, embodying the General Conditions by reference had been drawn up and adopted. The issue of Scale Charges remained somewhat contentious, however, and, after some debate at the AGM it was resolved that the Scale of Costs for house purchase over £600 should be re-examined.

The Library Again

One major task for The Society in 1926 was the reorganisation of the Library. There was a need for a full time Librarian in addition to the post of Honorary Librarian, and the existing part time holder of the former office was dismissed. The upstairs room he had occupied was taken over as additional space for meetings of The Committee, The Poor Man's Lawyer Scheme and the Law Students' Society. This released space on the ground floor for further book shelves. To replace the previous male part-time Librarian it was determined to appoint a woman, at a salary not exceeding £2.10s.0d (£2.50) a week. A Miss Craven was appointed to the post commencing on 26th April 1926. Her working hours were weekdays 9.30 am to 1 pm and 2.15 pm to 5.30 pm, Saturdays 9.30 am to 1 pm, later shortened to 12.30 pm. Offers of land in New Street were received in connection with a proposal to build a new Law Library. This undertaking was considered to be beyond The Society's means and the matter was not proceeded with.

On a more domestic note the Annual Dinner for 1927 was fixed to take place after the AGM on 14th January, but arrangements for the dinner were placed in the hands of a sub committee.

The Annual Dinner was a major topic of discussion at the AGM held on 28th January 1928. The Dinner Sub Committee raised again the suggestion referred to earlier that the Dinner should be 'more in the nature of a public function' with more guests invited on behalf of The Society and members being entitled to bring their own guests. There was some considerable discussion as to who might be suitable guests. In the outcome it was determined that members could invite guests provided they were members of the legal profession – which was defined to include articled clerks. In April 1928, however, the Dinner Account showed a loss of £7.1s.9d, approximately £7.07p – a not inconsiderable sum when it is remembered that The Society's Librarian was being paid £2.50 a week. The President, Mr W A Clarke, made good the deficiency out of his own pocket – a dangerous precedent it might be thought! When in April 1929 a deficit of £6.14s.3d (approximately £6.75) was reported on the Annual Dinner the loss was subsidised out of The Society's accounts.

Legal Education continued to be a topic exercising The Committee. The majority of local law students were attending courses at the University College, but the College was not covering the costs of providing these courses from fees. There was a considerable deficit on maintaining the College's Law Department and a continuing loss of £60 pa. The AGM resolved to pay £30 immediately towards reducing the historic deficit and a payment of £10.10s.0d. (£10.50) towards the running cost for the ensuing year. A similar sum was paid, as had become usual, to the Solicitors' Benevolent Association as the annual account showed a small balance in hand, but with a healthy capital sum in various Government Stocks.

The other by now usual items of report were contained in the 1927/1928 Report, including the continuing activity of the Poor Man's Lawyer Scheme which had dealt with 122 cases, and the Poor Persons Rules Committee which had dealt with 77 applications, yet again nearly all concerned with Divorce issues. The Committee was, however, pleased to report that a grant towards the running expenses of the Poor Persons Rules Committee had been received from The Law Society.

On a national level The Society joined in the creation of a special sub committee originated by the Executive Council of The Association of British Chambers of Commerce on the working of the Law of Property Act 1925 and The Land Charges Act 1925, both pieces of legislation having 'teething troubles' in their early years.

An unwelcome press appearance: the issue of advertising

From time to time the minutes of The Committee contain references to events and happenings which, over 80 years on, appear almost laughable, but which at the time must have been matters of grave concern. The minutes of The Committee meeting for 2nd March 1927 record two such instances. A letter had been received from Mr James Atter, a member of The Society from Melton Mowbray, claiming that certain other Solicitors in Melton had been 'touting for clients'. The facts of the allegation were considered but were thought to be insufficient to ground the complaint and no further action was taken. A much more serious view was taken of a photograph which had appeared in the *Illustrated Leicester Chronicle* of Mr Josiah Hincks describing him as a 'well known solicitor'. The Secretary was instructed to write to Mr Hincks informing him that The Committee had considered this picture and expressing their hope that the description had not been inserted with his consent, 'as they feel that it is undesirable in the interests of the profession that members should seek any publicity of this kind'. Mr Hincks subsequently wrote to say that he regretted the publication of the photograph and that he had not authorised its caption.

On 10th June 1927 The Committee had to consider a letter put before them by Mr Frearson, a Leicester member, purporting to come from 'The Legal Aid Society'. Inquiries made at The Royal Infirmary indicated that letters of this sort were 'freely circulated' amongst people who had undergone accidents. The Committee concluded 'something should be done' to stop this practice and the Hon. Secretary was asked to communicate The Society's concerns to The Law Society. At the next Committee meeting the Secretary reported that he had received a letter from The Law Society which stated that the activities of 'so called' legal aid societies were under constant consideration, and that calls had been made on the Director of Public Prosecutions to take action, but all in vain. The Committee determined that The Royal Infirmary should be asked to display a notice warning patients against employing a 'Legal Aid Society'. On the 16th September 1927 it was discovered that the solicitors purporting to act for 'The Legal Aid Society' were a firm just off Bedford Row in London. The Secretary was asked to inform The Law Society of this information.

In January 1929 The Committee wrote to Messrs Loseby Son and Hammond who had been so ill advised as to include in an advertisement for a clerk placed in a Market Harborough newspaper, the information that they had certain sums of money to lend on mortgage. The firm were informed it was not in the best interests of the profession to include such information in a job advertisement. The rules on advertising were indeed most strictly construed and applied.

It is interesting to speculate how Committee members from the 1920s would view pictures in glossy local publications of current members of The Society enjoying themselves at The Society's Annual Dinner and the degree of horror they would feel if they were able to see advertisements in the press and on television for various 'help line' services in connection with accidents!

Conveyancing Problems Again

These occupied a considerable part of The Committee's time in 1928. At the February meeting it was reported that The Law Society was proposing to produce a new form of contract for the sale of land and to sell these at 3d a copy (approximately 1p). It was realised that local law societies might be disadvantaged by this – the Leicester forms cost 6d (2½p) a copy – and lose income. The Secretary was deputed to attend a meeting at Chancery Lane, but he reported in April that an attempt to prevent the sale of the new cheaper forms had been lost. It is interesting to note from the 1928 Accounts that the sale of The Society's local form of contract brought in the second largest amount of income received, second only to annual subscriptions, approximately £139 as against £190 respectively. The Society therefore stood to make quite a loss in respect of this issue which is an example of influence passing from a local to a central organisation.

A particular problem had arisen with respect to the sale of council houses in respect of which Leicester Corporation was effectively acting for both sides in the transaction. Representations were made to the Town Clerk who agreed that all purchasers of property from the Corporation should be asked to go to their own solicitors. Within a few months, however, The Committee was informed that certain Building Societies operating in Leicester were stating that their solicitors would undertake work on the sale of properties on which the Societies would be making mortgage advances, and that the costs would be lower than local scale charges. Little could be done about national organisations such as The Woolwich Equitable, but The Society approached the Leicester Permanent Building Society (an ancestor of 'A & L') to request an undertaking that it would not circulate such 'propaganda'! A further initiative was taken in respect of 'The Perm' in April 1929. Subsequently the Building Society declined to pass a formal resolution desisting from circulating the offending 'propaganda', but gave instead an undertaking to their solicitors, Messrs Stone & Co, that they would desist.

The 1929 AGM and the report for 1928 otherwise reported, as had now become standard, the work of the Poor Man's Lawyer Scheme which had received 132 applications for advice, and the Poor Persons Rules Committee which had received 87 applications, nearly all of which were, as in previous years, concerned with Divorce proceedings. Few books had been purchased for the Library during the year because of the death on 1st August 1928 of the Treasurer, Mr S F M Stone, President in 1916. The AGM made the by now customary donation of 10 guineas (£10.50) to both the Solicitors' Benevolent Association and the Law Department of the University College – the latter had now achieved an annual working balance and had reduced its deficit considerably.

By 1929 The Society had 127 members, of whom 13 were 'honorary', generally because they were retired from practice. There were 4 members from Ashby-de-la-Zouch, 4 from Coalville, 3 from Hinckley, 15 from Loughborough, 2 from Lutterworth, 1 from Market Bosworth, 5 from Market Harborough and 3 from Melton Mowbray. The remainder were all from Leicester. The 1929/30 Annual Report, however, noted 'with regret that there are now several Solicitors practising in the City who are not members of the Society. It is obviously in the interests of the Society that all Solicitors practising in Leicester should join the Society and your Committee hopes that members will use their influence to persuade these gentlemen to become members at an early date.'

1929 was clearly a busy year for The Society. The by now well established professional structure for Solicitors was seen in operation when The Law Society approached all provincial societies about the issue of defaulting Solicitors. The established autonomy of the profession is here clearly seen with a national body consulting via local organisations who are deemed to be representative of Solicitors in their areas. The issue in question was the misappropriation of clients' funds during the previous few years, and this was causing some unrest. In the course of this history we have encountered only one such case so far in Leicester, and that was some years previously. It is not therefore surprising that The Society strongly opposed the proposal from a Law Society Special Committee that an indemnity fund should be created to cover cases of default. The Society was, however, in favour of a proposal from The Law Society for a voluntary scheme to provide pensions for Solicitors' Clerks. That scheme was duly implemented: the indemnity fund's day was, however, yet to come.

In October 1929 the Leicester Medical Society invited members of The Society to a joint meeting to consider medico-legal aspects of compensation cases. The discussion was considered a success, but the attendance of solicitors was considered disappointing. It was proposed to extend an invitation in future to the Medical Society and solicitors were urged to attend. The day when there would be a specialised Leicester Medico-Legal Society was still far in the future.

Continuing work on the Library

The 1929/30 report of course mentioned the work of the Poor Man's Lawyer Scheme, 170 cases, and the Poor Persons Rules Committee, 89 cases, again all relating to Divorce. A number of deaths were noted, including that of Mr J S Dickinson, President in 1904. A major part of the Report was, however, also devoted to the Library. Several new volumes had been acquired, and to make room for them a number of older titles had been offered for sale, realising a sum of £4.2s.6d. (£4.12½p). However, a number of older volumes – some of them very old – still remained unsold. In consequence of accessions and deletions it was felt desirable to produce a new catalogue. It is interesting to note in this connection that between 1928 and 1971 a Library Accession Book, which still survives in The Society's records, was maintained. Initially this does not give the cost of individual titles but normally brackets a number of volumes together at an inclusive cost. Thus in December 1934 some 19 volumes were acquired at a cost of £66.18s.0d. (£66.90p). The cost of individual volumes begins to be recorded in 1940, but then ceases until 1953. However, yearly expenditure totals do appear for a number of years though these, being dependent on the number of books published, do not give enough information to state what the average cost of maintaining the Library year by year was. One thing is, however, clear and that is the steady rise in the cost of books. In 1958 the 7th Edition of "Rayden on Divorce", for example, cost £5.17s.6d. (approximately £5.87½p) while the 11th Edition in 1971 cost £16.10s.0d (£16.50p).

We have somewhat moved ahead chronologically by considering increasing book purchase costs, but they point to an issue that occupied The Society in 1929, namely the inadequacy of annual subscriptions to maintain the Library. The annual subscription had not increased since before the Great War. It was proposed to increase subscriptions and to alter the Rules of The Society accordingly. The annual subscription for members practising in Leicester was, it was proposed, to rise to 3 guineas

(£3.15p). After some considerable debate during which it was argued that increasing subscriptions would deter younger men from joining The Society – a perennial concern nowadays for many organisations – the proposal was carried.

The Society's funds were, however, sufficient to support the annual donations of 10 guineas (£10.50p) to the Solicitors' Benevolent Association and to the Law Department of the Leicester University College. It was, however, in this connection noted that Law students in the Leicester area, especially those from Loughborough, were attending lectures in Nottingham, where classes were too large, in preference to Leicester where they were too small. It was stressed that the standard of tuition was the same in both Colleges and students were urged to support their local law school. The cry 'stay local' is still heard today in higher educational circles, with little effect it has to be added in the case of the 'brightest and best' of students.

Disciplinary Matters

As The Society moved into yet another decade it was once again concerned with the issue of defaulting solicitors. The notion of an indemnity fund was popular with London solicitors but unpopular in the provinces. The issue was, however, to be the subject of legislation and a special general meeting of The Society was held on 30th May 1930 to discuss the matter. This was poorly attended, but it nevertheless decided to support the proposal to promote legislation to make membership of The Law Society compulsory with that body having power to make regulations and rules relating to conduct and practice and to make grants to the clients of defaulting solicitors. This was something of a change in policy on the part of The Society which, in the light of hindsight, may be seen as bowing to the inevitable. From a wider historical point of view this development may also be seen as a further accretion of power to the centre at the expense of local organisations. The Law Society had also set up a special committee to consider the training of Articled Clerks: this had, however, consulted local law societies whereas the issue of defaulting solicitors had not been referred back. On the other hand The Law Society had been active in investigating the action of the Legal Aid Societies which we have previously encountered.

In connection with the regulation of local practice, however, the AGM of The Society on 20th January 1931 adopted a new practice rule designed to discourage local solicitors from acting for both vendor and purchaser in conveyancing issues which appeared to have become something of a practice amongst Leicester City firms.

The work of the Poor Man's Lawyer continued as ever, though there was a marked increase in the number of applications in 1930 to 206 while 87 applications were received by the Poor Persons Rules Committee.

The Library was the cause of some debate at the 1931 AGM. The Honorary Librarian (Mr S H Partridge) was of the opinion that the current premises at the rear of Messrs Owstons' offices were too small and were damp. He counselled a search for alternative premises but it was argued that this would entail the payment of additional rent. Extra shelving for books could be squeezed into the current premises, and in the event the Law Library did not move until 1960. The fate of the old books referred to earlier was quite interesting. Many had belonged to Sir Nathan Wright, Recorder of Leicester 1680-84. It was resolved that no old books should be sold or destroyed, but that they should be retained, reconditioned and repaired.

1931 was, on the whole, a comparatively quiet year for The Committee with generally only the by now regular items of business such as conveyancing costs coming before it. One item of interest, however, was a proposal to engage an entertaining speaker for the Annual Dinner. Mr Gillie Potter was approached to speak at a nominal fee of 5 guineas (£5.25p).[26]

The Committee otherwise got on with a considerable expansion of Library stock, including the rolling replacement of Halsbury's Laws of England, and overseeing the Poor Man's Lawyer Scheme whose workload increased considerably with 270 applications being made, while the Poor Persons Rules Committee received 83 applications.

A storm, however, was to break at the AGM. The content of the Solicitors' Bill promoted by The Law Society was revealed to the meeting. Clause 1 which gave power to the Council of The Law Society to make rules to govern the profession was objected to by Mr P J Hammond as being too vague and placing too much power in the hands of the Council. Mr G E Bouskell, the Vice-President, replied that the Council were all experienced solicitors who would be expected to act in the best interests of the profession. Mr M R Simpson objected on the basis that the Bill was an example of the tendency 'towards bureaucratic legislation', while Mr E G B Fowler, the President, also considered the Bill objectionable as giving The Council a 'blank cheque', though he did not object to legislation

---

[26] Gillie Potter's name is now largely forgotten, but he was a very popular broadcaster on 'the wireless' in the early 1930s. His catch phrase was, 'Good evening, England, this is Gillie Potter speaking to you in English' which was designed to debunk the rather pompous BBC announcers of the day. Gillie claimed to speak from Hogsnorton. Some of his work has been reissued on CD..

which would require Solicitors to keep two bank accounts. In the end The Society approved of 'the principle of every solicitor being compelled to keep proper accounts and, in particular, two Bank Accounts', but objected to the wide scope of Clause 1 of the Bill.

Once again looking back from a time when the vast majority of working practices in all walks of life are minutely and bureaucratically – if not always effectively – regulated it is hard to realise that less than eighty years ago there were no national rules regarding the keeping of solicitors' accounts, particularly the separation of office and client accounts. No doubt The Society and its members felt at the beginning of 1932 that their honour and ethical standards were sufficient to ensure protection for clients, but the onward march of regulation had started and was to continue. Even so at its first meeting in February 1932 The Committee considered that Provincial Law Societies should be consulted before the Council of The Law Society made any rules under the proposed legislation, though it was argued that it would be better to be regulated by The Law Society than to 'allow steps to be taken by other persons not connected with the legal profession'.

The 1932/1933 annual report having reported the death of Mr W J Freer, President in 1901, contained the usual statements on the growth of the Library; the work of the Poor Man's Lawyer Scheme – the workload here had increased steeply to 366 cases and it was further reported that a similar scheme to that in Leicester had been started in Loughborough – and the Poor Persons Rules Committee which had dealt with 48 cases. Other matters that had occupied The Committee were the submission of views to the City Council on whether compulsory registration of title should be applied in Leicester, this having been recommended by The Law Reform Association, a body that had become active in the district. The City Council had not taken any action on the matter. The Society had also been asked to support the fund for the meeting of the British Association which was to be held in Leicester in 1933 and a sum of £25 was voted by the AGM.

Changes to the Annual Dinner

It was, however, the issue of the Annual Dinner which caused the greatest debate. Once again the, by now, old argument was raised that the dinner should be a more public affair, that it should be moved to the time of Assizes so that the Assize Judge and members of the Bar could be invited, together with guests representing aspects of civic life and enterprise. One member argued such a change would put up the price of tickets and thus deter younger members from attending. Another argued to the exactly opposite effect that a more public dinner would attract more of the younger members. One view was put forward that inviting outside guests 'savoured of advertising' – the old bogey again! In the end it was determined that the dinner should have a more public character, but that members should not be allowed to bring private guests.

Disciplinary Issues Again

The 1933/34 annual report began gloomily with five deaths to report, including that of Mr W Simpson, Hon. Secretary 1884-1904 and President in 1912. There was also the unwelcome news that under The Rent and Mortgage Restrictions (Amendment) Bill the local authority would be empowered to publish information and give advice to both landlords and tenants on their rights and duties. The Committee had viewed this proposal with some alarm. The Committee argued that advice on legal matters should only be given by professionally qualified people and that the particular provision concerning the giving of advice should be opposed. Seven MPs representing the City and County of Leicester had been lobbied accordingly. The Committee had also been consulted with regard to the draft professional conduct rules made under the new Solicitors Act, and these had been considered satisfactory. Steps were also recommended to counter the actions of Legal Aid Societies, organisations we have encountered before. These, as we would now say 'Ambulance Chasers', employed agents 'who, aided by Press reports of accident cases, induce patients at hospitals to employ them to undertake the settlement of their civil claims on the footing that the legal aid society is to receive a percentage of the compensation paid'. Following the example of schemes in Folkestone and Middlesex The Committee hoped to persuade The Leicester Royal Infirmary to accept a rota of local solicitors to advise hospital patients. This scheme was set up and at the 1935 AGM it was extended to hospitals in Loughborough and Melton Mowbray. While The Society was clearly concerned at the 'poaching' activities of Legal Aid Societies, the need for cheap legal services was clearly growing as the Poor Man's Lawyer Scheme had received 429 applications during the course of the year, which must be contrasted with 270 in 1931, itself an increase on previous years, while The Poor Persons Rules Committee had received 93 applications, once again the overwhelming majority relating to Divorce.

The 1933 AGM was particularly concerned with, yet again, the Annual Dinner. A powerful argument was put forward that excluding private guests was not in The Society's interests as what was needed was more publicity for The Society so that the public should know it existed. Was that an early indication that The Society feared it might be becoming marginalised? In the event it was determined that private guests could be invited, but ladies were excluded 'other than lady members of the profession' – not that there were any in Leicester! These proposals were put into effect, and with the Dinner now taking place at Assize Time and being a much larger event from 1935 it was determined to hold it at The Grand Hotel rather than the much smaller Leicestershire Club in Welford Place.[27]

In 1934 The Committee was concerned with proposals from The Law Society on the questions of touting and undercutting, both of which could amount to criminal offences under Section 5 of the Solicitors' Act 1932, and in respect of which successful prosecutions had been mounted elsewhere. The Society took its own action in informing all solicitors practising in the area, whether members or not, of the need to avoid touting and undercutting. The Society did, however, make considerable progress with a new scale of charges and revised regulations in connection with conveyancing matters. However, it had to be stated that: 'this revised scale ..., if approved by the Society shall [not] come into force unless and until an undertaking to abide by the same has been signed by all the members of the Society who have signed the existing agreement'.

A new scale of charges was needed because the scale introduced in 1920 was no longer appropriate in the context of both the undercutting problem and rapid changes in the provision of new houses for sale. 80% of the new housing estates being built were being developed on the basis of free conveyancing provided by the developers. House prices had also risen so the older scale which charged higher fees on more expensive properties was out of date: even 'working class' people were now purchasing houses costing over £500. Having agreed a new scale of charges, however, The Society had to gain the agreement of members to it. On 7th March 1935 The Committee was informed that of the 128 members, there were, leaving aside the honorary members, 79 practising in the City and 36 in the County, but of these only 39 City members and 12 County members had signed the new undertaking as to costs. By July 1935 only 5 City members had failed to sign up to the new undertaking, and despite the original intention that unanimity was required for the new scale to become effective, it was determined that it should come into force. By the time of the 1934/35 Annual Report all but 4 members of The Society had signed.

---

[27] The Club has of recent years undergone a number of changes of identity, from a rather up-market restaurant, Welford Place, to its 2008 rebranding as 'a club cum disco'.

A special sub committee had to be formed to encourage City members to sign. The need for such a scale was even more imperative in view of the draft rules issued under the Solicitors' Act in 1933, to which the 1934/35 Annual Report referred. These forbade touting and undercutting either statutorily authorised scales of charges or those adopted in particular localities. They also forbade profit sharing with any person who was not a solicitor, and joining 'Legal Aid Societies' many of whose members were not professionally qualified. The term 'ambulance chasing' in connection with the activities of such organisations was now regularly in use.

The workload of the Poor Man's Lawyer Scheme had increased dramatically with 560 applications being made. The rota of solicitors manning the Monday night advice sessions had increased to 26, while those who were prepared to take referred cases on for further action numbered 21. 104 applications had been made to the Poor Persons Rules Committee. Those members of The Society undertaking this voluntary activity were clearly meeting, at least in some measure, a real need in Leicester. A similar workload was undertaken in 1935, and again in 1936 by which time the '1st Rota' consisted of 30 names, and the '2nd Rota' of 21.

The 1936/37 annual report relates to a year of considerable importance to The Society. The new practice rules made under the Solicitors Act finally came into force. These differed from the initial draft in that the prohibition on undercutting scale fees was made to relate to the scale in force in the area where the property in question was situated as opposed to the scale in force for the district in which the charging solicitor practised. This was not a real problem in the City of Leicester (one or two diehards objected to what they regarded as being railroaded into adopting a new scale of charges, but it was the compulsion not the actual scale to which they objected), but it was a problem in the County where there never had been the same degree of unanimity as to conveyancing charges. The Committee therefore had to spend much time trying to determine what the scales of charges were in the various county districts. When agreement could be reached these could then be approved locally then sent to The Law Society at which point they would become the rates below which undercutting could not legally take place. Even so the 1936/37 Report had to admit that no final agreement had been made in respect of all County members. The new 'Scale of Costs and Regulations for Conveyancing Matters' was printed at the end of the 1936/37 Report.

In May 1936 the Hospital Advice Rota came into effect in both the City and County. 31 firms and sole practitioners joined the rota in Leicester, and 14 in the County districts. The scheme, which was designed to choke off the incursions of Legal Aid Societies, worked by hospital secretaries communicating to a central office the names of people in hospital desiring the assistance of a solicitor. The central office – the practice of Messrs Bray & Bray – then referred cases on, strictly by reference to the rota – a 'taxi cab' rule. This scheme operated separately from the Poor Man's Lawyer Scheme and the Poor Persons Rules Committee, with those seeking assistance being liable to pay costs. Even so The Committee could report: 'The number of cases referred would appear to indicate that the Scheme is supplying a need'. (15 cases had been dealt with by July 1936, and 47 by October). The existence of the scheme had been notified to the Leicester Chamber of Commerce which had given its support.

Gathering Clouds of War

At the end of 1936 The Society was approached by the Commanding Officer of the 4th Battalion of the Leicestershire Regiment asking for assistance with regard to raising the peacetime establishment of the 44th Anti-Aircraft Battalion. A list of members was despatched and the officer was further advised to contact members directly with regard to volunteering for this form of military service. Despite this somewhat ominous event The Society's life continued on an apparently even keel so far as routine issues were concerned. In 1937 The Committee had met on only three occasions. There had been a number of deaths, including Mr J L Douglass, President in 1925. The Library was maintained, and the Poor Man's Lawyer Scheme and The Poor Persons Rules Committee continued to operate with the generally higher application rate that had developed during earlier years. The Annual Dinner for 1937 was, however, moved from the early part of the year into October. It was considered that this had been a beneficial change.

However, there were still continuing problems with scale charges and the activities of Legal Aid Societies. With regard to the former uniformity had not been achieved in the County districts. There was a particular problem in Ashby-de-la-Zouch consequent on the fact that much of the conveyancing work there was affected by the operation of the Warwickshire Law Society's scale of costs. The issue (and Leicester was not alone in experiencing difficulties) had been referred to The Associated Provincial Law Societies who had resolved that it was desirable to have standardised local scales of charges and conditions of sale and that all local societies should collaborate to bring about such scales. Even this modest proposal had, however, met with opposition from Liverpool, Manchester and Newcastle – another example, one fears, of the historic inability of the profession to secure unanimity. The need for unity was, however, highlighted by the increasing practice of using banks and other non-professional agents to complete conveyances, especially where this enabled the purchaser's solicitor to avoid a journey. It was pointed out that this practice was dangerous as it 'tended to encourage bankers and other non-professional agents to transact a solicitor's work'. The need to protect litigation from the incursions of Legal Aid Societies was also a feature of the 1937/38 Annual Report. The Hospital Advice Rota had dealt with 146 cases since its inception and damages had been recovered in 21, but the results of other cases were unknown and members were urged to keep Messrs Bray & Bray informed of the progress of any litigation. The Annual Report for 1938/39, the last full year of peace, also dwelt on the Hospital Advice Scheme. By then 352 patients had been referred to solicitors on the rota, 336 from the City and 16 from the County. 81 cases had been reported as reaching a conclusion. In 48 damages had been recovered. In 33 patients had been advised they either had no case or one so doubtful that they decided not to proceed. It was, however, once again stressed that the continuing efficacy of the scheme in combatting the incursions of Legal Aid Societies was to a degree dependent on members reporting the outcome of cases.

One issue affecting The Committee should be noted. On the 15th December 1938 a Committee meeting was held whose minutes were for the first time typewritten, though copperplate made a brief comeback a short while later! Inter alia, this meeting also increased the weekly salary of the Law Librarian, then a Miss Borwell, by 10/- (50p) a week, and urged member firms to take concerted action as to the periods of closure of offices at the Christmas, Easter, Whitsun and August holidays.

The usual round of local domestic issues is recorded in the 1939/40 Annual Report, but while books were still being purchased for the Library, and while the Poor Man's Lawyer Scheme had dealt with 465 applications, and the Poor Persons' Rule Committee had dealt with 99, and while the Hospital Advice Rota had in 1939 dealt with 154 cases, the document is inevitably influenced by the outbreak of war.

There had been continuing efforts to create an acceptable local scale of conveyancing charges, a task rendered more urgent by the proposal from The Law Society to bring in new Conveyancing Charges Rules, and the reluctance of the Master of the Rolls to approve too many local variations from national models on the basis that 'there is no justification for any variation of scales in respect of districts where the conditions are similar'. The Warwickshire Law Society had taken an initiative in trying to bring together the schemes of various Midlands Law Societies and a drafting sub committee was created in July 1939. However, the outbreak of war had disrupted work on this matter.

The run up to the outbreak of war had also seen The Law Society compiling a register of all solicitors in connection with National Service. By the end of 1939 11 members of The Society were on service with His Majesty's forces. The annual subscriptions of members on active service were suspended and no annual dinner was held.

The inter war years were a period of rapid social, economic and political change. In some ways The Society appears to have been able to operate in this changing context by pursuing the even tenor of former times. Its local cohesiveness, its continuing strong family structures and the centrality of the Library were all links back to an earlier and less hectic age. The Society also had a number of successful initiatives including the operation of the Poor Man's Lawyer Scheme and the Poor Person's Rules Committee both of which, as we have seen, experienced a massive increase in the demand for their services. The Hospital Advice Rota was also a notable success and clearly met a real local need. On the other hand the period in question saw an increasing accretion of power to The Law Society and away from local law societies. The real regulatory 'clout' now lay with Chancery Lane which could no longer be considered in any way a 'primus inter pares'. More locally The Society was finding it harder to persuade all local solicitors to become members, and this was compounded by the obvious difficulties in the 1930s in setting, and then securing compliance with, conveyancing scale charges, especially in county areas. At the same time it can be seen that banks, estate developers and other bodies such as the Legal Aid Societies were attempting to 'muscle in' on work traditionally done by solicitors, and that is still a current concern. Touting for clients and undercutting fellow professionals were major concerns both nationally and locally at this time. Seventy years on they are simply known as advertising and competitive business practice.

Chapter 5

The Second World War and Post War Reconstruction in the 1950s

Kelly's "Directory of Leicestershire and Rutland for 1941" lists some 74 firms of solicitors in the City and County of Leicester, 48 being in the City. 10 years later Kelly's "Directory of Leicester" (only) recorded some 53 firms, though as with previous editions of this publication it is often hard to distinguish places of work from private residences: a degree of double counting remains inevitable. The years following saw a slight increase in firms in Leicester to 56 in 1954 and 59 in 1960. Most of these firms remained small with only a few partners, and many solicitors were in sole practice. Over the same period the membership of The Society grew from 142 in 1940 to 195 in 1961 (the latter year's figures exclude 7 honorary members). In both cases it may also be added that nearly all members were also members of both The Law Society and The Solicitors' Benevolent Association – The Committee's efforts in urging members to join throughout the 1920s and 1930s had clearly been successful.

This, however, is somewhat to jump ahead of our narrative. How was The Society faring in war time? Initially, as the war time phrase had it, it might have appeared to be 'business as usual'. During 1940 The Committee noted with sorrow two deaths, including that of Mr W Harding, President in 1927. New books were purchased for the Library, 87 applications were made under the Poor Person's Rules and 307 applications were made to the Poor Man's Lawyer Scheme, 20 of these were, however, noted as being directly attributable to the war. The hours of operation of this Scheme had also, in view of 'The Black Out', been altered to 12.30 pm to 1.30 pm. What was now known as 'The Infirmary Scheme' had received 125 applications. The Committee had also received a request in July 1940 from Chancery Lane by which local solicitors were asked to give legal advice to Citizens' Advice Bureaux. A branch of this organisation had been set up in Leicester. The Committee put considerable effort into devising a cooperative scheme. On the one hand it was felt that strict supervision needed to be exercised over the giving of legal advice, while on the other hand it was clear that the relationship between the new initiative and the existing Poor Man's Lawyer Scheme and the Poor Person's Rules Committee needed to be sorted out as it would be undesirable to have different types of scheme in operation. In the outcome a system of assistance based on that operating at The Royal Infirmary with a rota of members prepared to assist the Bureau was developed. Once again the coordinating office was that of Messrs Bray & Bray. A further item of domestic business was effected at the 1941 AGM, held in March, and that was a further revision of the local scale of conveyancing charges.

However, the war was impinging on the work of The Society. Members became involved in a special 'War Weapons Week' in which all sections of Leicester society were asked to raise a sum of £1m to aid 'The War Effort' – the sum is still vast, but must be considerably increased to take account of inflation to realise the implication of the request. There was also the issue of whether solicitors and their clerks should be exempted from military service at the age of 30. The Bury and Manchester Law Societies had urged the Government to adopt such an exemption, but Leicester was of the opinion that 'reservation at that age for Solicitors and their Clerks was neither in the best interests of the nation nor the profession'. Indeed by the end of 1940 25 members of The Society were on active service. Interestingly one of these was Mr Alfred Halkyard who, as previously noted, had won The Military Cross in The Great War. Indeed it is believed that Mr Halkyard was the only member of The Society to see service in both World Wars. During the war Mr Halkyard was promoted to Colonel.

By the time the 1941 annual report was made to the AGM, held now in May 1942, the impact of war is clearly physically shown in the truncated form of the Report. The death of Mr J Parsons, President in 1918, was noted, membership stood at 137, books and reports had been purchased for the Library, the Poor Man's Lawyer Scheme had continued, though now only on alternate Mondays as the number of applications had fallen off. On the other hand The Committee minutes of 12th May 1941 had recorded a response to a letter from The Law Society that the local Citizens Advice Bureau scheme was working well; maybe the need for the Poor Man's Lawyer was diminishing. Applications continued to be made under the Poor Persons Rules and interestingly a number were transferred to the Services Divorce Department. The Infirmary Scheme continued to operate successfully under the coordinating aegis of Mr C F Bray. The continuing influence of the war was, however, seen in the creation of a Friar Lane Fire Watching Group and the permission granted to men in the armed forces who were qualified, or who were articled clerks or who intended to take up the law after the end of the war to use books in the Library to advance their education. On the other hand The Society appeared to regret its earlier generosity in suspending totally the annual subscriptions of members who were on active service as it had become clear that in some cases at least their practices were being carried on and so were able to bear costs. Instead it was resolved that a reduction of 50% should apply.

The annual reports for 1942 and 1943 were presented to the combined 83rd and 84th General Meetings which were held together in 1944. By then the war had clearly taken its toll. The reports are typewritten and reflect the somewhat sparse nature of the underlying Committee minutes. From August 1942 there had in addition been early closing of the Library at 3.45 pm daily to enable Miss Borwell, the Librarian, to undertake War work. Messrs Owston undertook to facilitate use of the Library during the early closing period. Nevertheless The Society tried to maintain its life as normally as possible by continuing purchases for the Library, by operating The Poor Man's Lawyer Scheme which continued to operate fortnightly and which had dealt with 475 applications over two years. It was, however, desired to increase the number of advising solicitors from 16 to 26 as that would mean that each person would only have to do duty once a year. The Poor Persons Rules Committee continued to operate, dealing with 210 applications over two years, 27 cases being transferred to the Services Divorce Department, and Mr C F Bray reported the continued successful operation of the Infirmary Scheme. Mr Charles Squire had also retired in 1943 as Registrar of Leicester, Loughborough and Ashby-de-la Zouch County Courts and a sum of £105.10s.6d (£105.52½p) had been raised from members to make a presentation to him. This was a very considerable sum to raise in war time when other calls were being made – and heavy rates of taxation levied – on members' incomes. The Society had also been concerned with the recommendation made by The Scott Committee[28] that compulsory registration of title should be extended. The Society was in favour of this once machinery was put in place to achieve it, but other local law societies carried the day, at a meeting of the Associated Provincial Law Societies held at Chancery Lane on 15th January 1943, with their argument that compulsory registration was 'impracticable and undesirable'. Compulsory registration did come, but it had to wait a while.

---

[28] This was one of three Committees, the others being Barlow and Uthwatt, set up to consider the future of public and private land law after the end of hostilities. Out of these came our modern systems of Planning, Compulsory Purchase and Registration of Title - but only after some lapse of time.

The 1942 and 1943 reports noted the deaths of, inter alia, Messrs G E Bouskell, K McAlpin and W A Clarke who had been Presidents in, respectively, 1917, 1926 and 1928. The death on active service of Mr C R George was also noted. He had been killed in an air operation in North Africa and was the first, and indeed the only, member of The Society to lose his life on active service in the current conflict. He had been a member of The Society since 1935.

In 1944 Mr E Percy Smyth a member from Melton Mowbray, assumed office as President and retained that post until 1946. The Committee appears to have been able to meet twice in 1944 and once again in 1945, and the life of The Society seems to have become very constrained indeed. However, some business was transacted. A new Librarian, Mrs Hoggs, was appointed in 1944. The 1944 Committee meetings considered the initial views of The Rushcliffe Committee, which was to lead to the creation of The Legal Aid Scheme after the War, and initially deputed two members to attend a conference to be held in London on 7th September 1944 to further consider the proposals.

At the following committee meeting in October 1944 The Committee was broadly in favour of the principle of a 'Legal Panel Scheme' but was opposed to the details of income limits and the proposed scale of charges. The Committee also felt that Conveyancing, Probate and Administration should be in general outwith the scheme. By the time of the 1945 Committee meeting on 15th June 1945 The Rushcliffe Report had been issued and the 'general feeling of the meeting [was] that the scheme should be accepted and to be thankful it was no worse'.

New technology and other innovations

All was not entirely gloomy, however, for it was proposed that 'a machine for the purpose of photographing documents' should be purchased. This would be located in the Library and 'could be used for copying accounts, abstracts and correspondence, and that no doubt after instruction a clerk from the various firms would be able to work the apparatus'. Mr Partridge, the Hon. Treasurer from 1935, together with Mr M G Pearce were deputed to look into the cost of obtaining such a machine. One photocopying machine for the whole of the profession in Leicester; it is today inconceivable.

In 1945 The Committee received a communication from The Law Society regarding the creation of a new Law Department in Nottingham

University College, this would also be approved under Section 32 of The Solicitors Act 1932 for the provision of the 'statutory year' of legal education for articled clerks. Once more the old hostility towards 'things Nottingham' on the part of Leicester arose, and The Committee considered that 'Nottingham was not a suitable centre having regard to the other adjoining counties and that the best interests of the profession would be served by having a ... University within easy reach of the profession'. Quite how such a negative view would have been received in Nottingham is not recorded. In due course the Nottingham Law Department was opened and many would now consider it, *pace* Leicester University, as maybe the best in the Midlands, and certainly one of the best.

The 1945 Committee meeting also received further news of the proposed extension of town and country planning laws. However, just to show that past problems were still able to rear their heads once more the issue of scale charges was again referred to a sub-committee!

The Return of Peace

On the 10th October 1946 a special general meeting of The Society was held at which the President, Mr E Percy Smyth, expressed his hope that The Society should occupy 'a more prominent position amongst the profession and in the life of the City and County of Leicester ... unless the Society was to fade away .. an earnest effort [had] to be made to revive and increase [its] activities'. To this end the Constitution was recast so as to encourage more solicitors to join by, inter alia, providing that any person who had served with the armed forces during the War should not be required to pay an entrance fee on election – a first step towards The Society's post war reconstruction. However, the same meeting also heard that the annual subscription for existing members needed to be increased, and that entailed further changes to the rules of The Society. The functioning of The Committee was considerably overhauled at this time. Committee meetings were scheduled to take place monthly, save in August, and a sub-committee structure was adopted consisting of The Finance & General Purposes Sub-Committee (F&GP), Costs Sub-Committee (C), Public Relations Sub-Committee (PR) – which was later authorised to create an Annual Dinner Committee – and the Poor Man's Lawyer Sub-Committee (PML). The Committee on 7th November 1946 also authorised expenditure on new books for the Library and, continuing The Society's interest in Legal Education appointed Colonel Halkyard to be its representative on the Law

Studies Committee of University College Nottingham. It would therefore appear that earlier opposition to Nottingham being the centre for legal education in the East Midlands had evaporated with the war's end.

1947 saw The Society undertaking a recruitment drive amongst solicitors practising in the City and County of Leicester. This involved sending a letter inviting non-members to join, and where that proved fruitless members of The Committee proposed to 'pay a call' on the gentlemen in question. But while this new initiative was undertaken there were also old concerns to be dealt with, and the first committee meeting of 1947 dealt with recommendations with regard to conveyancing scale charges. It is interesting to note that these reflected a considerable increase in the price of homes with sums of £10,000 being mentioned, though any such property would clearly be on the top end of 'luxury price range'. This change, of course, had to be approved by a further special general meeting; but this had to be adjourned when held on 6th March 1947 as only two county members were able to attend. Once again we see the need for The Society to secure the cooperation of county members in relation to what continued to be a somewhat vexed matter. The reconvened meeting was held on 24th April and the wide divergence of views amongst members present led to the resolution proposing the new scale of charges being lost. The Committee was forced to circulate a questionnaire to all members of The Society asking for their views and suggestions on scale charges. A further special general meeting was convened on 30th July 1947 after this consultation exercise and this resulted in a revised scale of charges being adopted. A further problematical issue with regard to conveyancing, and one still capable of causing difficulties, exercised The Society in 1947/48. This was the alleged slowness of Leicester City Council in dealing with Local Land Charge Searches. Considerable discussion ensued with the Town Clerk.

The AGM of The Society on 30th October 1947 was told of the work that had been undertaken by The Committee and its Sub-Committees, and that members were showing an increased interest in their profession and its activities. The same meeting was informed that the work of the Poor Man's Lawyer Association had been carried on throughout the period of hostilities by 'a devoted few', but Mr C F Bray appealed for more volunteers to carry on the work in peacetime. At the committee meeting of 8th January 1948 it was reported that the response to this appeal had been good. The same meeting learned, however, of the proposed inception of the Legal Aid and Legal Advice Scheme consequent on The Rushcliffe Report, and a sub-committee was formed to undertake a special study of the issue.

An illegal practice and the defence of members' interests

April 1948 saw The Committee acting on behalf of Society members to protect their interests. A local solicitor in sole practice had died and it appeared that The Law Society had been somewhat slow in appointing a qualified person to assume responsibility for the practice, while the practice itself was being carried on irregularly by unqualified clerks. The Committee determined to protest to The Law Society while the President, Vice-President and Secretary were deputed to speak to the clerks and take such other action as was necessary to deal with their illegal activity. The Committee also resolved to protest to the Bankruptcy Department of the Board of Trade which had proposed to discontinue the presence of an Official Receiver in Leicester and to concentrate the work in Nottingham – as ever the proverbial red rag! The protest, however, proved unavailing and Leicester was to lose its Official Receiver in November 1948. The Committee determined then to lobby local MPs to take the issue up with the Board of Trade. The Committee did, however, in May 1948 agree to cooperate with The Nottingham Incorporated Law Society in the formation of a North Midland Law Society (later to be The East Midlands Association of Law Societies) which was to be specially formed to undertake the implementation of The Rushcliffe Report on legal aid and advice. Further promotion of the interests of members was undertaken in the holding of a series of two lectures by the, then, Mr R E Megarry, on the Town and Country Planning Act 1947 – non-members were to be excluded. The Committee also took action to prevent estate agents in Leicester and Leicestershire from preparing contracts for the sale of properties, and letters were prepared to send to local estate agents warning them of the dangers they ran if they pursued such a practice.

The 1948 AGM was held on 28th October which, unfortunately coincided with the Autumn Assize, but by way of compensation it was attended, for the first time, by 3 members of The Council of The Law Society and they addressed the meeting on topics of current interest to the profession. Unfortunately it is not recorded what these topics were.

By 1949 membership had increased to 142 from the previous year's 136 and the annual report for 1948/49 expressed the hope that more solicitors could be encouraged to join. The report makes it clear that The Society with its new committee structure was functioning well and had recovered its vigour following the problems of the war years. A considerable amount of work had been put into preparing for the implementation of the Legal Aid Scheme, and the creation of The East Midlands Association of Law Societies was, it was thought, likely to 'ensure that the views of solicitors practising in the East Midlands area will carry more weight than in the past on professional matters of national importance'. It was added, however, that the local law societies making up the Association would retain their autonomy.

One area where autonomy was under threat was the ever vexed topic of scale costs. The Law Society had recommended adoption by all local societies of the West of England Scale of Minimum Costs with a view to approaching the Lord Chancellor to approve a rule making it an offence to charge less than the minimum amount. In Leicester it was thought that unanimity on this issue could not be achieved.

The various sub-committees made their own reports. 'Costs' had been largely concerned with applications from members to charge less than the prescribed conveyancing scales. The PR Committee informed The Society that it had been successful in shortening the length of time taken by the City of Leicester in processing local land charge searches. F&GP had been much concerned with continuing the tenancy of the Library and in securing improvements to its heating. A special sub-committee had considered purchasing premises in Millstone Lane to provide a freehold home for The Society but an architect's report on the state of the building was adverse and this proposal was not further considered. Cost issues also precluded the employment of a salaried secretariat for The Society, a decision altered later, but not for many years. The Society did, however, pay part time salaries to clerks who assisted the Secretary and Treasurer. In 1949/50 this was altered so that the Secretary received an honorarium of 100 guineas (£110) a year towards the cost of staff performing secretarial services. The PML committee reported that it had dealt with 684 applications, 360 of which related to 'husband and wife' issues. The work of the Poor Man's Lawyer Scheme was considered to be a fitting prelude to the inception of the new national legal aid scheme, but The Committee as a whole felt that the effect of the scheme on the profession could not possibly be predicted. The Committee undertook to provide at least one lecture on the new scheme and to circularise all members with relevant information. There can be little doubt, however, that the inception of this scheme, which was designed to make justice available to all irrespective of means, was a welcome boost for The Society and was seen as the beginning of an important new era in the life of the profession locally and nationally.

The 1949/50 annual report indicates that the work of The Committee and its sub-committees had continued apace. Attempts had been made to improve the professional lot of members by, inter alia, asking the Leicester County and Ashby-de-la-Zouch Justices to cease the practice of holding courts on a Saturday morning. These requests had not been successful, but there had been more success in obtaining the use of The Members' Cloak Room at The Town Hall in Leicester for solicitors at times when the Assizes and the Quarter Sessions were being held. The Committee had also informed The Law Society of its view that 'the present requirements as to compulsory attendance of Articled Clerks at a recognised Law School and the nature of the tuition given there require drastic revision'.

Mr C F Bray, who had given such stalwart service with regard to the work of the Infirmary Scheme, became President of The Society for 1949/50, and to mark his year of office he presented a President's Jewel to be worn on a collar ribbon by his successors.

Increasing Membership

This distinctly 'upbeat' annual report also contained news that membership had risen from 142 to 150. Indeed this increase was to continue generally throughout the next decade, 162 in 1950/51, 166 in 1951/52, 168 in 1952/53, 171 in 1953/54, 173 in 1954/55, 182 in 1955/56, and by 1960/61 the membership totalled 195. This evidence of vigorous growth is an indication of the health and activity of The Society during the first decade of the 'New Elizabethan' era.

The increasing size of The Society was reflected in an attendance of 50 members at the 1950 AGM which was held in the Board Room of The Leicester & County Chamber of Commerce, then situated at No 3 Granby Street, Leicester. This meeting was honoured by the presence of the President of The Law Society, Mr L S Holmes, who spoke on the activities of The Law Society and of its President in particular. The incoming President of The Leicester Law Society, Mr G Day Adams took the opportunity to urge all members to attend The Law Society's Annual Conference as this was a way of meeting solicitors from other parts of the country and of discussing issues of common concern.

The 1950/51 annual report again recorded the vigour of The Society in protecting its members' interests. The Committee had, for example, complained to The Law Society about the practice of Nationalised Industries and large companies who allowed their legal departments to act privately for employees. This was regarded as unfair competition against solicitors in private practice. Further, but sadly unsuccessful, attempts had been made to persuade the Leicester County Justices to cease holding courts on Saturdays. On the 'social side' the Annual Dinner on 29th January 1951 had been honoured with the presence of Mr Justice Lynskey and Mr Justice Finnemore, The Lord Lieutenant of Leicestershire, The Lord Mayor, The President and Secretary of The Law Society and many other distinguished guests. The 'public nature' of the Annual Dinner was then by now well established. A golf competition organised by Mr A D Foxon had taken place and 15 members had competed.

Legal Aid and other matters

The PR Committee reported that it was hoped to complete a set of photographs of all past Presidents for hanging in the Library Committee Room. The PML Committee reported that its work had continued despite the beginning of the Legal Aid Scheme as there were matters outwith its remit. 467 applications had been dealt with. The inception of Legal Aid was, however, dealt with in a special appendix to the Report. The first provisions of the Legal Aid Act 1949 came into effect in October 1950 and the first meeting of the Leicester Local Committee to administer the local working of the Scheme was held on 13th October 1950. The Committee consisted of 35 solicitors and 7 barristers. It also had a Certifying Sub-Committee of 4 solicitors and, where practicable, 1 barrister. That committee clearly undertook much of the business side of the Scheme for it had held 13 meetings by 30th June 1951. The local profession had clearly embraced the new era in funded advice, for 73 solicitors in Leicester, 7 in Loughborough, 5 in Melton Mowbray, 4 in Market Bosworth, 7 in Market Harborough, 4 in Lutterworth, 4 in Hinckley, 8 in Ashby-de-la-Zouch and 6 in Coalville were empanelled for the Scheme.

The Society's accounts were also clearly in a healthy condition for the profit and loss account showed a surplus of £131.5s.1d. (approximately £131.25) while the balance sheet disclosed healthy deposits at the Trustee Savings Bank and The Leicester Temperance Building Society, with a premises reserve fund which had been created with a view to cover the contingency of having to find new premises. The new decade had begun well and war time blues seemed to be dispelled.

The mood of optimism in the 1950/51 Report was continued in that for 1951/52. Once again the President of The Law Society had addressed the AGM. He took the opportunity to thank members for their work with regard to Legal Aid and stated that the Scheme was working well. Locally a full time secretary had been appointed to the Legal Aid Committee and some 37 applications for legal aid were being received each month. 375 applications had been received for the period in question, 273 being granted and only 61 refused. The certifying Committee had met 15 times. Despite this the PML Sub-Committee still reported that it was dealing with matters falling outwith the Legal Aid Scheme, though the number of applications was falling, some 411 being received in the year ending 30th June 1952. The work of the Poor Man's Lawyer was set to continue with the permission of The Law Society until the extension of the Legal Aid Scheme took place.

While the work of the PML Association continued into 1953, with 411 applications being received and with 42 members of The Society attending from time to time to give advice, the new Legal Aid Scheme was developing rapidly. As from 1st August 1953 the local secretary for Leicester took on the task of servicing Northampton, while a new office was set up at 10 Salisbury Road, Leicester in December 1952.

Once again the topic of cases being taken from Leicester to Nottingham for trial had exercised The Committee. It was feared that long defended divorce cases would be transferred and that this would cause considerable hardship to litigants, witnesses and solicitors and could lead to no divorce business being heard in Leicester. A protest was made to the Lord Chief Justice and the President of the Probate, Divorce and Admiralty Division. The reply was that there was no intention to transfer all such cases to Nottingham, but that it was geographically convenient for an additional judge to sit as a Special Divorce Commissioner in Nottingham for some long defended divorces and this was needed to accelerate the hearing of petitions, the volume of which had increased quite dramatically in the years immediately following the end of the Second World War. The Society's Committee nevertheless hoped that continuing representation could be made to secure the appointment of a similar Special Commissioner for Leicester. By the time of the 1952/53 Annual Report these representations had been successful in securing the appointment of a Commissioner to hear divorce cases from Leicester and also from other neighbouring towns.

The increasing importance of The Society

At the 1952 AGM Mr W B Frearson was elected President. He had been Secretary of The Society for a period after the Great War and he made special comment on how greatly the volume and importance of The

Society's work had increased. One may add to that the increasing diversity of issues for consideration. In 1952/53 The Committee had to deal with: a proposal to abolish the District Probate Registry in Leicester and transfer the work to Nottingham (which was averted following representations to the Secretary of the Principal Probate Registry); the preparation of new Conditions of Sale; the introduction of new scale fees by The Law Society (an issue on which the President of The Law Society addressed the local Society at its AGM in November 1952); the problem of fees paid to solicitors for police prosecutions in the Leicester Division of The Leicestershire and Rutland Constabulary as these appeared to be lower than in other divisions; legal education classes for unadmitted clerks which were given by Mr Grey of the Law Department of Nottingham University and which attracted an initial average attendance of 90. The Society also continued to maintain its Library which by 1952 contained more than 4000 volumes and had dealt with 20,172 borrowings, the most popular titles were "Megarry on the Rent Acts", "Phillips on Divorce", "Dymond on Death Duties", and "Emmett on Title". This perhaps gives an indication also of the type of work undertaken by Society members.

Socially speaking The Society was saddened by two deaths in 1952, one being that of Mr W E Richardson, President in 1922, but it rejoiced in the appointment of Mr Geoffrey Barnett as Lord Mayor of Leicester. Mr Barnett was, of course, later knighted thus joining Sir Thomas Wright and Lieutenant-Colonel Sir Frederick Oliver, D.L., as knighted members of The Society.[29]

The 1953/54 report carried the sad news of the death of Mr E P Smyth who had served on The Committee for many years and had been President for much of the Second World War and its immediate aftermath from 1943 to 1947. The Report stated: 'He was largely responsible for the amended constitution of the Society and Rules which were unanimously approved at a Special General Meeting held in October 1946. The vigour of the Society since that day and the respect with which its representatives are received both by The Law Society and other Provincial Societies is a fitting tribute to his zeal and foresight.'

---

[29] His wife, Dr, subsequently Lady, Isabel Barnett was even more publicly well known as a panel member of the popular 1950s television programme 'What's My Line?' She appeared alongside Barbara Kelly, David Nixon and Gilbert Harding under the chairmanship of Eamonn Andrews. Older readers may remember that the panel and chairman wore evening dress in those highly proper days. The present author can remember one memorable contestant whose clue to the panel as to her occupation was: 'I strip, expose and develop', which was rather risqué at the time. It transpired she worked with films!

The speed of conveyancing and the advance of Legal Aid

One matter which has become an almost perennial problem was the speed of the conveyancing process. The Leicester Auctioneers and Estate Agents Association had asked The Committee how best to avoid delay in the exchange of contracts as there were complaints that delays had led to sales 'going off'. The PR Committee had met representatives of the estate agents and had explained that enquiries of both the vendor's solicitor and the Local Authority had to be made before a purchaser's solicitor could properly advise his client to sign, and such enquiries took time. It transpired that a major reason for delay was the failure of vendors to instruct solicitors to begin preparations for a sale at the same time as placing their houses with an estate agent. As has frequently been the case it is not always the cruel delay of the law that is to blame for the cumbersome moving of the house sales system.

The Legal Aid Scheme was by now running well, though the first amending regulations were made in 1954 to further improve the Scheme, for example with regard to applications from infants and lunatics. The Leicester Local Office had received 391 applications for aid between August 1953 and July 1954 of which 280 were granted. Even so there was still a considerable demand for the services of the Poor Man's Lawyer which was back to operating on a weekly basis, though arrangements were also in place to see applicants on an ad hoc emergency basis. The PML had received 422 applications, 208 of which had been referred to a solicitor, a number of these being processed via the Legal Aid Scheme. In the Report for 1954/55 it appeared there was some falling off in the number of applications to 336, and that was partly attributable to a decline in applications relating to matrimonial problems. The same Report indicated that it was hoped that the Legal Aid Scheme would be applied to the extended jurisdiction for the County Court planned under the County Courts Bill. On 1st January 1956 Legal Aid was extended to the new jurisdiction and the 1955/56 Annual Report indicated that 418 applications for aid had been received between August 1955 and July 1956, of which 273 were granted. Even so the PML scheme continued to receive applications, some 351 in the year in question, of which 17 were passed over to be dealt with under the Legal Aid Scheme. The Report, however, noted that despite six years of operation, the Legal Aid Scheme still did not apply to Magistrates' Courts and Advice and Aid in Criminal Cases.

With regard to legal education the Report for this year recorded the formation of an interviewing panel in Leicester for intending articled clerks. This, of course, gave The Society a real degree of involvement with recruitment to the profession and was a further sign of the vigorous life of the organisation and the growing range of its activities. Lectures had also been arranged for unadmitted clerks on both Contract and Tort. The lecture series were repeated the next year and at the 1954 AGM urged The Committee to continue the practice, and in 1955/56 the subject of the lectures was conveyancing.

Of Meals and Premises

The Annual Dinner had been held on 7th February 1954, and there was a record attendance of 274 members and guests. 'The result was some lack of space and a consequent inability of the waiters to provide adequate service.' Obviously complaints had been received. The Dinner Sub-Committee concluded the only way forward was to limit the number of 'unofficial guests' to two per member. However, the fact that there had been a problem indicates how successful an event the dinner had become, a marked contrast to the earlier years of the century when pleas had been made to members to attend. The Grand Hotel, however, was able to cope with 270 diners at the 1956 Annual Dinner. The 1954 AGM also heard that The Society might have to vacate at least part of the space rented for the Library and Committee room from Messrs Owstons. It was resolved that The Committee should have a permanent home, that members should pledge financial support to acquiring such a home and that The Committee should be authorised to acquire premises in the New Walk or some other suitable area. The issue of premises became critical shortly thereafter as Messrs Owstons requested The Society to relinquish the use of the committee room over the Library. A search for a property to purchase was begun and a £100 option to purchase was obtained on No 40, Friar Lane. However, the sale fell through as the owner's asking price was considered to be far too much in excess of the value of the property together with the cost of the necessary alterations, though as we shall see No 40 was subsequently purchased. Accordingly a further five year lease was concluded with Messrs Owstons at a rent of £70 p.a.

Sadness, Regrets and Working hours

The 1955/56 report records the deaths of three members, including Mr E G B Fowler, for 48 years Coroner of Leicester, Clerk to the Leicester County Justices and Rutland County Justices and President in 1931. The Committee also regretted that some solicitors in the area were still not members of the Solicitors' Benevolent Association which was to reach its centenary in 1957/58: 'it would be a commendable gesture if our Local Law Society could record 100% membership of the Association, which carries out such valuable and humane work'. In the meantime the 1955 AGM voted a donation of 15 guineas (£15.75) to the Association, and it was pointed out that while there were causes for regret in Leicester over the percentage level of SBA support, 'London had one of the worst percentages'! Sadly, by 1957 Leicester was still below the 100% membership mark.

The AGM was also urged to adopt a five day working week with offices closing on a Saturday morning, but this was lost, 23 to 6. Saturday mornings also figured with regard to sittings of the Justices. Only in Leicester and Ashby-de-la-Zouch did the Courts sit on a Saturday morning. The AGM resolved that the Justices should, once again, be asked to refrain from Saturday opening. The Committee reported that it had attempted to persuade the Board of Trade to appoint an Assistant Official Receiver for Leicester on the basis of the volume of work, but no such appointment had been made. It would appear, however, that the Board of Trade had at least relented with regard to its earlier proposal to deprive Leicester of an Official Receiver.

Congratulations and New Horizons

Alderman A Halkyard had been elected Lord Mayor of Leicester, a fitting crown to a long career of military and public service and the 1955/56 Report carried The Society's congratulations to him. It was also proposed to extend membership of The Society to Rutland solicitors (though in the event most felt initially unable to accept) and to deal with the claim of Warwickshire Law Society that its area extended into those parts of Leicestershire within a 10 mile radius of Coventry. The greatest new venture on the horizon was the application by Leicester University College to receive full University Status, and the launch of the University Appeal Fund. The 1955 AGM resolved to support the application and to organise the support of members for the Appeal Fund. It was also considered desirable that the University once established should create a Faculty of Law for granting Law Degrees and also to become an Approved Law School under the Solicitors Acts. It was considered undesirable for Leicester Law Students to have the trouble and expense of travelling to Nottingham. Subsequently the Principal of The University College while hoping that a Law Faculty could be established was unwilling to give a guarantee with regard to the near future. A Law Department was, of course, established in 1965 at The University of Leicester, but it was a somewhat different creature from that envisaged 10 years earlier by The Society's AGM.

A New Constitution, New Avenues and the Centenary Years

On 24th October 1957 The Society adopted a revised constitution. In many ways this reiterated the original constitution, but it also incorporated the various changes that had been made down the years, especially the new committee structure brought into place in the 1940s. There were, however, certain departures from the original rules. Thus the maintenance of a Law Library was 'demoted' below the promotion of honorable practice and the encouragement of legal education. It was joined by the aim of forming a club for the use of Society members. The basis of membership also moved towards being individual. The old requirement that no member of a firm could be a member unless his partners (if any) also became members was modified. In its place came a rule that: 'The Committee shall exclude from the Society a member practising in co-partnership each of whose partners or principals (as the case may be) practising in the City or County of Leicester is not and has not for upwards of six weeks been a member or candidate for membership of the Society ...' That allowed solicitors resident in Leicester or Leicestershire but whose practices were entirely elsewhere to be members. Joining fees and annual subscriptions still, however, reflected a City/County divide with the entry fee being 5 guineas (£5.25) and £2.12s.6d (£2.62½) respectively. The size of The Committee was fixed at 9 together with the President, Vice President, Treasurer, Secretary, Librarian and (if any) members of The Council of The Law Society. The rule was maintained that in every year those 3 members of The Committee who had been longest in office were required to retire, although eligible for re-election without nomination. Committee meetings were to take place monthly, save in August. Eligibility for election as President was fixed as being only past President or Vice President, or a person who had held one or more of the offices of Secretary, Treasurer or Librarian, or who had been a Committee member for not less than two years. The standing sub-committees were fixed as (1) Finance and General Purposes (F&GP) which consisted of the Treasurer, Librarian and three other committee members, (2) Costs (C), (3) Public Relations (PR), (4) Poor Man's Lawyer (PML) and (5) Clerk's (CSC), all of which consisted of three members of The Committee, though the President, Vice President and Secretary were also ex-officio members of each standing sub-committee. Of these F&GP was clearly the most important with powers to supervise the finances, staff and Library of the Society, to consider and report to The Committee on matters arising between The Society, The Law Society and any other Provincial Law Society, unless the matter fell within the remit of another sub-committee, and to consider, and in any case of urgency to deal with, any matter referred to it by The Committee, the President, Vice President, Secretary or Treasurer. The 1957 Rules also made provision for scale charges though one of the most important features of these was the reference to the overall requirement fixed by The Law Society for the minimum charge to be not less than the ad valorem scale fixed from time to time under the Solicitors' Remuneration Orders made under the Solicitors Remuneration Act 1881. These particular rules were further revised in 1960 where the minimum charges – referred to as 'authorized fees' – were again set by reference to the Solicitors' Remuneration Orders. The significance of this is that charging for conveyancing and cognate matters was based not on a local but on a national scale.

Some of The Committee's work in 1958 was concerned with the ongoing search for premises to be a home for The Society. A property at the corner of New Walk and Museum Square was available at a rent of £300, but was rejected on the basis that it could fall victim of a town planning scheme. In the meantime a suggested room for Committee Meetings was found at the Leicester Trustee Savings Bank, though meetings continued to take place at Number 10, New Street. 40 Friar Lane was then considered, and in March 1958 F&GP were instructed to consider how to raise funds to purchase this property, and the proposal was further carried forward by another committee meeting later the same month. By April The Committee had been informed that the acquisition of new Library premises was essential as many older volumes had had to be placed in store in member firms' offices, while Messrs Owstons could not guarantee the Library's current home for a period of ten years, though the cost of acquisition would involve an increase in annual subscription to 8 guineas (£8.40). By August 1958 a price of £4,500 had been agreed for the purchase of the rear part of 40, Friar Lane, subject, of course, to planning permission and the provision of appropriate lavatories complying with sanitary bye-laws. By December

1958 The Society was in a position to sign the contract of purchase with a view to completion in January 1959, though, perhaps predictably, there was some delay with regard to this matter. As the process of purchase went ahead there was some discussion of incorporating The Society as opposed to having No. 40 Friar Lane owned by trustees. This went so far as the creation of a sub-committee to draft the Memorandum and Articles of Incorporation, though there were counter proposals for setting up a trading company, to provide duplicating and plan copying services, which would also own the new premises. In the meantime acquisition had taken place and by September 1959 the work of conversion could be discussed with the architects, with the tenders for the work being received in December 1959. The necessary notice to quit the old premises was given in June 1960. Closure of the old premises took place on 14th September 1960 and the opening of the new took place on 20th September with a formal ceremony on the evening of 19th September. The Society's Library moved into new premises that had originally been designed and built as a Turkish Bath!

It should not be supposed that the work of The Committee was at this time entirely concerned with the acquisition of premises. There were other important issues, such as the winding up in June 1959 of the Poor Man's Lawyer Scheme when the final provisions of the Legal Aid Act 1949 were commenced, and the ever vexed issue of the date and cost of the Annual Dinner, the price of which rose to £2.15s.0d (£2.75), with post-dinner drinks *not* being included in the price of a ticket. The creation of a special programme of events for young members, ie those under 36, was also actively considered. More ominously, bankruptcy proceedings against a member, Mr Clifford Buckley, were reported on 1st October 1959 and that matter was referred to The Law Society. Mr Buckley had previously dishonoured an undertaking and had ceased to answer all correspondence. He was a sole practitioner in Bowling Green Street elected into membership in 1947 but admitted as a solicitor in 1930. Mr Buckley had ceased to be a member of The Society by 1961.

By the time of the 1960 AGM on 28th April thought was being given to the Centenary Dinner which would have speeches, a feature of the occasion which had been omitted some few years previously. It was suggested that a number of judges with Leicestershire connections should be invited to the event, together with the Presidents of neighbouring Law Societies and other local dignitaries. It was also suggested that a Centenary Fund be opened to receive requested donations of £2.2s.0d (£2.10) per member to defray the cost of the Dinner while a separate Dinner and Dance should be held to which ladies could be invited: it might have been strange without them! This dinner dance was held on 14th April 1961, but the Centenary Dinner itself was held in The Queen's Hall of the University of Leicester as this was considerably larger than the King's Room at the Grand Hotel. The dinner, held on 6th January 1961, was honoured by the presence of Mr Justice Paull, Mr Justice Wrangham, Mr Justice Marshall, The Lord Mayor, The Lord Bishop, and The President of The Law Society. In all some 450 members and guests attended. One issue had been whether the event should be 'dinner jackets' or full evening dress – 'Top Hat, White Tie and Tails' to quote Fred Astaire. It may seem odd today that should be an issue as few people now possess full evening dress, but it was an issue in 1960/61, and was only decided by the information that the judges who would be attending would be on circuit, and they preferred in such circumstances to travel with 'DJs' rather than tail coats.

A further feature of the Centenary Year was the proposal to donate a piece of civic plate to The City and to raise the cost, some £300, mainly from members practising in Leicester. This took the form of a silver candelabra with the City Coat of Arms engraved thereon. It was presented to the Lord Mayor on 3rd May 1962.

At the end of its first century The Society could look back with a justifiable sense of pride. It had weathered the difficult years of the Second World War and had radically overhauled its operating systems. The old bickering over systems of conveyancing charges had effectively disappeared, and while the reason for this was the power of The Law Society, the Leicester Law Society had found new roles for itself, particularly with regard to interviewing would-be articled clerks, and the administration of the Legal Aid Scheme. Indeed the influence of the Legal Aid Act 1949 in helping to revive The Society's life and vigour can scarcely be overstated. At the same time the long and honourable tradition of the Poor Man's Lawyer Scheme had been brought to a peaceful close as the 'legal aid net' widened. Perhaps even more important for the future was the fact that by the end of the 1950s all but one of the solicitors practising privately in Leicester as principals in sole or partnership firms were members of The Society, and there was 100% membership amongst County principals. All save one of the principal solicitors employed by Leicestershire local authorities were also members. Such a high level of membership gave The Society enormous influence, while many of the old ties of social and family cohesion that had characterised The Society's earlier years continued to operate. Influence thus combined with cohesiveness. Who could have foreseen the revolutionary changes that were to begin in both The Society, The Profession and the local area in the next decade?

Mr Thomas Ingram
1868

Mr Joseph Harris
1861

Mr Joseph Harvey
1877

Mr H. A. Owston
1883

i

Mr William Napier Reeve
1869

Mr W. J. Freer
1901

Sir Thomas Wright
1902

Mr T. H. Wright
1920

Vera Stamenkovich
1995/96
(Photo: Leicester Mercury)

Linda Lee

Prakash Suchak
2008/2009

Imogen Cox
2016/2017

Chapter 6

An interlude with The Law Students

We encountered the Leicester Law Students' Society in Chapter 2. Sadly very few records of this organisation appear to survive. However, The Society has in its possession one volume (which bears a label 'for the edification of future generations') detailing the activities of the students' society during the 1950s. This is an important record as not only does it contain details of many, now senior, local practitioners in their early days, but it also reinforces the impression that in the 1950s the profession locally was vibrant, active and confident. The students were clearly quite a vigorous body and many were to go into local practice adding their strength to that of their elders. Interestingly the students' society had female members long before The Society did, though none seem to have progressed into local practice, and one must wonder whether they gave up the law before qualification or decided to move elsewhere. At least one of the female members married one of the men and, as was the custom then, appears to have given up the practice of the law.

The volume opens in 1952 when the Honorary President was H H J Wrangham and the Committee included Mr K V Holmes, Mr J D McKinell, Mr J B Ervin (later to form McKinnell, Ervin & Holmes), Mr J M Barlow (Evan Barlow, Son & Poyner), Mr D A H Law, who was with Messrs Bartlett, Walters & Parry of Loughborough before setting up his own sole practice in Leicester and Mr M Turner who also later set up his own practice in Leicester. From that committee Mr Jeremy Barlow has provided us with some reminiscences. He had arrived at his firm in December 1951 and was articled to his father, E Morgan Barlow, qualifying in 1957. One of his earliest memories was the death in 1952 of King George VI. Firms gave their staff an hour off to watch a procession go along Horsefair Street in honour of the late King. There were also inter firm cricket matches between Barlows, Freer Bouskell and Harding & Barnett. To play one football match against the Derby Law Students – a highly trained squad – the Leicester Students, however, managed to include Derek McBean, a senior office boy from Barlows who at one time had been on Leicester City's books. McBean scored six goals in Leicester's 6-1 victory!

The first recorded meeting for 26th November 1952 was held at the Saracen's Head Hotel (now Molly McGuire's on the Market Place) and consisted of a debate, as, it will be remembered from Chapter 2, was this society's tradition, on the topic: 'That this House considers that Law and Order is Better Preserved by a Policy of Reform not Retribution'.

The case for the motion was put by Superintendent Kelly of the County Constabulary. 18 Law Students attended, including a Miss J M Bowes, together with 11 police officers and three guest adjudicators. Fearless comment was clearly in order as one speaker referred to Mr Justice Avory as having a mind as sharp as a needle and as broad! Other judicial variations were also the subject of comment such as the practice of Mr Justice Lynsksey to bind over those who committed the then illegal acts of homosexuality, while Mr Justice Stable would impose sentences of up to 15 years for such offences. There was clearly a lively debate and the motion was carried 2:1 by the adjudicators. At the next debating meeting 16 local solicitors were present and the topic for debate was 'That the present form of Recruitment to the Legal Profession needs Radical Alteration'. The problems then encountered were those of difficulty of entering the profession unless one had the money to support oneself during training and the family or social connection to gain a foothold initially. Social equality demanded reform. The opposition, led by Colonel Freer, understandably spoke up for family tradition and the commitment which having to pay a premium on entry to articles induced. There was a long debate, but the motion was carried 20:15.

Debates were, of course, not the only activities of the students' society. On 30th January 1953 at The Barley Mow Hotel, Mr Barnett Janner (Lord) MP (a famous name in Leicester local history and father of Greville (Lord) Janner Q.C. MP) addressed the society on the Rent Acts, while Mr J A Grieves spoke on Criminal Law and Advocacy at The Saracen's Head on 4th February 1953. On 17th February 1953 a Moot was held at The Saracen's Head on the issues of a landlord's duty to repair premises and his liability for the negligence of an independent contractor.

The Students' Society was clearly a very active body which engaged in a wide range of activities, including joint meetings with other similar organisations, such as those in Coventry and Derby. They also organised teams to play rugby, soccer, skittles and cricket. In addition they organised sherry parties, dances and carol singing for charity. In 1953 the dance tickets were priced at 7s.6d (37½p) and it was planned to sell 300. Their minutes are also replete with highly derogatory references to the character and ability of the officers, one being described as: 'plainly intended by nature to be the world's most fraudulent financial operator ever, and the wonder of all those who are aware that he passed his Trust Accounts and Book-keeping Examination at the first attempt'. Student wit was clearly then of a rather higher order than is generally nowadays the case, while the City's public houses were obviously suitable for activities which today would be unthinkable. One should also remember that meetings commenced at 7.30 pm and were usually over within an hour and a half with some food and drink provided. No doubt some members stayed on for further liquid refreshment, until 'last orders' at 10.30, but most would have made their ways home by a respectable hour on foot or by public transport.

It is interesting to reflect on the cost of activities over half a century ago. The Saracen's Head in 1953 charged £6 per annum for hiring a room throughout the year and regular expenditure on food and drink at the meetings was some £20. There were two social evenings planned at a cost of £10, and three lectures out of which a visiting speaker would be dined at two; cost £3.10s.0d (£3.50). A sherry party was planned at a cost of £13. These items together with a County Cricket Club Member's Ticket at £2.5s.0d (£2.25), travelling expenses, £8, Sporting fixtures, £10, and miscellaneous expenses, £3, brought the estimated budget for the year to some £75.15s.0d (£75.75). What might that purchase today? Perhaps a meal for, say, four at one of Leicester's curry houses. We must, of course allow for inflation, but the costs of running the students' society also appear to have been modest.

On 27th October 1953 the students' society departed from its usual venue (going to the De Montfort Hotel) and its usual practice of debate and lectures, and hosted a two part evening based on popular radio programmes of the day, 'Any Questions' and 'Twenty Questions'. An interesting topic for the December 1953 debate was: 'This House considers morals to be a handicap to a Solicitor's success'. The proposition was defeated, but only by 16:12, not a great margin in favour of morality. Rather more credit for the students was reflected in their victory in a Law Notes Moot against six other societies in November 1953, the first time for over twenty years the Leicester students had competed. Leicester won again the following month and again in January 1954, and once more in November 1955. Again this is an indication of a vigorous group of young people.

January 1954 commenced with a social evening held jointly with accountancy students; there was a table tennis match and a debate on the evils of morning coffee, while Mr C L Hale MP, an erstwhile member of the students' society, gave an address on 'Law and Laughter' on 22nd February 1954. Mr Hale had been articled to Mr Evan Barlow and claimed to have spent much of his time in articles either at the County Cricket Ground or at Osborne's Snooker parlour at the lower end of Friar Lane – now redeveloped as apartments – between 1917 and 1922. Oddly enough he passed his final examinations and then decided he was worth more than £150 to £200 p.a. in salary and so set up on his own account in Coalville. By 1954's values the sums in question would be about £1000 to £1500. Mr Hale became a member of The Leicester Law Society in 1924 and his practice subsequently became Hale & Mander. Mr Hale's jokes and anecdotes that evening included:

'A solicitor ... descended to the nether regions where he found his old cronies laughing and joking with the devil; he was amazed at this, as the only persons he could see in the inferno were solicitors. He enquired about this and the devil, taking him aside, pointed out a hill on which there were thousands of people stretched out, drying in the sun. On enquiring the reason he was told: "They are too green to burn; you should know that"...'

'A solicitor had died in comparative poverty and a collection was being taken to bury him. A County Court Judge, who was not fond of solicitors, was informed of the circumstances and asked to contribute a shilling (5p). "Here's five shillings; go and bury five of 'em" was his reply.'

The 1953/54 accounts reveal, inter alia, that a sherry party had cost £19.15s.5d (£19.75½) with 18 bottles of sherry being consumed together with some 300 cigarettes. To redress the clear health and safety implications of such excessive consumption it is gratifying to note that 30 bottles of soft drinks were also consumed. Rather more serious was the debate on National Service held on 12ᵗʰ October 1954. The motion which decried National Service as a 'major social evil' was defeated 8:4. It was, however, subsequently recorded that none of the evening's speakers had actually done National Service. The year 1954/55 otherwise maintained the usual round of debates, social and sporting events. The annual carol singing resulted in a sum of money being despatched to 'Dr Barnadoes' (sic), but the principal feature of the event appears to have been the amount of alcohol consumed which led to only five 'finishers' out of a 'field of about forty or so starters'. It is interesting to note that law students, then as now, were both great consumers of alcohol and also not always accomplished spellers.[30]

The pattern thus established continued into 1955/56. There was again the annual ball held at The Bell Hotel – where Jonny Lester's band cost £25.14s.0d (£25.70p) – what might entertainment cost nowadays?

---

[30] The same report for 1954/55 includes the appalling howler 'obiter dictur'.

In addition the law students had a successful sporting season in cricket, rugby and some strange sport named 'Association Fottball' (sic)! A sign of the times, however, was the Treasure Hunt of May 16th 1956, an event which indicates the presence of a number of car drivers. 10 members and 12 guests took part, and seven cars are recorded as being used. With considerable indifference to the effect of alcohol on driving some members had to be 'dragged' from the bar of The Cedars at Evington to get the hunt underway at 7.00 pm. The terminus was The Fox and Hounds at Skeffington via The Fox and Goose at Illston. The majority of participants arrived well before closing time to enjoy supper.

The students were in more serious mood on 9th October 1956 when Mr David Witcomb, their Librarian, reported on the provision of books for law students in The Society's Library and the vote of a grant from The Society to keep this up to date. Mr Witcomb asked for suggestions for new titles to be added – no ribald ones were made. Mr Whitcomb then led for the proposition in the evening's debate 'that the two branches of the legal profession should be fused'. Mr Whitcomb envisaged that after qualification every lawyer should do two years general practice and should then specialise, with clients being able to go straight to an appropriate specialist without having to consult a generalist first. It is not recorded whether the motion was won or lost, but it is interesting that an issue which has for so long been an item of contention should be under discussion.

1956/57 is the year from which printed membership lists for the Law Students' Society survive. The Committee consisted of Messrs P A P Astill (C Norman Astill), J F Tillotson (Toller, Pochin & Wright), J C Pyper (Harding & Barnett), P H F Carr (John A Carpenter), B G Ruddock (A D Foxon), P Gibson (Loseby & Moore) and J A Holland (Harvey, Clarke & Adams). The members were: Miss J M Bowes (Oldham, Marsh & Son), J P Day (G Stevenson & Son), R O A Dixon (A H Headley), R Dixon (Sprigge, Pollard & Co), C Fraser (Owston & Co), M H Gardiner (Sawday, Wright & Co), P Gilbert (Crane & Walton), A M Gooch (Stone & Co), K J Gyles (Harding & Barnett), Miss D A Hammond (P J Hammond), J D Hammond (Stone & Co), K Lacey (Chapman & Goddard), M E Lewis (Edward Hands & Lewis), G Myerson (A H Headley), G E Parkinson (Freer Bouskell & Co), C J Partridge (Moss, Toone & Deane), Miss C Pilling (Hawley & Rodgers), P A Simpson (Freer Bouskell & Co), B T C Small (Toller, Pochin & Wright), Miss A D Smith (Barradale & Haxby), P G Smith (Freer Bouskell & Co), A G Spence (A D Foxon), M Turner (Whetstone & Frost), D B Witcomb (Freer Bouskell & Co), S Woodward (Crane & Walton), M W Young (Bray

& Bray). That is a membership of 33, with most coming from Leicester City firms. But the presence of four female members should be noted and also the 'spread' of firms. Freer Bouskell & Co with 4 members certainly appeared to be recruiting lawyers for the future.

The meeting for 13th February 1957 was held jointly with the County Police Force – a debate between law students and The Police was established as an annual event. The topic for debate on this occasion was: 'the criminal is more to be pitied than blamed'. The usual social evening held jointly with accountancy students followed a fortnight later. 1957's events followed the pattern established in previous years with, amongst other activities, a balloon debate in April and a car treasure hunt in July. There were 11 cars for this event, though the minutes record these as being borrowed! In October 1957 there was a most adventurous meeting when members paid a visit to Desford Pit, descending at 5.00 pm from the dusk of a Leicestershire evening to the blackness 800 feet below. Having been shown some of the old workings the members elected to travel to a working coal face. 'They travelled along miles of dusty tunnel until they arrived at an extremely small aperture, into which they were instructed to crawl. This aperture proved to be the face itself, and the party crawled for some 200 yards along the face immediately next to thundering machinery and straining men to the accompaniment of muffled bangs as the explosives in the mine were detonated'. The evening concluded with sampling Botcheston Beer 'which succeeded in washing away an accumulation of four hours coal dust from tired throats.' A rather more 'normal' event followed in November 1957 when Mr Justice Donovan addressed the law students on the topic of 'The High Court'. This event took place in The Town Hall – presumably The Saracen's Head was not thought appropriate to the dignity of the speaker. The students then retired to The Royal Hotel – another of Leicester's sadly vanished hostelries, the front of which is now preserved as part of Lloyds TSB in Town Hall Square. The conclusion of that evening seems to have been less dignified than the beginning involving a 'scrum down and bumping outside the hotel'.

1958's events commenced on 15th January with a debate on government by political party, while in February in the Courtrooms of Leicester Castle the law students staged what was recorded as being another annual event, namely a Mock Trial. A trip to Kenilworth Rugby Football Ground on 12th February proved to be the occasion for the consumption of ale which continued after the meeting as the bus on which the members travelled was blown by a strong wind to The Blue Pig at Wolvey and the return to Leicester was delayed until 11 pm. Nowadays many of the current generation of law students are just starting their evening jollifications at such an hour, but over half a century ago 11 pm had a decidedly naughty air about it. However, it is clear that as the decade of the 1950s wore on the gatherings of the law students appear to take on a rather more relaxed and less formal tone. The annual report for 1957/58 records that 'the ... annual booze-up (officially sherry party) took place at the Market Bosworth Rectory. The refreshments both liquid and solid were top class and the last guest finished running round the drive to sober up about 12.30 am'.

By 1958/59 the Students' Society had 32 members, of which 3 were female. Once again there was a full programme of events including golf, soccer, rugby and cricket fixtures. The annual car treasure hunt and mock trial were also held as were 'two hops' – which for those unfamiliar with the slang of the day means two dances of an informal nature. Another established feature of the year was The Tall Story gathering at which the 'best received story of the evening was that of Ann Smith concerning a frustrated spinster who wanted warmth on the long winter evenings'. This was in addition to the usual round of debates and joint meetings with the Police and Accountancy students. Carol singing took place on 24th December 1958 beginning at The Cradock Arms in Knighton and £5.5s.0d (£5.25) was raised for Dr Barnado. The annual sherry party had certainly become a more general drinking event as the expenditure of over £30 on 12th April 1959 included a 'pin (small cask) of Worthington E'. There was dancing in plenty – a mixture of Rock 'n Roll and Chris Barber – and the last guest was evicted at 2 am. That sounds distinctly more like a modern student event!

The last surviving annual report in the archives, that for 1959/60, records the established pattern of debates and sports events, though the increasingly mobile nature of society is, perhaps, reflected in the number of these held at 'away' venues. Interestingly the May debate at Loughborough College (now University) was on the establishment of a Ministry of Arts and Sports – over forty years later such an arm of government now exists. A joint debate was also held with junior members of the Chartered Auctioneers and Estate Agents' professions on the issue of the level of professional fees. While the Law Notes Moot, in which Leicester students had done well in the past, had been allowed to lapse, members travelled to a local moot in Birmingham. There were also a number of lectures delivered including one on the discrepancy between the ideal and the actual in prison organisation, while the Bishop of Leicester (Dr R R

Williams) later addressed members on Natural Law and Canon Law. The mock trial also took place in March and the Treasure Hunt in July. There were two 'hops' held in Oadby Church Hall, and while they were social successes they were financial failures – members did not sell enough tickets, a familiar lament. However, the Annual Ball at The Bell Hotel held on December 30th was a great success.

The last membership list surviving is for 1960/61 and it records the names of 25 members, once again 3 of them being female. A number of new members have been pencilled into the printed list while a number of others have been pencilled out as 'qualified'. One of those was Miss A Smith of Messrs Barradale & Haxby, but she does not appear to have joined The Leicester Law Society, at least not in her maiden name. It had by then become the policy of the Students' Society to invite those who had to leave by virtue of qualification to become Associate Members. In this respect we can see the origins of the 'Young Solicitors'. One other feature of note is the existence of a new class of 'special members'. These were one bar student and two intending solicitors who were pursuing their legal studies at University, Mr A K Hawley at Cambridge and Mr J McLauchlan at Durham. There is considerable significance in this: the traditional pattern of legal education based on articles and 'the statutory year' was beginning to alter. While there had been a number of Leicester solicitors with degrees even from the early days, the overwhelming majority of practitioners until 1950s and into the 1960s still qualified in the way that had been established earlier in the 20th century. The Students' Society played a most important role in that process. It provided a stimulating educational and social forum for its members, and its fortnightly meetings were 'musts' to attend. It created a collegial atmosphere for students while also introducing them, via the good offices of those solicitors who assisted its work, to professional ethical standards and local practices and conventions of behaviour. There can be no doubt that the Students' Society was a most valuable 'feeder' into the principal Society and much of the success of the senior body in the 1950s probably stemmed from the regular influx of keen new members already familiar with organisational life from the ranks of the law students. The names on the surviving membership lists clearly show that the majority of members stayed in Leicester on qualification.

However, as stated earlier, the pattern of legal education was to undergo major changes in the 1960s. The expansion of higher education after 1965 following the Robbins Report led to the creation of more Universities, more student places and certainly an increase in the number of University law students.[31] Leicester itself saw the creation of a University Law Department whose first intake arrived in 1966, while the creation of Leicester Polytechnic at the end of the 1960s saw the establishment there of degree level study, albeit for the London external LLB. The days of 'traditional' professional study and qualifications were thus numbered and the scene was being set for the radical proposals of the early 1970s that the Law should become a graduate only profession.

It is to those developments in the 1960s and 70s and their impact on the Leicester Law Society that we must now turn.

---

[31] The author's own matriculating year at the University of Liverpool in 1964 comprised 48 students. The next year's intake soared to 70, low by current standards, but very high then.

Chapter 7

The Swinging 60s and beyond

We left The Society having completed its first century and its move into new Library premises. Mr M G Pearce of Messrs Straw & Pearce in Loughborough had undertaken to write in his own time a history of The Society and he had been supplied with all the records. It was agreed that The Society would publish a limited edition of 300 copies of this work. Mr Pearce, who had been admitted in 1927 and elected to membership in 1929, sadly died in 1963. The task of writing a history was subsequently passed to another member of The Society, but no progress appears to have been made with the project.

The annual report for the year ending 31st December 1962 gave the membership of The Society as 192. This was a creditable figure for a surviving Waterlow's Solicitors' Diary for 1964 gives the following number of solicitors in the City and County: Ashby-de-la-Zouch, 11; Coalville, 2; Hinckley and Market Bosworth, 15; Leicester, 160; Loughborough, 20; Lutterworth, 6; Market Harborough, 10; Melton Mowbray, 9. That is a total of 233 so a membership level of 192 for 1962 represents a very high proportion of participation amongst local solicitors. Incidentally the same diary records the name of a woman solicitor, that of Judith Coupland, who was at The Gas Board. She does not, however, appear to have been a member of The Society. Indeed the decade of the 1960s was some years advanced before women joined The Society, the first three being Miss Janet Fortune, who was admitted in 1965 and elected in 1966, Miss Ursula Wild, later Mrs Donald Hubbard, who was admitted in 1963 and elected in 1967, and Miss Barbara Orbell, later Mrs Jeremy Stafford, who was admitted in 1966 and elected in 1967. [Mr and Mrs Stafford were the first Leicester Solicitors to marry each other.] It was only in the 1970s that women began to enter The Society in any real numbers, and we shall return to that later. For the moment, however, The Society continued to be very much its traditional self and the early years of the 1960s record the well established pattern of concerns and activities.

New initiatives in 1962 included the issue of a new form of Particulars, Conditions of Sale and Agreement which won the approval of members and generated a profit of £862.15s.11d (£862.80 rounded up). There was also an Articled Clerk's Prize to be awarded to someone from the City or County achieving, in the opinion of The Law Society Examiners, the best result in the Qualifying Examination Part II then held in August of each year. In connection with service as an Articled Clerk it was also announced that Leicester City Education Authority had decided to give grants to students attending the College of Law at either London or Guildford. The days of such enlightened educational generosity departed in the 1970s and 1980s and are now the merest memory.

In defence of members' interests The Committee made representations to The Law Society about the proposed new Accounts Rules which were considered to impose heavy burdens and greater accountancy charges on solicitors, and also urged members not, in general, to accept conveyancing agency commissions below particular rates. There was also the perennial problem of work being sent from Leicester to Nottingham Assizes, and then, to add injury to insult, not being dealt with at Nottingham; resulting in delay while the matters were once more remitted to Leicester! The Committee asked members to inform them of any such instances so that appropriate reports on the functioning of The Assizes could be sent to Chancery Lane.

The Library continued its work with the acquisition of, inter alia, a set of Nichols "History of The County of Leicester", a gift from Mr Albert Herbert, and student books for the new Law Society Examination Syllabus. Legal Aid continued to flourish especially as for the first time it was available in the Magistrates' Courts and the number of Legal Aid Certificates issued rose from 710 in 1961 to 900 in 1962.

Two points of interest arose from the 1962 AGM. The first was an issue encountered earlier, namely Saturday closing. It was clear that the majority of members practising in the City were in favour of opening on a Saturday morning, so no recommendation about closure was made. On the other hand, Mr H M Lloyd, Under Secretary of The Law Society, in his address to members argued that solicitors should not be so overworked as to be unable to play their part in local affairs, social services and activities outside the profession. Saturday closing is now, of course, the general rule, but are solicitors in general overburdened so as to be unable to have a wider social and public life?

1963's report contained news of an increase in membership from 192 to 194 and added: 'This Society has the largest membership of any in the East Midlands Area and enjoys the support of nearly 100 per cent of practising Solicitors in the City and County'. The report otherwise contained the usual items relating to the maintenance of The Library, which had made 5000 loans in the year, the need to continue support for the Solicitors' Benevolent Association, and the onward march of Legal Aid, with some 974 certificates being issued in 1963. The age-old problem of securing compliance with conveyancing scale charges reasserted itself, this time not in Leicestershire but on a wider regional basis. The Committee had urged that charges in the East Midlands should be as uniform as possible. The Committee had also investigated allegations that certain local estate agents were engaging in the practice of getting parties to house purchase to sign contracts in their offices. The Leicester Association of Auctioneers and Estate Agents had banned such a practice, but there were some agents who were not members of this body and so were outside its control.

The 1963 AGM was, however, the occasion for some serious heart searching. The most contentious issue was that of postal voting for election to the Committee. It was argued that though The Society had the best part of 200 members only 50-60 attended the AGM, and thus elections took place on a less than ideally representative basis. Some members took the view that a system of postal voting should be introduced. Others argued that such an innovation would lead to even fewer members attending the AGM, and that such a change would mean considerable work for The Secretary. It was, however, determined that The Committee should consider introducing such a change. In the event The Society determined not to proceed with postal voting in 1964. Another contentious issue was that of institutional advertising. Some members argued that while solicitors could not advertise individually, they could see no reason why general advertising on behalf of the services solicitors could offer should not be undertaken. It was agreed that The Society would in general support the investigation of institutional advertising.

Saturday opening continued as a vexed issue and this was coupled with complaints about the continuance of court sittings on a Saturday morning. There was also concern expressed over the number of vacancies for articled clerks. The Law Society had undertaken a recruiting campaign and as a result 'more and more young men [sic] both graduates and non-graduates are seeking articles in offices and it is very difficult to place them'. This plea was reinforced in 1964 by a further request for information about the availability of positions for school leavers seeking clerkships.

There was also concern over the collection of photographs of past presidents. Reference was made to the time at which Mr C F Bray had presented The Society with the Badge of Office which all subsequent Presidents have worn at official functions during their year of office. Mr Bray had been asked to form a collection of photographs of all past Presidents. These had been brought together but were currently languishing in the strong room of a particular firm. It was argued that this collection should be displayed in the new Library. The fate of this collection will be detailed in a later chapter!

On a less contentious note the AGM agreed that there should continue to be occasional series of lectures for members provided speakers of sufficiently high calibre could be obtained. It was also determined that there should be an annual dinner dance in addition to the annual dinner.

Sad news and Complaints

The 1964 Report contains news of the deaths of Mr C F Bray, President of the Society in 1949/50, and of Alderman Halkyard, a former Lord Mayor of Leicester.

More ominously for the future there were complaints about the speed and cost of conveyancing. The Law Society had proposed a national form of contract for use in all domestic conveyancing issues on the basis that this would expedite transactions. The Committee argued, quite truthfully, that delays in conveyancing were (and still are) largely due to purchasers being unwilling to commit until they have themselves sold their own properties. However, one suspects, then as now, that myth is more potent than reality with regard to the alleged slowness of solicitors in respect of conveyancing. At the AGM particular mention was made of mounting press criticism of conveyancing charges. It was clear that the most vocal complaints came from those areas of the country experiencing the highest house prices, and thus the highest conveyancing costs because of the scale charge system. It was recognised that press criticism could not be ignored and that the profession as a whole should try to improve public knowledge of the amount of work involved in conveyancing. With the benefit of hindsight we know this was all in vain. Ever increasing house prices ultimately led to the death of scale charges.

A further blow to solicitors was the House of Lords decision in *J Brown v Inland Revenue Commissioners* in which it had been determined that a solicitor was not entitled to retain interest on client account monies placed on deposit.

On a more positive note The Committee was able to record that Ashby Magistrates would cease to sit on Saturday mornings as from 1st January 1965. The Legal Aid Act 1964 had also come into force and had extended legal aid to Care, Protection and Control proceedings and to Protection from Eviction. It was still too early to say whether this would lead to any particular increase in applications, but applications for aid were generally up.

A Year of Change?

The 1965 report contains information on a miscellany of matters all of which point to a quickening of pace in relation to many matters affecting solicitors and their practices. The impact of the new technology of the day was considered in respect of a memorandum from the West Essex Law Society urging all solicitors to subscribe to the Telex System which could lead to reductions in postal charges as 40% of all solicitors' outgoing letters were to other solicitors. The Committee declined to agree on the basis that Telex could not cope with enclosures to letters and that its installation cost, some £160 p.a., would be uneconomical for smaller firms. Technology has, of course, moved on substantially and documents can now be sent by fax or electronically while 'E Conveyancing' has also come to stay: but these things were a long way in the future in 1965. Technology also enabled tape recorded lectures to be made available to members, legal executives and articled clerks. Leicester City Council had also proposed to create a register of house owners having properties for sale to enable prospective purchasers to negotiate directly with vendors and thus speed up transaction times. An investigation of the proposal discovered that the City Council would not accept responsibility for the accuracy of particulars supplied by prospective vendors. This was a major defect which, along with the possibility of unscrupulous estate agents taking advantage of the scheme and the lack of opportunities for both vendors and purchasers to be given independent advice on price, etc, led The Committee to oppose any such innovation. Despite this the Corporation pressed ahead with its Register, but before doing so sought the advice of The Society about a form of disclaimer to relieve the Council of all liability following use of the service and 'stressing the necessity for the [user] to seek advice from a surveyor and solicitor before deciding to sell or purchase and before signing any document'. It is interesting to speculate how far any such scheme operating nowadays with such a disclaimer would fall foul of the legislation governing unfair business contract terms.

The 1965 report further mentions the creation of The Law Department of Leicester University which was to admit its first students in October 1966. Professor J K Grodecki, the foundation Professor of Law, had spoken to the Committee about the problems of creating a new Law School and in particular the foundation of a Law Library. He had appealed for donations of unwanted text books and reports, and this appeal had led to the acquisition of many volumes.[32]

The Society recorded a number of deaths in 1965, inter alia that of Mr J T Bouskell who had been admitted in 1929 and had become a partner in Messrs Harris, Watts & Bouskell which had amalgamated with Messrs Freer & Co in 1943. Mr Bouskell had been Coroner for South Leicestershire from 1942, and Clerk of the City of Leicester Valuation Panel. He had been President of The Society in 1959/60 and Treasurer from 1954 to 1965. On a happier note membership of The Society increased from 181 in 1964 to 191 in 1965, almost back to 1962's level.

1966 was an exceptionally busy year for The Society with two special general meetings in addition to the AGM. The first of these special meetings was concerned with a change of rules in the constitution regarding the expulsion of members. Provision was made to ensure that any member over whom the shadow of improper conduct hung would be given a statement in writing of the conduct imputed to him, and an opportunity of giving an explanation to the Committee either in writing or in person. That was an important amendment reflecting the House of Lords' decision a few months earlier in *Ridge v Baldwin* which reinvigorated and reinforced the need for any disciplinary action to comply with the rules of natural justice: audi alterem partem and nemo judex in causa sua potest.[33] The second special meeting returned, yet again, to the vexed issue of scale charges. This was in response to a consultation exercise from the Non-Contentious Business Committee of The Law Society. Various schemes of remuneration for such work were put forward for consideration, including the retention of scale fees: the vote was overwhelmingly in favour of retaining them.

By 1966 membership had increased to 202 from 191 the previous year and this had implications for the Annual Dinner. The 1965 dinner had been attended by 128 members, 38 articled clerks and 123 guests. The principal guests had included The Lord Chief Justice, Mr Justice Waller, Mr Justice James, The President of The Law Society, The Lord

---

[32] Gifts from firms not only helped to stock the main University Library Collection but also to found an internal departmental library which was in the care of the present author for a number of years. These volumes are now to be found in the Harry Peach Room at Leicester University.

[33] Despite the regrettable decline in the currency of Latin amongst the profession, the present author respectfully refuses to translate these memorable phrases!

Lieutenant, The Recorder of Leicester, The Lord Bishop of Leicester and the Vice Chancellor of Leicester University. At the AGM it was pointed out that the increasing membership of The Society and the popularity of the annual dinner were putting pressure on capacity at The King's Room of The Grand Hotel which could comfortably hold only 300. The Committee considered a move to larger premises such as The Queen's Hall at Leicester University. In the event the dinner stayed firmly emplaced at The Grand (now the Ramada Jarvis) for many years, but for a while restrictions had to be placed on the numbers of those attending.

The standing of The Society at this time was reflected in the request of the Sheffield Regional Hospital Board for nomination of members to act as Chairmen of Mental Health Review Tribunals. Messrs C E J Freer, B F Toland, C H Jones and I D McKinnell were nominated. The Committee had also had a meeting with the Leicester and County Estate Agents' Association at which much mutual misunderstanding had been resolved and a Joint Standing Committee created to deal with matters of joint concern. The Society as a whole had been invited to attend Professor J K Grodecki's inaugural lecture to mark the formal inception of the Law Department of Leicester University. Because Leicester now had its own University Law Department, and with the cessation by Leicester articled clerks from attendance at lectures at Nottingham University, The Society withdrew from its membership of the Advisory Committee for Nottingham University Law Department. The Society was also consulted on arrangements for the conduct of civil litigation during the annual long vacation. Interestingly enough in making its response The Committee drew on the expertise of two senior legal executives experienced in High Court and County Court litigation. Might this be an indication that in Leicester such business was largely in the hands of legal executives while solicitors were more concerned with probate, conveyancing and criminal matters?

The Society continued its educational activities by again providing a series of tape recorded lectures in the Law Library, for which purpose a Tape Recorder had been purchased.[34] In addition Professor Wheatcroft had been engaged to deliver a lecture on Capital Gains Tax, and a two-day seminar on the same issue at Leicester University had been held addressed by Mr G Williams of the Midland Bank Executor and Trustee Co. Ltd and Mr S Bates, a barrister. The Library continued to be much in use and was the subject of £1,645.6s.9d (£1,645.35 approximately) expenditure in 1966. Books and bookbinding constituted the principal items of expenditure,

---

[34] Younger readers may not be familiar with such devices. They ran on a reel to reel basis, and were the ancestors of cassette recorders. These, of course, have now been largely replaced, save for dictation, by digitally based equipment.

while the Librarian's salary rose from just over £477 to £517 p.a. The possibility of installing a telephone in the Library was considered as this would benefit County members and those whose offices were not in the City Centre. This was, however, not taken forward as it was thought the installation of a telephone would increase the Librarian's workload and distract her from helping those seeking volumes. The heating system of the Library was also considered with a view to switching to an alternative form of heating, but the capital cost was not justifiable in view of only a small decrease in operating costs.

The annual report recorded, inter alia, the death of Mr C E Crane aged 83, senior partner of Messrs Crane and Walton who had been admitted in 1904 and who, in addition to many local and central government appointments and involvement in local building society and banking concerns, had been President of The Society in 1947/48 and 1948/49. 1966 was also the year of election of the first female member of The Society, but this event passed without special comment.

1967 saw membership of The Society rise to 217 and the annual dinner on 8th March was attended by 288 members and guests with 26 official guests including The Lord Mayor of Leicester, The Recorder of Leicester, H A Skinner, QC (subsequently His Honour Judge Skinner and then Mr Justice Skinner), The President of The Law Society, The High Sherriff of Leicestershire and the Provost of Leicester Cathedral. Despite such a heavy 'chain gang' representation on 'the top table' the number of speeches was kept to two. 1967 might otherwise be considered another 'business as usual' year, but it is important to note the volume and range of matters considered by The Committee. These included: nominating members to sit on the Local Rating Valuation Panel; seeking rights of audience for solicitors at the City and County Quarter Sessions; obtaining cloakroom facilities for solicitors attending cases in the Town Hall; setting up a joint committee with the local bar to discuss matters of common interest; consideration of changes to The Law Society's constitution to create a new constituency for council election purposes consisting of Leicestershire, Rutland and Northamptonshire; the expense of sending deeds to the Land Registry in Nottingham; the appointment of a new Law Librarian and the raising of a retirement subscription presentation in respect of the retiring Librarian; considering the impact of the Misrepresentation Act 1967 on conditions of sale and liaising in particular with estate agents in respect of this matter; formalising arrangements for placing prospective articled clerks as there continued to be increasing numbers seeking articles; setting up a Legal Education Sub-Committee to review the provision of tape recorded lectures and Law Society 'Crash Courses', and making representations in respect of the Leicester Corporation Bill, local legislation then being promoted in Parliament. This last issue is worthy of mention for the Bill as proposed would have given the Corporation very extensive powers of compulsory purchase for the benefit of its employees way beyond the normal provision of the general law, as well as to acquire shares in development companies and to suspend the operation of restrictive covenants on land acquired by the Corporation. The objections of The Society were successful in persuading the Corporation not to pursue the particular clauses in question.

Considerable changes were also made in 1967 in The Society's investments and the presentation of its accounts to take account of liability to Corporation Tax and Capital Gains Tax. The Society's investments nevertheless stood at £2000 and the outstanding mortgage on the Library was only £875.

Between December 1967 and December 1968 membership of The Society rose from 217 to 220. The subsequent annual dinner was held on 19th February 1969 and was attended by 140 members and 180 guests including 48 articled clerks, with 31 official guests including a number of judicial and civic dignitaries. While the attempt, referred to earlier, to seek rights of audience at Quarter Sessions had been unsuccessful, The Committee was in 1968 much concerned with the work of The Royal Commission on Assizes and Quarter Sessions. This ultimately led to the creation in the early 1970s of the current system of Crown and Circuit Courts with High Court Judges coming on circuit from time to time in place of the former Assize System. Interestingly while The Committee was strongly in favour of a District Criminal Court in Leicester it was opposed to County Court Judges having jurisdiction there as they already had too much work. The Committee also organised a Cocktail Party for second year students and staff from Leicester University. This was organised in conjunction with The Society's Young Members Group, the body later known as 'The Young Solicitors'. The Committee also agreed to give support to the work of the newly formed Radio Leicester, and participation had taken place in a discussion on the issue of warranties.

An Important AGM

The meeting on 30th April 1968 was, inter alia, concerned with a number of important issues. It must be remembered that during the 1960s the general incidence of taxation rose while the Labour Government of Harold Wilson, in power from 1964 to 1970, was much concerned with issues of equity (in the widest sense) with regard to prices and incomes throughout society. To this end a Prices and Incomes Board had been created which had examined the incomes of solicitors. 700 firms throughout the nation had been issued with a voluminous questionnaire in this connection. 8 local firms had been surveyed. The Board concluded that solicitors received less remuneration than doctors, but more than architects and dentists. Probate and Conveyancing provided two thirds of the profession's income with most of this coming from domestic conveyancing. Litigation brought in some 20% of the profession's income, but took 30% of its expenses. It is clear that most firms were cross subsidising litigation from probate and conveyancing. Furthermore there was no real national scale of charges for contentious work, while scale charging for both registered and unregistered conveyancing was coming under increasing attack. It was doubtful whether the subsidisation of contentious business could continue. It was, however, found by The Board that, outside London, practices in the Midlands were the most remunerative, with sole practitioners earning more than individual partners in two-man practices, though 'incomes were higher the greater the number of partners in the practice'.

The President of The Society, Mr A D Foxon, addressed at some length the problem of recruitment to the profession and its public image. Some years previously The Law Society had concluded a further 5000 solicitors were needed, with an annual intake of 1700. This figure had not been met, with the intake reaching only 1500 p.a. by the late 1960s. (How strange these figures now seem in the light of the mushroom growth of the profession over the last 30-40 years.) There was also a change in the nature of practices with the rapid disappearance of the old style managing clerk and his replacement by admitted staff. Mr Foxon argued that members must do more to take articled clerks so as to alleviate the shortage of admitted staff, particularly at assistant level. Mr Foxon acknowledged the cost burden of taking an articled clerk, then amounting to some £3 a week. (The figure seems nothing now but was substantial then when a bus ride from Oadby into Leicester cost less than 3p in modern terms.) Mr Foxon argued, however, that members were under a duty to take articled clerks. So far as the image of the profession was concerned, he further argued strenuously that the public did not, in his experience, think ill of solicitors, despite there being a general impression amongst the profession that it was unpopular. However, he acknowledged that when a solicitor did wrong it was only slightly less newsworthy than a Bishop being taken in adultery. Mr Foxon's conclusions should be noted for their wisdom has been shown down the years and is a basis for good practice still:

'The profession [in Leicestershire] enjoyed the respect and confidence of the public. [I stress] the part played in preserving good relations with the client by not only doing the work expeditiously but also by keeping the client informed as to what [is] happening. In the absence of such information the client often [tends] to imagine that nothing [is] being done on his behalf and this often [means] that the solicitor [is] unfairly blamed for delay.'

Mr Foxon further voiced his disquiet over the issue of costs in undefended divorce cases. A scale of costs had been imposed in respect of such actions by the Lord Chancellor against the will of solicitors, and while The Law Society did not recommend strike action, and while District Registrars had to apply the scales, there was considerable disquiet about this development. Mr Foxon was particularly concerned by a statement from the Lord Chancellor in which it had been claimed that solicitors could do a dozen undefended divorces in a morning at £60 a time. This, of course, ignored the fact that the £60 charge covered the entire case from beginning to end, while very few solicitors then had a dozen such cases at any given time. Similar misleading remarks had been made by the Attorney General. These, of course, are instances of government ministers berating the legal profession as a convenient whipping boy, but they also indicate a breakdown in the relationship between the profession and the government which had been established following the inception of the legal aid scheme. This, coupled with the intrusive investigations of the Prices and Incomes Board, marked, in the light of hindsight, a very important change in the standing of the Solicitors' profession. Nearly all subsequent developments with regard to charging, funding, competition and regulation relate back, in the present author's view, to this period of history.

The issue of remuneration was to be the subject of a special general meeting of The Society held on 16th January 1970. The Prices and Incomes Board had reported on solicitors' remuneration and The Law Society had requested the views of local associations. It was pointed out that the Board had considered the profession to be a commercial undertaking – another indication of a changed governmental attitude towards solicitors. There had been particularly acute and protracted discussions between the Prices and Incomes Board and The Law Society over the issue of conveyancing scale charges over a period of 2½ years. This delay had not assisted the public relations image of the profession.

Members were considerably exercised by the issues involved. Some favoured giving way over conveyancing scale fees as the public wanted value for money, but argued instead for better legal aid rates. Others counselled against any formal admission that the current scales were too high, and pointed to recent increases in solicitors' overheads, including selective Employment Tax – a payroll tax. Some members were absolutely opposed to any reduction in scale charges and pointed to the politically loaded terminology of the Board's report which used expressions such as 'excess remuneration'. (Governmental reliance on the easy image of the 'fat cat lawyer' is nothing new.) Some more radical younger members argued for dropping scale fees altogether, contending that solicitors should refuse to cross subsidise litigation, and that the government would not dare allow this to result in the public failing to gain legal representation when needed. Yet others opposed this seeing the scale fee as a guarantor of professional status. The meeting was declared closed without any consensus being reached, but Mr B E Toland, The Society's Law Society Council member, no doubt had much information to submit to his fellow council members!

On a more domestic level there had been a further special general meeting on 28th April which extended, finally, the sphere of The Society's operation to include Rutland.

At the end of December 1969 membership stood at 215, a slight increase on the previous year, but nevertheless the subsequent dinner on 18th February 1970 was attended by 137 members and 175 guests of whom 43 were articled clerks. The usual large number of dignitaries were also present, including three High Court Judges. Shortly before this the annual dinner dance had also been held at the Grand Hotel on 5th February. Continuing the social theme a Cocktail Party was again held for Leicester University Law Students on 10th March 1970. In connection with this annual event the present author cannot resist recounting the following incident which occurred, either in 1970 or 1971. A number of Past Presidents of The Society were present on the occasion, including the redoubtable Mr A D Foxon whom we have before encountered. He had suffered from alopecia and was thus completely bald, but such was his commanding presence that he carried his condition with aplomb and dignity. From the University one of the guests was E J Griew, subsequently Professor of Law at both Leicester and Nottingham Universities.[35] 'EJG' had also suffered from alopecia. When he entered the reception room 'Colonel Foxon', as many knew him, pointed to 'EJG' and exclaimed with enormous glee: 'Snap!' That was the start of a very liquid evening the hungover consequences of which the current author remembers rather too well.[36]

---

[35] Edward Griew's wife, Marion, subsequently became a member of The Society in 1971. She was in matrimonial practice at Messrs Bray & Bray.

[36] That is also why the exact date cannot be remembered!

Apart from this social business The Committee considered matters as varied as the proposed creation of a Crown Court in Leicester consequent on the Report of the Royal Commission on Assizes and Quarter Sessions, but did not think the volume of civil litigation in Leicester warranted a protest over the proposed removal of what would otherwise have been civil assize work to Nottingham. In the light of hindsight a protest might have been made as the concentration of higher level litigation in Nottingham has tended to stress even more the dominance of that City as the East Midlands Regional Capital. The Committee did, however, protest over the proposed closure of County Courts in Market Harborough and Oakham as this would cause inconvenience to those members of the public who used these courts. The Committee made a complaint to the Governor of HM Prison, Welford Road, about the lack of proper accommodation there for interviewing clients and witnesses. This bore fruit as a temporary interview room was provided in the former chapel while an undertaking was given to include more permanent provision as part of a new gate complex. The Committee was also successful in securing enhanced remuneration for solicitors undertaking police prosecutions before Leicester City Justices.

Pausing at the end of the 1960s we find The Society in good health financially and in terms of membership with many potential members amongst a buoyant number of articled clerks. The Society's influence and prestige were clearly still highly potent features of local civic life. A pronouncement from The Society would carry great weight with other local professional bodies, local authorities, commercial, governmental and financial organisations. Even so, there were dark clouds on the horizon. The government of the day was clearly not sympathetic to solicitors as a profession and had chosen to make a particular investigation into their remuneration. In addition the whole notion of scale charges was under attack. The emergence of the profession of solicitor had been intimately bound up with the notion of scale charges which rested on a statutorily recognised footing. Gradually, as we have seen in previous chapters, the entire nation had come under the aegis of charging schemes which became more unified and homogeneous as the years progressed. Scale charges went hand in hand with prohibitions on undercutting and touting for clients and the ban on individual advertising. In these ways the profession of 'Solicitor' distinguished itself from those who were 'in trade' and who competed in the market place of commerce. Such notions were to be increasingly called in question in the next decade.

But such issues may not have been of great moment in 1970. Membership of The Society had increased from 211 in 1969 to 216 in 1970. The 1971 annual dinner was attended by 147 members and 207 guests, 32 of whom were clerks articled to members, while the annual dinner dance had, yet again, been held a few days previously. The Committee was consulted by The Law Society on the issues of complaints procedures against solicitors and the practice of acting for both vendor and purchaser on a conveyance. The issue of minimum scale fees refused, however, to go away and there was considerable concern when a case was referred to The Committee with an allegation that a firm had offered to make no charge for completing a Building Society mortgage to attract business. This was considered a clear breach of the Solicitors' Practice Rules.

Efforts were made to establish enhanced links with *The Leicester Mercury* in order to get better publicity for The Society. A number of articles had been prepared on current legal issues and on the work of The Society. Members had also spoken, albeit anonymously, on Radio Leicester on legal subjects of public interest. The Secretary had also dealt with a number of issues referred to him by social agencies, such as the Citizens Advice Bureau, and had been able to disabuse a number of people with regard to misconceptions about solicitors and their role.

There was certainly no shortage of people wishing to enter the local profession. The Society maintained a register of firms offering articles and asked for applications for such posts to be channelled through that register. In 1970 there were 20 people seeking articles, rather more than were available, so firms could be somewhat selective. It appeared there was a slight preference for graduates while a number of applicants were graduates who had already passed various heads of The Law Society's Part II Examination.

Two interesting issues at the 1970 AGM were the use of the 24 hour clock to denote the time of the meeting and the alteration of The Society's rules to take account of decimal currency – the guinea finally disappeared!

By the end of 1971 membership had increased to 230 and this was hailed by The Committee, especially as most of the new members were either recently qualified or had commenced sole practice. The Society was seen to be a vital link in the chain of communication between The Law Society and individual solicitors.

The usual round of social events, including the annual dinner, the dinner dance and what was now called a 'Conversazione' for Leicester University Law Students and staff, was held, while there was a continuing public relations drive and good contact maintained with *The Leicester Mercury*, Radio Leicester and the Citizens Advice Bureau. It was again stressed, however, that the best publicity for the profession was the efficient and expeditious handling of clients' business and the maintenance of regular communication with clients. Contact was made with a number of Parent Teacher Associations, and talks were given by The Hon. Secretary at Schools' Careers Evenings. 3 pupils from Public Schools had been allowed to spend a week of their Easter holidays in member firms' offices to see what went on – a modest beginning for the notion of work placements in which many firms nowadays participate.

Various improvements were made to The Library, including the installation of electrical lighting in the basement and a new Librarian, Mrs J M King (of whom more later), was employed when Miss C E Borwell retired. The Society also organised lectures on The Industrial Relations Act 1971, the foundation of the modern system of employment law which was greeted as a new sphere of work for solicitors in place of the Victorian concept of Master and Servant.

Questions at the AGM

The AGM for 1971 reverted to the 12 hour clock to denote the time, but the march of events could not otherwise be ignored and the meeting was particularly concerned with the old issues of conveyancing scale charges and the increasingly questionable practice of acting for both sides in a conveyance. The Lord Chancellor wished to abolish such a practice.

Someone must have asked what the purpose of a local law society was. Various answers could have been given arising out of the business of the AGM which dealt with a range of issues such as recruitment to the profession locally, relations with the Leicester Law Students' Society, and Rights of Audience in the new court structure proposed under the Courts Bill. However, particular reference was made to the maintenance of the Law Library and the way in which it had been able to function as a mail exchange point during a recent postal strike. While it was not possible to create an alternative postal service because of the Post Office Monopoly, the idea of a form of document exchange service was floated at the AGM as this had already been created in Bradford. In later years The Society re-examined this proposal but it was overtaken by the implementation of the 'Doc-Ex' system which was of much wider application.

A Year of Change

While the year 1972/73 saw a further increase in membership to 242, and while the traditional annual dinner and annual dinner dance were both held, signs of change were in the air even at social events. The response to the toast to The Legal Profession at the annual dinner was given by the President of the Nottingham Law Society, Miss Nora Healey. She was the first female President of a neighbouring Law Society to attend The Society's dinner and was the second woman to become President of a local law society. Leicester had to wait for a number of years for its first female local law society President, but it is worth mentioning that between 1970 and 1978 17 women were elected into membership.

Perhaps of more immediate import was the need to consider the provision of legal services for all sections of the community. Despite the existence of the Legal Aid Scheme it was clear that many people were unwilling to consult solicitors in their offices. It was clear that meetings needed to take place on neutral ground. Two Society members were already assisting the Citizens Advice Bureau by attending on one evening and one Saturday morning each week. The Committee proposed to set up a rota of solicitors to attend at the CAB two evenings a week between 6.30 pm and 7.30 pm and to obtain the necessary leave from The Law Society for this purpose. There had also been discussions with members of The Law Department at Leicester University about the proposed creation of a Legal Advice Centre in Highfields. These were the tentative beginnings of what subsequently became The Highfields and Belgrave Law Centre. That was superseded by the Leicester Legal Advice Centre with the voluntary participation of local practitioners, an issue to which we shall have reason to return in a later chapter. Readers may also see in these developments a return to the days of the Poor Man's Lawyer Scheme. The Committee was also much involved in the proposed creation of a Duty Solicitor Scheme to come into effect on 30th April 1973 whereby the Number One Magistrates' Court, then sitting at Leicester Town Hall, would be served by a rota of volunteers to give advice to anyone requiring such assistance. The cost of the scheme was to be borne by the public purse under The Legal Advice and Assistance Act, 1972.

This proposal was the subject of some discussion at the April 1972 AGM when there was disquiet voiced about both the principle of such a scheme – would clients be 'guided away' from a solicitor of their own choice – and its workings. It was determined to refer the issue to an ad hoc committee of those prepared to operate the scheme. At the same time it was resolved that The Committee should also consider the recent institution of afternoon court sittings which were making it hard for solicitors specialising in full time criminal practice to make appointments to see clients. One year on it had to be conceded that afternoon sittings in Leicester had to continue as there simply were not staff and rooms available to deal with all the work of the magistrates in the morning. On a happier note between 1972 and 1973 the Duty Solicitor Scheme had been set up and a further scheme offering advice via the Citizens Advice Bureau had also been created, while advice had also been given on the creation of the Highfields Legal Advice Centre and another in Loughborough.

A further 'straw in the wind of change' was the notion that there should be a generally accepted scale of remuneration for articled clerks graded according to age, experience and qualification. The days when an articled clerk paid a premium to be taken on had long since disappeared. The dreaded topic of VAT had also become part of the lingua franca of the profession and The Society's lecture on the tax drew a record number of 207 attenders in November 1971.

However, the main preoccupations of 1971/72 were the proposals for a new Solicitors' Remuneration Order. This led to two special general meetings, one in July 1972 before the order was made and one in October after its making. This marked the final end of conveyancing scale charges, and a prohibition on acting for both vendor and purchaser, or lessor and lessee, in 'for value transactions' between strangers. The abolition of the old scales as from 31st December 1972 led to many questions being asked. Could, for example, solicitors operate an unofficial extra-statutory scale of charges based on the practice of the Building Societies? Could they, indeed should they, give quotations for conveyancing over the 'phone? Should they agree a conveyancing fee in advance of a transaction? Should different types of fee be charged for different types of conveyancing? How to reflect the cost of doing the job in the fee charged? The fact that many of the questions then raised have long since been answered should not blind us to the degree of concern felt by non-contentious practitioners. They would in future have to cost out each transaction rather than rely on a prefixed scale.

The future of Legal Education

1973/74 witnessed a continuing increase in the size of membership to 254 and a highly successful annual dinner, with 157 members and 207 guests attending, and the annual dinner dance with 276 attenders, together with the usual reception for second year Law students at the University of Leicester. However, having begun to come to terms with the changes consequent on the abolition of scale charges, The Society now had to consider the radical proposals of the Ormrod report on the future of legal education and a proposed funding levy. A special general meeting was held on 26th March 1974 to consider these issues. There was a strong argument put forward by one member against the idea of placing a levy on practising solicitors in order to fund legal vocational training. In answer to this it was argued that once the principle of a levy was accepted, the only way of collecting it was as part of the annual practising certificate fee and that meant that only solicitors needing such a certificate would pay. There was also concern at proposals to replace articles with the notion of 'associate solicitor' status following completion of the new vocational qualification, and over the proposal to entrust the universities and polytechnics with running that course. There was further concern over the relationship of the new training scheme with those for members of the Bar and for Legal Executives, especially in relation to how Legal Executives could qualify as solicitors in future.

They may seem commonplace now, but the Ormrod Committee's initial proposals were so radical when made that they shook many in the profession to the core. In essence Ormrod proposed that the Legal Profession as a whole should by 1980 become graduate only, and that the degree should be in law, with the universities and polytechnics having responsibility for providing both the academic and vocational training stages of qualification. The argument supporting this was the need for lawyers to have a much better command of the law than that provided by the then current professional examinations for both the Bar and the Solicitors' profession.

In the long term, of course, the Ormrod proposals were considerably modified. Both branches of the Legal Profession did become graduate only, (with some allowances made for qualification by non-graduate legal executives) but the degree did not have to be in law and provision was made in the Common Professional Examination to enable non-law graduates to obtain the necessary grounding in law. There are many individual solicitors and firms who still prefer trainees to have a degree in another discipline. The notion of articles was retained, though we now speak of training contracts and trainee solicitors. The Law Society did not give up either providing the vocational stage of training or its oversight of those organisations otherwise providing such courses, and has retained a voice in relation to the content of degrees in law. Only one institution has so far succeeded in offering a 4 year law degree with the vocational content being taken as one 'all through' package. This is the University of Northumbria, formerly Newcastle Polytechnic. In all other institutions the academic law degree has remained separated from the vocational stage of training. The 'old' pre 1992 Universities offer only academic legal education, while vocational training is offered by the post 1992 Universities, The College of Law in various locations, and various commercial providers.

With the benefit of hindsight a great opportunity was lost in the 1970s to reform legal education in a more logical fashion. The greatest regrets have to be that there was so much heat generated over the issue of non-law graduates and the failure to ensure a greater role for local law societies in the vetting of potential trainees. While there can be no doubt that a non-law graduate can become an extremely fine practitioner, it is sad that the notion of a two year common professional examination was not pursued. The University of Sheffield had a 2 year 'senior status LLB' which could be gained by graduates in other disciplines and this, in the present author's opinion, should have become the norm. It would have prevented the jibes frequently heard in some academic circles about 'one year lawyers'. So as far as vetting is concerned, it was proposed initially that would-be entrants to the vocational course should be subject to much greater scrutiny than had hitherto been carried out by local panels of solicitors. Had this been developed it would have given local law societies a much enhanced role with regard to legal education, and might well have prevented unsuitable candidates from wasting money on the cost of the vocational course when this does not lead to a training contract. As it is, the basic qualifications for gaining a place on a vocational training course have become the possession of a 'qualifying degree', generally at not less than 2:2 standard, and an ability to pay the fee. Whether the aspirant trainee would make a good solicitor is not a rigorously pursued issue at the stage of entering on the vocational course. Solicitors do, of course, need to be able to handle the law, with all its increasing complexity, but they must also be able to handle clients and run successful businesses in a highly competitive market place. The opportunity to address the issue of commercial aptitude was effectively lost in the 1970s.

The report for the year 1974/75 stated an increase in membership to 275 together with the usual round of social events. On the Library and education fronts a lecture had been held on Capital Transfer Tax, attended by 200 people, while Library holdings had been extended to include The Road Traffic Reports and Industrial Tribunal Decisions. The Duty Solicitor

Scheme was by this time well established as was the Citizens Advice Bureau Scheme, which had 42 members on the rota who had, between November 1973 and March 1974, provided advice to 140 people. There was clearly a continuing need for this form of legal service provision. The Committee had also been asked to nominate members to various local committees including The Liaison Committee on [Housing] Improvement Grants, The City of Leicester Local Valuation Panel and the Consultative Committee for Law of Leicester Polytechnic. The Leicester Law Society Form of Contract for Sale of Land had been revised in the previous year and had been welcomed, but its cost had to be raised to 6p a copy to meet the increased costs of running The Society.

Much of the business of the 1974 AGM was taken up with concerns over contentious business. A number of issues were aired such as: the continuing issue of afternoon court sittings; the question of costs in the Crown Court being settled by untrained staff, and matter of supervision of the Duty Solicitor Scheme. It was proposed that The Society's rules be amended so that a Contentious Business Sub Committee could be formed in order for there to be a forum in which matters of concern to litigators could be discussed and views forwarded to The Committee. Such a committee did exist unofficially. It was decided to investigate whether this could in some way be brought under the auspices of the existing Public Relations Committee to avoid having a change in the rules.

One matter of interest are the gloomy predictions of the outgoing President, Mr R D G Williams: 'training of solicitors could be handed over to the State to be dealt with in a Department of the University Faculties of Social Sciences, legal aid could be placed under the Ministry of Health and Social Security, the Disciplinary Committee could be a lay body, and [the Trades Unions] could secure substantial membership amongst members' clerks and typists'. None of these outcomes actually occurred in the precise way Mr Williams predicted, but the tenor of his remarks shows the increasing strain being felt by solicitors. He urged members to make their views known to The Law Society on topics of concern and to press The Council of The Law Society to take action, irrespective of whether this was acceptable to The Lord Chancellor. He further urged members to examine the work they undertook, to adopt new activities and to abandon unprofitable ones and finally 'to ensure that solicitors remain within the community and in touch with all members of it whether with or without payment'.

1975 was the year in which The Society lost one of its longest serving members. Arthur Shirley Atkins was a partner in Messrs Atkins, Stone and Co. of Hinckley. He was admitted in 1897, having been born in 1875, but did not become a member of The Society until 1926. He reached his century a few months before his death, still in practice. It is believed he was at the time of his death the oldest practising solicitor in England. Despite this sad loss and a number of other deaths the membership of The Society continued to increase and the usual round of social events was held. This was also the year when the 'Doc-Ex' system to which earlier allusion was made came into effect. The Society also involved itself in regional affairs and there was continued liaison and exchange of views with various local law societies, particularly those in Birmingham and Nottingham. The Society continued to bring members up to date with new developments in the law and a lecture was given on The Community Land Act 1975. Fortunately members would never have to put what they learned on that occasion into practice as that particularly complex and byzantine bit of legislation was never effectively commenced. Considerable effort by the Committee, and a special general meeting, was applied to the question of whether some form of institutional advertising should be undertaken. This would utilise the columns of *The Leicester Mercury* and was likely to cost over £2000 for a quarter page advertisement, with between 6 and 10 variations, each one to be used twice, to be displayed every night or every other night for a fortnight. A similar scheme in Bolton had produced good returns. There then arose the question of how such an advertising campaign was to be financed. The rules of The Society were altered to allow a general meeting to raise a levy on members and this power was then utilised to raise a levy of £7.50 per member to pay for an institutional advertising campaign.

One other highly contentious issue arose in 1975, namely the state of The Society's finances. Book price inflation was making it impossible to purchase all the books that were thought necessary and economies had to be made by reducing the number of periodical subscriptions. Even with economies The Society needed more income, and this could not come from the sale of contract forms only. The F&GP Committee came to the conclusion that subscriptions would have to be raised. The annual accounts for 1975/75 showed a deficit of £409.53, and that did not bode well for the future. The result was that a supplementary special general meeting had to be held on the same day as the 1976 AGM to increase subscriptions. These had not been increased for some seven years, despite the considerable inflation which voraciously ate away the value of money in the early 1970s. The result was an increase in annual subscriptions from £9.30 to £14.00. As a further boost to income membership increased to 288 in 1976 with seventeen new members elected during the year.

The Society also lost its representative on the Council of The Law Society consequent on the retirement of Mr Brian Toland after 24 years' service. His place was taken by a representative from Northampton who, while not a member of The Society, was invited to be present as an observer at Committee meetings and who was thus able to maintain liaison between The Society and Chancery Lane. The Society's rules were subsequently changed in 1977 to allow any person who represents on the Council of The Law Society the constituency in which The Society is situated to be a member of The Committee.

Continuing Concerns

By the latter part of the 1970s a number of issues of continuing concern emerged which cut across the pattern of yearly reports.

The notion of Neighbourhood Law Centres had established itself and a Leicester Law Centre was under discussion in 1975. The Committee were not convinced that such a centre was needed given the existing voluntary arrangements alluded to earlier but, somewhat reluctantly, agreed to assist and cooperate with the Centre should its funding be approved. At the same time, however, the Duty Solicitor and Citizens Advice Bureau schemes continued to operate satisfactorily. The Society was less successful initially in taking forward its proposed scheme of institutional advertising and it was realised that assistance from professional 'ad men' would be needed. This prompted a move to set up a joint scheme with the Northamptonshire Law Society with further assistance from Chancery Lane. By 1977 The Law Society was operating a national scheme of Institutional Advertising and the Committee adopted this as the basis for local advertising. One dark omen for the future was the proposal in 1976/77 to remove legal aid from certain categories of work, namely certain matters in connection with undefended divorces.

Articled Clerks continued to be an issue with the proposals alluded to earlier in respect of education and training giving continuing cause for concern. It was becoming ever clearer that articles in Leicester were becoming harder to find year by year. A register of people seeking articles had been running for some years and in 1977 75 applicants were added to it, while only 2 found articles through it. Members were urged to utilise the register whenever a vacancy for an articled clerk arose.

The maintenance of The Library and in particular the cost of heating it was also a continuing problem. Indeed financial pressures continued to mount. Various suggestions were considered to raise additional income to meet increased outgoings on The Library and entertaining. One proposal which got nowhere was for The Society to go into the business of selling appropriate professional stationery. A rather more fruitful proposal was that a series of low cost lectures could be mounted. In 1977 following discussions with the Law Faculty at Leicester University a series of such lectures were begun.[37]

On a more positive note the membership of The Society continued to increase and in 1977/78 for the first time exceeded 300; 298 ordinary and 4 honorary members. During the same year the Leicestershire Branch of The Young Solicitors Group was established as a forum for those aged under 36, and the initial membership was 35.

The AGM voted in favour of organising a second annual dinner each year on a 'closed' basis, ie members of the local profession only, and requested The Committee to investigate the possibility of holding this over the summer months. In due course, after initial abandonment in 1978/79, the 'members' closed' became a popular annual feature of The Society's calendar for many years, though there was a degree of debate over its location in either the North or the South of the County and thus it tended to be peripatetic. More recently this event has been replaced by more informal gatherings such as curry and quiz evenings.

Less happily the 1977 annual report and accounts was the last to be printed in booklet form; no doubt an economic sign of the times.

1978/79 proved to be quite a momentous year. Membership decreased for the first time in many years to 291 ordinary members, for while 14 new members were elected the membership of 21 others ceased. Furthermore the annual accounts for the year ended 31st December 1977 revealed a deficit of £990.56. Much of this was due to increased Library costs, but an ongoing deficit could not be borne.

Externally a Royal Commission had been examining, inter alia, the provision of legal services and that had already caused The Committee to shoulder a considerable burden of work with regard to answering consultation requests. This continued into 1978/79. The litigators on The Committee continued to be particularly vocal at the AGM about the costs

---

[37] The present author contributed one on The Housing (Homeless Persons) Act 1977, and prefers to remember it as being well received!

paid to solicitors acting as advocates when attending the Crown Court and the fact that these were determined (by non-qualified staff) at very low rates. Furthermore these same staff too often took it upon themselves to determine who should be dealing with a particular job within a solicitor's office in the determination of fees. There was further general concern on the part of many members at the rapid rise in the number of solicitors. Whereas a few years previously there had been a shortage of solicitors there were at the time 32,000, an increase of 8000 over the figure some years before. Each year 1200 new solicitors entered the profession when, it was contended, only 800 were needed. It was argued that the cost to the taxpayer of producing a graduate was £8000 and that the economy could not stand that cost. One member criticised the Universities for turning out too many undergraduates and argued in favour of accepting only men [sic] who had undergone the traditional five year articles. Of course that pass had long been sold. By 1978/79 some 90% of entrants to the profession were graduates, but only some 50% of Law Graduates actually entered the legal profession.

The Future of The Library and Society Events

The cost of maintaining the Library in the face of revenue problems, and the matter of salaries and other incidental expenses affecting the Library premises had been increasingly pressing problems for some years. While a referendum of members held in 1978/79 was overwhelmingly in favour of retaining a Library, The Committee was of the opinion that the Library premises would have to be sold and an alternative home found.

On the social side the annual dinner had been attended by 334 members and guests and the annual dinner dance by 270. The traditional cocktail party for Leicester University Law Students was again held, and by way of innovation The Society held a buffet lunch for members on 14th March 1979 at the Leicestershire Club. This proved such a success that The Committee hoped to make it an annual event.

The lot of a would-be articled clerk

Mr Peter Duffin of Jones Duffin and Co has kindly submitted this reminiscence of his experiences in seeking, and then holding down, articles at the end of the 1970s.

'[My] earliest memories of being Articled started just before I got lucky when following numerous letters of rejection I decided to walk the streets (literally) knocking on Solicitors' doors seeking work. It was quite dispiriting and I will always remember a place on New Walk where the receptionist opened a glass hatch and asked what I wanted. On being told I was looking for Articles she promptly said there were no vacancies and smartly slammed the hatch in place. OK, I will reveal all ... Headleys!!

It was late in the afternoon when I called at Hammonds on Friar Lane. One of the partners actually took the trouble to leave his desk to speak to me. I think this was the first solicitor I actually met on my travels. He told me that a vacancy was pinned to the notice board at the Law Library across the road.

I attended an interview a short time later with Mr Maxwell Waite of Parsons Waite and obviously said the right things to be offered Articles at the princely sum of £1500 p.a. This was in 1978.

My first duty was to go to the document exchange at the top of Pocklingtons Walk. I felt quite important taking and delivering important documents as all my previous jobs had been in factories and of a manual nature, or driving trucks or vans.

John Waite would encourage me when on occasions I moaned at being perpetually in debt by saying: "One day, Peter, one day, now pop down the shops and get me some fags!!"...'

It is certainly no easier nowadays to get a training contract, indeed it is probably even harder and more dispiriting a search. However, health conscious principals are currently unlikely to send their trainees to buy cigarettes – well, one hopes not!

The End of an Era

The Society had entered the 1960s in buoyant mood. Much of the framework of family and social connections which had served it so well was still in place. New entrants to the profession locally came in by well established routes which ensured they were imbued with the traditional ethos of Leicester practice. The Society had a clear set of reasons to exist, and these were reinforced by the success of the Legal Aid Scheme which did much to ensure that litigation was no longer so considerably dependent by way of cross subsidy on probate and conveyancing. The Scale Charge system also appeared to be working well.

Twenty years on and the entire picture has changed. The profession as a whole had become unpopular with the Government and some sections of the public – part, perhaps, of a general impatience with anything not seen to be 'technologically white hot' engendered under the Wilson government of 1964-1970. Wide changing reforms were recommended in the law and its administration and The Law Commission was set up in 1967 to undertake wholesale reform of 'lawyers' law'. The Scale Charges were abolished; the Universities and Polytechnics began increasingly to 'muscle in' on legal education. One by one the old certainties were swept away. There was, moreover, the beginning of what we now call 'consumerism'. This was not articulated at any of the AGMs during the period under discussion, but members must have been aware that the days when clients nearly always took and acted upon their solicitor's advice were passing. Clients were becoming less deferential and more demanding with regard to the standard of service offered and the costs incurred. Indeed the very notion of a 'client' began to be replaced by one of a 'consumer of legal services': in other words a person who purchased a particular 'product' eroding the concept of a Solicitors' profession and replacing it with the concept of a service industry.

In these circumstances it is easy to understand the very real expressions of dismay and even anger (albeit politely expressed) that surfaced at a number of general meetings throughout the 1970s. There were many members who clearly felt they were being railroaded into new ways they did not like and did not understand. There were unavailing calls to restore some sort of status quo or to hold a particular line. Domestically The Society also faced revenue problems and considerable difficulty with maintaining what had been the core activity for over 100 years, the provision of a Library.

How would The Society meet these very real new challenges in the next decade?

Chapter 8

The Thatcher Years

As The Society moved into yet another decade The Committee recorded sadly that there were many solicitors in both City and County who were not members and urged all principals to persuade newly qualifieds to seek membership on admission. Even so in 1981/82 there were 11 new members and the total active membership was 304, a slight decline of 1 on the previous year. The annual report recorded the continuing work of both the Duty Solicitor Rota and the Citizens Advice Bureau, while there was a continued regular monthly appearance by members on the then well known Radio Leicester programme 'Cross Talk', which had begun some two years earlier. The Society had participated in what was also a well established feature of Leicester life, The Home Life Exhibition which was held in the now demolished Granby Halls next door to Leicester RUFC. Socially The Society had enjoyed a good year with the first Members' Closed Dinner at Loughborough University on 27th November 1981, a general knowledge quiz against Northamptonshire Law Society (who won!) on 20th October 1981, and a successful annual dinner, though numbers attending were recorded as 'less than usual', there having been 335 attenders at the 1980 dinner. There also appeared to be long term declining support for the annual dinner dance, though this had attracted 284 attenders in 1980.

With regard to professional concerns The Committee had been in discussion with Leicester City Council over the issue of whether more Law Centres were needed in Leicester. The Council favoured the creation of a new centre in Belgrave but there was no consensus between City and Society over the level of 'unmet need' – nor indeed on how to define it. The Society had also made recommendations as to yearly salary levels for articled clerks in Leicestershire. These were £1,800 for a school leaver, £2,750 for a graduate and £3,250 for non graduates over 25, though it was again recorded that the flow of written and oral applications for articles had increased and greatly exceeded the number of places available in the area.

The Library

This dominated the work of The Committee in 1981/82 as it had for a number of years. It is necessary at this point to backtrack a little. We saw in the last chapter how the Library had given cause for concern towards the end of the 1970s. By the last years of that decade the maintenance of the 'old Turkish baths' could no longer be supported and negotiations took place with Leicester University for the removal there of the Library and its operation.

At the end of the 1940s the then University College had erected a new Library by building The Worthington Extension across the rear of the two front courts of its premises. Following the building of the new University Library in the early 1970s, this structure housed, from 1975, The Law Faculty, and the Harry Peach Room became the base for the Faculty Library, over which the present author had oversight. There was ample room in those premises to house The Society's Library and so in 1979 Mrs King, the Librarian, Mr Richard Bloor, the Society's Librarian, Mr Rashid Siddiqi, for Leicester University Library, and the present author spent much time overseeing the installation of the books in specially reserved bays of the Harry Peach Room. It was a particularly happy encounter for the Law Faculty as not only was The Society's Library well stocked, but Mrs King soon adopted a disciplinary-cum-grandmotherly role with regard to law students using the rest of the room.[38] The move also enabled The Society to sell its premises in Friar Lane. For the first time in over 120 years The Society was homeless. Sadly the move did not work as the location of Leicester University made it hard for members to use the Library and within a few months its future was again in doubt. A number of solutions to the problem of maintaining the Library had been examined such as changing its financing, reducing its size or even disposing of it altogether. These issues also loomed large at the AGM in June 1981 when an emergency levy was raised on members to keep the Library solvent. There was clearly a lively debate with some members of the opinion that the Library should be disposed of; but then it was pointed out that some of those who held to that opinion were regular users of the Library! In the end a levy of £12.50 was imposed on City members, £5.00 on County members and £6.25 and £2.50 on City and County members respectively

---

[38] Mrs King held strong views on the social and legal abilities of some of her 'customers'. There were those, who shall remain nameless, who rang in to ask whether the Library held 'idiots' guides' to particular issues: such practitioners did not receive her approbation. There was also the distressing, at the time, incident when Mrs King found herself locked in the Ladies' Lavatory in the Law Building. This led to a local version of the somewhat ribald 'rugby club' version of 'Oh dear, what can the matter be'. The author assures readers, however, that Mrs King was *not* left there from Monday to Saturday but was extricated with as much dignity as was possible in the circumstances.

who were assistant solicitors. It was also determined to increase the annual subscription levels to £36 for City members and £12 for County members to avoid a continuing annual deficit consequent on a reduction in the sales of contract forms. It was reported that some firms might resign in consequence of this increase, indeed Messrs Stone & Simpson had already done so – a sad loss given the historic association of The Society with Samuel Stone.

The difficulties with the Library continued into the next year and ultimately forced the most radical solution of sale. At the 1982 AGM it was reported that the burden of keeping the Library had become too great. The Leicester Society was not alone in facing this difficulty, other local societies who maintained libraries had been forced to consider closure. Leicester University had been unable to take the Library over, while Leicester Polytechnic could only offer to house it, but not maintain it. It had therefore been determined to sell the collection, and a price of £15,200 had been obtained from Professional Books Ltd of Abingdon.[39] This money was invested to retain its value.

The Society Rethinks its Role

Membership in 1982/83 stood at 324 ordinary members with 22 new members being elected. Mr D W Godfrey as President was able to state that the year had been a much happier one for The Society as, following the sale of the Library: it was no longer 'dominated by questions of expense and the desperate struggle to make ends meet'. He was also able to report a considerable increase in attendance at the annual dinner which had been held at Leicester University. At just under 300 members and guests the University's dining facilities had been filled. However, attendance at the dinner dance continued to fall and only some 150 people attended the 1982 event, slightly up on the previous year it was true, but largely because one (unnamed) firm contributed a substantial number of attenders.

With regard to professional matters, however, The Society recognised, following the closure of the Library, that it had to find other means to provide a service to members in return for their subscription. The first fruit of this was the re-introduction of an initiative essayed some years before of the Members' Newsletter which later became one of the main features of The Society's life. In addition The Society began

---

[39] The present author remembers only too well the denuded condition of The Harry Peach Room after The Society's books were moved: it was not a happy time, and it involved him in considerable effort in rearranging the Law Faculty's books to try to 'flesh out' the shelves, a doubly unpleasant task bearing in mind that he had been required to move many of those very same books some three years earlier to create a space for The Library.

to examine the acquisition of an information retrieval system for the use of members. That was the forerunner of modern 'on line' computer based legal information systems such as Lexis-Nexis and Westlaw. Many member firms will nowadays have their own commercially charged access to such services, while there is, of course, a very considerable amount of legal information freely available from the Government and the Courts and various Law Libraries, via the Internet. Indeed such has been the growth of these services that, in the light of hindsight, disposing of the Library was quite not the disaster it might have been!

The Society by this time also had an Education and Training Sub Committee and this had been much concerned during the year with changes to the training regime which introduced the notion of 'the second stage of training' to follow the academic stage, and which involved passing the final examination (now replaced by the Legal Practice Course), serving articles and completing any other course prescribed by The Law Society – the current pattern of training had effectively emerged. This Committee had also recommended local commencing salaries for articled clerks, and these were to be £3000 pa. The F&GP had also been concerned with the continuing debate about the need for another Law Centre in Leicester. The Committee's view remained that there was not sufficient unmet need to warrant such a centre. The Society was also concerned that its members' interests might be adversely affected by the proposed creation of a Police Prosecution Department for Leicester and Leicestershire as this would take prosecution work away from local practitioners. Ultimately of course such proposals resulted in the creation of The Crown Prosecution Service, and while this has removed some work from local private practitioners, it has also provided another employment stream for solicitors, and indeed for specialist non qualified staff.

Despite all this activity, the future of The Society was questioned at the 1982 AGM. One member was concerned that The Society had no disciplinary function. For many years there had been complaints about solicitors. In the early years of the 20th century many of these, as The Society's records indicate, had come from other solicitors and frequently related to the issue of the old conveyancing scale charges and allegations of failure to adhere to these. But there were additionally complaints from the public, and by the early 1980s these were running at the level of some 5 or 6 a week. These were received by the Hon. Secretary and The Committee then dealt with them as it thought best in order to filter out complaints from proceeding to the formal stage of being made to

The Law Society. However, the lack of a clear disciplinary role for local societies was a perceived problem. While nowadays the whole issue has been transferred to an effectively independent system of complaints and disciplinary bodies, such developments were some way in the future in the early 1980s.

The End of the Conveyancing Monopoly

By 1983/84 proposals to open up the market in conveyancing to firms of Licensed Conveyancers were greatly concerning solicitors the length and breadth of the nation. While in retrospect the impact of such competitors has not been great, and certainly does not justify the somewhat inflated claims that were made for them by their proponents, at the time the furore within the Solicitors' profession was intense and this led to a considerable change of attitude with regard to advertising. A special general meeting of The Society was held on 22nd March 1984 at County Hall in order to gather the views of members so that these could be forwarded to The Law Society. The Leicester Law Society stressed that if Licensed Conveyancers were to be permitted, the enabling legislation should require high standards of competence, integrity, financial security and independence of interest. The Society at the same meeting resolved that The Law Society should relax the restrictions on advertising by solicitors, and should appoint a Director-General to promote the public image of solicitors.

It is interesting to note these resolutions. In the 1980s the influence of Thatcherism was increasingly directed towards the ending of monopolies and the creation of a much more competition based economy. While the forces of competition thus unleashed led to some unforeseen developments, chiefly the emergence of the great supermarket chains as the new near monopoly suppliers of food, so far as the lower branch of the legal profession was concerned the effect was to erode the resistance of solicitors to the argument that they were 'in trade' and could, and should, behave accordingly. If the professional status of solicitors was to be eroded by the ending of the conveyancing monopoly, why should they not accept the practice of advertising their services in the same way as other service providers?

More domestically the Report for 1983/84 recorded the election of 24 new members, and the launching of a number of new initiatives. These included the formation of The Continuing Education Partnership in conjunction with The Northamptonshire Law Society, The Faculty of Law and the Department of Continuing Education at Leicester University and the Law Department at Leicester Polytechnic. This was partly a response to The Law Society's proposals that all solicitors should undergo continuing education – Continuing Professional Development as it is now known. It was hoped that the Partnership would become the designated vehicle for the delivery of this service in Leicestershire and Northamptonshire. Once again events have overtaken this hope. The forces of competition have ensured that the majority of 'CPD' points now emanate from commercially provided courses, and even DVDs. Even so The Society committed itself to the notion of continuing education, and on its own initiative arranged for 60 trainee and new qualified solicitors to view videos on advocacy presented at County Hall on 5th October 1983 – an interesting hark back to the practice in previous years of having tape recorded lectures, and the precursor of solicitors watching DVDs at home via television and home computers.

Another new initiative was the inception in Leicester of The Law Society's scheme whereby accident victims could receive half an hour's free advice in referral from various sources, such as the CAB.

The social life of The Society continued along its well established lines, with both a closed dinner and the annual dinner, the latter being once more held at Leicester University. Attendance at the annual dinner dance, however, fell to 140, one third of those being a party organised by Messrs Josiah Hincks, Son & Bullough. However, The Society enjoyed a very successful barge trip 'for members and their ladies' (a reminder that membership of The Society was still overwhelmingly male) from Foxton to Smeeton Westerby and return. There was also the annual cocktail party for law students at Leicester University which had continued for many years to be a feature of The Society's calendar, though the Annual Report stated: 'whether many of the law students derive any long term benefit may be questionable ...'.

Amongst the reports of the various sub-committees, which by now included The Education and Training Committee, The Contentious Business and Non-Contentious Business Committees and The F&GP, there is an item relating to the previous mentioned Information Retrieval System. Discussions had taken place with Leicester Polytechnic to make access available to members in respect of the Eurolex Service. This then contained full text reports of 44,000 cases, 23,000 items of legislation and 75,000 digest and summary reports. This, of course, is quite small in relation to the current data bases available on Lexis-Nexis, which bought out Eurolex, and Westlaw, but it is a further example of how The Society was adapting itself to the pressures and demands of a rapidly changing world.

A Female Committee Member

Amongst the features of the year 1984/85 was the presence on the Committee of its first female member, Miss L M Rolling who had been nominated for membership the previous year, and that was a small, but significant, further sign of change on the part of The Society.

The year was further marked, nationally, by the Administration of Justice Bill and the reports of the Farrand Committee on Conveyancing which paved the way for both the creation of Licensed Conveyancers and dealing by solicitors in house sales. While house selling had long been a feature of legal practice north of the border, there was considerable apprehension expressed locally that there would be all sorts of problems including conflicts of interest and the erosion of professional standards should such a development occur in England and Wales. Once again it is interesting to note that, as with Licensed Conveyancers, the local impact of the ability for solicitors to deal in houses has not been great. There are some firms in Leicestershire who have successfully embraced the notion of a 'solicitors' property shop', but, by and large most have chosen not to enter that field of activity. It might have been Thatcherite economic philosophy to argue that entrenched monopolies with respect to particular practices were wrong, but the reality remains that the overwhelming majority of houses are sold by estate agents and the overwhelming majority of conveyancing is carried out by solicitors. That is a measure of the gap between the reach of government policy and its grasp.

The Committee was also much concerned this year with the issue of proposed relaxations of the rules relating to advertising and the proposed reconstruction of The Law Society following the Cooper & Lybrand Report. It is heartening to note that The Society was in favour of the radical proposal that the 'disciplinary' and 'pastoral' functions of The Law Society should be separated. Subsequent events have proved the wisdom of that position.

Amongst other developments the statutory duty solicitor scheme came into effect this year, and preparations were in hand for this to become a 24 hour service. Concern was, justifiably, felt about the level of remuneration to be paid for those called out in the middle of the night. Indeed The Contentious Business Sub Committee had a busy year in general, trying, unsuccessfully, to establish regular meetings with the local county court registrars, but noting, with thanks, an improvement in the administration of local court business.

In the Autumn of 1984 The Law Society permitted solicitors to advertise, albeit in a strictly regulated fashion. Initially few local firms 'took the plunge' and the feeling was that everyone was waiting to see what others would do. Little use had been made of newspaper advertising, but some use had been made of rural news media, magazines and brochures. It was thought, by The Public Relations Sub Committee, that few firms were likely to spend considerable sums on advertising when the income from conveyancing was under attack. The sub committee issued a directive against individual advertising in the Leicester area, but was not averse to institutional advertising of the type encountered in earlier years.

Socially the events of 1984/85 included the annual closed dinner which was entertained by the then well known wit, raconteur and actor, Mr David Kossof, but sadly, this event was not well attended. Attendance was also down at the annual dinner and the writing was clearly on the wall for the annual dinner dance which attracted only 80 people. A much more vigorous social life was enjoyed by The Leicestershire Young Solicitors' Group whose annual report was included for the first time in the Annual Report. They had held a closed Christmas dinner, an annual dinner, a dinner dance and other social events including a treasure hunt, a brewery trip and a wine appreciation event – echoes of The Law Students' Society in the 1950s and 60s. The Group had also engaged in more serious activity, particularly in connection with the Trainee Solicitors Group, and especially with regard to projects to introduce school pupils to the law and the creation of Business Start-up courses. It is interesting that the Group appears to have been much more favourably inclined to the notion of solicitors running property selling agencies than was the parent body!

A Year of Change and Hopes

1985/86 witnessed continuing confusion with regard to changes in conveyancing. A meeting held in 1985 at County Hall enabled The Society to gain information from other local societies about how their members were responding to change. The President, Mr J E Adams,[40] opined that 'some of the more exotic ideas produced outside Leicestershire would certainly not work here', and time has proved him right. He also hoped that for the future The Law Society would rely more on provincial societies – this was perhaps not the way things have gone. He was, however, happy

---

[40] Mr Adams is unique amongst Society Presidents in that, having begun his career as what was known until the early 1960s as a 'Managing Clerk', a post then retitled as a 'Legal Executive'; he had held office as National President of ILEX. He thus served two societies in the office of President.

to announce a successful annual dinner which had returned to The Grand Hotel, a revivified members' newsletter, the inception of quarterly luncheon meetings for the exchange of views on topical issues and also to involve members more in the work of The Society, and a revision of The Society's rules – long overdue in consequence of the sale of the Library.

With regard to contentious business it was reported that, despite the commencement of the Police and Criminal Evidence Act 1984 in January 1986, there was no county wide 24 hour duty solicitor scheme in Leicestershire, largely because local practitioners were unhappy at the rates of remuneration on offer. However, The Society had been instrumental in creating 24 hour schemes for Ashby, Coalville, Hinckley and Bosworth and hoped to have a scheme running in Leicester in May 1986. The commencement of The Crown Prosecution Service was also noted, though it was hoped that some agency prosecution work would be available at not less than legal aid rates. More happily it was reported that enhanced listing of cases procedures had been adopted by the County Court and that the 'Court under His Honour Judge Jones ... actively encourages the co-operation of solicitors'.

The Bulletin

The Society began to issue a regular bulletin to its members in February 1983,[41] though initially it was effectively typewritten and brief in character. Nevertheless as Mr K P Byass, President at the time, opined it was 'intended to be a means of communication between the Committee of the Leicester Law Society and its members. It is hoped that the Bulletin will appear on a more or less regular basis every three or four months.' The Newsletter soon established itself as a useful as a useful means of communicating topical information to members, as well as reminding them of important changes in law and practice they should be implementing, for example increases in the salaries of articled clerks which rose in the provinces to £3850 pa from 1st August 1985.

Issue Number 12 of March 1985 reflected the changing times through which The Society was going and argued: 'As a profession we are experiencing difficult times. The nature of a solicitor's practice is changing very quickly. To survive we are having to review our methods and objectives. At the same time competition is fierce ... from the point of view of the Leicester Law Society the closing of the Law Library was a watershed. Until then the prime objective of the Society had been to

---

[41] An earlier 'one off' had been issued in January 1979.

maintain the Library. The Committee ... now feel the Society should review its objectives and in so doing be more active in assisting its Members.' This was the reasoning behind the idea of Members' quarterly lunchtime meetings for the discussion of issues of common interest and to encourage more communication between Members who, it was felt, had rather retreated behind their desks.

Legal aid issues also bulked large at that time and attention was drawn to the decision of The Law Society to seek judicial review (successfully as it turned out to be) of the Lord Chancellor's decision with regard to restrictions on Criminal Legal Aid. Sadly this was a feature of a continuing issue – the erosion of trust and cooperation between the government and the profession, part of the general antipathy towards the professions which was characteristic of the Thatcher years and which continued a decade later under Mr Blair. Even so considerable changes in the administration of Legal Aid were introduced by Statutory Instruments in 1986 and in particular the Legal Aid Committee structure for administering the scheme was drastically modified. The next issue of the Newsletter announced the appointment of the first 9 members of the Council for Licensed Conveyancers, a sure sign that the end was in sight for the conveyancing monopoly.

At the 1986 AGM a further female member of the Committee was elected in the person of Miss Vera Stamenkovitch who was, of course, to go on to become The Society's first female President. Another development of national import was a Practice Direction giving solicitors, for the first time and in very limited circumstances, rights of audience in uncontested matters in the Supreme Court. This was a faltering first step towards the notion of the Solicitor Advocate. Further developments at a national level in 1986 included the proposed creation of a new regime for dealing with complaints against Solicitors in the form of The Solicitors' Complaints Bureau. The likely cost of this scheme would, of course, have to be borne by the profession and was estimated to lead to an increase in practising certificate costs of £45 pa. At the same time professional incomes were likely to be further squeezed by the proposed introduction of fixed fees in criminal legal aid cases and the proposed abolition of 'green form' advice. Even so there were arguments that firms could survive if they made use of the new freedom to advertise and marketed themselves effectively – it was all a very far cry from the last days of the previous century when competition and advertising would have been absolute anathema to The Society's members. Furthermore there was the prospect of the further erosion of conveyancing work not just because of the end of the monopoly but also as a result of legal developments whereby Building Societies were enabled to take on such work.

To update its structure in the light of all the changes going on round about The Society determined to revise its rules. The principal changes were the deletion of references to the Law Library and the substitution of references to continuing legal education, the redefinition of the roles of the various sub committees, an ability to allow proxy voting at meetings – an issue of some contention in previous years – a new power for The Committee to fix entrance fees and annual subscriptions consequent on rapid changes in other costs, and authority for The Committee to co-opt up to 4 additional members during the course of a year.

By the end of 1986 The Society had successfully introduced its quarterly lunchtime meeting scheme, and had been much concerned with the future of conveyancing, especially the issue of a new Conveyancing Protocol. There was also good news to report about reductions of delays in hearing times at Leicester County Court, even though that body was understaffed. Members were urged to assist court staff by not 'chasing cases which are not urgent'. There was also some satisfaction that The Lord Chancellor had agreed to some increases in rates for criminal legal aid, while the Green Form scheme of interim legal advice appeared to be reprieved. On the other hand the Solicitors' Complaints Bureau had commenced its work on 1st September 1986 and had taken over the work previously done by The Law Society's Professional Purposes Committee. The new structure involved an Adjudication Committee, mixed professional and lay, and an Investigation Committee, predominantly lay, to monitor the investigation processes of the Bureau. This was also the first year in which solicitors were asked to include their ethnic details on applications for Practising Certificates. The information thus gathered was to be used solely for monitoring and analysing trends in professional development. The times were changing, rapidly and radically, and the profession as a whole was moving in the direction of a regulatory model increasingly adopted for industry following the privatisations of the Thatcher Years, ie the notion that there should be an independent external regulator to act in the interests of consumers of the service offered by an enterprise.

The Leicestershire Law Society

The new rules referred to above were adopted at a special general meeting on 21st January 1987. At the same time The Society's name was changed to 'The Leicestershire Law Society'. The Society was then one of 126 local Law Societies in England and Wales at a time when there was debate about the pros and cons of decentralization of power from Chancery Lane to regional associations. Some such measure of coordination was needed in relation to issues such as the 24 hour duty solicitor scheme which was just about operating nationally but where there was disagreement between urban and rural areas over levels and methods of payment. There was also a perceived need to ensure the Crown Prosecution Service did not operate without private practitioner input. More locally there was concern at the beginning of 1987 about delay in the processing of Local Searches and Enquiries. At the end of 1986 members had been asked to comment on this issue. This led to correspondence between The President and the chief executive of one local authority who promised to amend their ways – a good example of the efficacy of collective action. Nationally such action had resulted a few months earlier in the holding of a dinner for Leicestershire MPs at the Leicestershire Club on 28th November 1986 at which Committee members were able to voice concerns over, inter alia, the future of conveyancing and the issue of legal aid. Such an event has now become a regular feature of The Society's year, though the dinners are held at Westminster for the benefit of local members of both Houses of Parliament and the need for properly planned Parliamentary Liaison is accepted.

Another issue which had caused some concern in previous years received its quietus in May 1987. Previously the attitude of The Society was that advertising was not in the interests of Members. Following deliberation by The Committee this policy was altered and The Society became neutral with regard to advertising, leaving this as a matter for individual member firms. Advertising and public relations continued to be matters of note throughout 1987 as The Law Society emphasised that there were three main issues facing the profession as a whole – competition, recruitment and appearance – the latter not being confined merely to matters of apparel! It is, however, interesting that recruitment was back on the agenda, this time not because of an over supply of candidates but because of numbers of solicitors leaving practice. Between 1978 and 1982 there were many female entrants to the profession and the perception was that they were now leaving to begin families. One way in which the issue was addressed was the creation of 'women returners' courses at which women solicitors who had been out of practice could update their skills and knowledge with a view to re-entering practice. Such events have been promoted by a number of Universities, The Association of Women Solicitors and commercial providers over the years. At the time of writing, however, some of these events appear to be under-subscribed. It may well be that once a woman has been out of practice for more than a year or two it is increasingly hard for her to return, even with assistance. The problem of attrition amongst women solicitors remains unsolved.

By the start of 1988 the quarterly lunchtime meetings of The Society were well established and that on 21st January 1988 was attended by some 40 members where the issue for consideration was the impact of the Financial Services Act led by Walter Merricks, the Assistant Secretary General of the Law Society. Another successful feature of The Society's activities was the operation of a local Conveyancing Protocol which particularly dealt with Preliminary Inquiries. 49 local firms had declared their adherence to the Protocol and other member firms were invited to join. The Committee reported that the operation of the Protocol would be kept under regular review.

On a more downbeat note The Society was informed of the somewhat doleful national news concerning complaints against solicitors and the work of the Solicitors Complaints Bureau. In 1987 the SCB received 17,000 complaints and 20,000 other referrals. There was then one complaint for every two solicitors annually, 80% of which deserved investigation, though only 5% were serious. The issues to avoid were firms acting beyond their capacity, not exercising sufficient supervision of staff, ignorance of conduct and/or the Solicitors' Accounts Rules, allowing insufficiently experienced staff to act in matters, and simple 'rotten management'. There was also a particular issue of lack of liaison between the SCB and local law societies.

These ill tidings were somewhat confirmed in the May 1988 Newsletter when local Law Society Council constituency member, Alan Coles, drew attention to increasing competition between firms for conveyancing work, while domestic conveyancing fees represented an ever smaller proportion of the cost of the houses on which they were paid. While he detected a note of confidence in his area he pointed to a growing number of mergers as firms sought to share costs, attract suitably qualified staff and develop specialisms. He noted also, however, growing disparities of remuneration between the fortunate 'head hunted' practitioners and those who appeared prepared to accept inadequate pay and other rewards.

On a happier note in April 1988 a flyer was sent to all members announcing that a Summer Ball was to be held at the City Rooms in Leicester on 10th June 1988 with a buffet, cash bar and dancing to the Bunny Graham Band. This was an attempt to revive in a more attractive form the old dinner dance which had been a winter function. The event was a success and was repeated in the summer of 1989. The Newsletter also began to carry lists of those elected to, or ceasing to be members of, The Society. It is interesting to note that in March 1988 of 11 new members, 7 were female while the leavers were all male.

Complaints – Again!

In 1988 the Hon. Secretary, Mr A P Smith, apparently known as 'the scourge' of the SCB, paid that body a visit and reported back in the July 1988 Newsletter. The SCB was, in his estimation, hardworking but understaffed and finding it hard to train and keep staff. One new development he noted was the proposed inception of a conciliation service whereby conciliation officers would speak to solicitors against whom a complaint had been made by 'phone in the hope of expediting dealing with minor complaints. The Society was also urged to nominate members to the SCB's negligence panel, ie solicitors willing to give initial free advice to complainants in cases of alleged negligence. This service was designed to counter the public perception that solicitors 'stuck together' and would not advise a lay person alleging negligence against other solicitors.

One year later in June 1989 the Hon. Secretary once again visited the SCB. He was concerned to see increases in the number of complaints which were likely to rise from 18,000 to 25,000, but he was pleased that the telephone conciliation service was working well and clearing a backlog of minor issues. He also reported an experiment in East Anglia whereby lesser complaints could be dealt with by an area based team, and, if this was successful, it was likely to become the national pattern. The SCB, however, stressed the need for preventing complaints in the first place, and where local societies had suspicions about any solicitors' cheques not being met that these should be reported immediately. It was also stressed that *all* conversations and messages to/from clients should be recorded.

The November 1988 Newsletter brought news of further changes made nationally which were to have continuing divisive effects. As from 1st September 1988 under the 'Solicitors' Introduction and Referral Code', arrangements between solicitors and third parties, such as Estate Agents, were made possible in respect of the regular introduction of clients and their business. At about the same time The Law Society made some progress towards regionalization by the appointment of two regional secretaries on a three year basis. East Anglia and the Southern area of England was to be serviced from Chancery Lane, but it was hoped that the regions would have a major say in the work of the regional secretaries and that there would be closer liaison with local law societies with particular regard to professional education and public relations.

Socially 1988 closed with a further Wine and Buffet evening at Leicester Guildhall for members, spouses and guests at a price of £6.25 per head, exclusive of wine. This was organised by a social sub committee of The Society.

Sole Practice

On 23rd November 1988 the Secretaries of Local Law Societies attended a meeting at Chancery Lane at which, inter alia, the issue of sole practitioners was raised. There was evidence that there was a high level of claims in respect of solicitors practising alone and there was the possibility of higher contributions to the Compensation Fund by sole practitioners and a more costly practising certificate. There was also the possibility of an enhanced regulatory regime in respect of sole practice. This news cannot have been welcome in some parts of Leicestershire which has always had a sizeable number of sole practitioners. Indeed it has been a feature of local practice life since the 1960s for some firms to fragment, and then recombine in other forms, maybe with some new personnel, while others have decided to set up entirely on their own account. Leicestershire still remains an area served to a considerable extent by small firms, despite the growth of larger concerns. One explanation for this is the large number of 'small to medium enterprises' (SMEs) in the local economy, and it is arguable that 'small businesses like to deal with other small businesses'.

On the 28th November 1988 the Parliamentary Dinner was held, but this time at the Lansdowne Club in London. There was a very full agenda for discussion with local MPs. This included:

- Transfer of Conveyancing work from solicitors and licensed conveyancers to a small group of financial organisations offering one-stop property services;
- The acquisition of estate agencies by large corporations who charged high commission fees and 'pushed' the use of particular forms of mortgage finance;
- The threat to branch offices and small firms should conveyancing be taken away from solicitors and the consequent diminution in the availability of legal services to the community;
- Changes to the Legal Aid System which were having a detrimental effect on the level of service offered;
- The possibility of introducing a contingency fee system as an alternative to legal aid;
- The future of the Crown Prosecution Service and Law Centres and the general lack of local success in Leicester in creating a Property Centre (or Solicitors' Property Shop).

It was expected that some of these issues would be addressed in a Government Green Paper due in January 1989.

While some of the issues outlined above have become part of daily legal life, for example contingency fees, others have not, particularly 'one stop conveyancing shops' operated by banks and building societies. It must be asked whether anyone in government seriously believed that such a development would be in the public interest, and whether they had investigated whether and how the financial institutions would be able to find the space in their premises and sufficient staff to enable them to take over conveyancing. It must also be remembered that at the time the nation was nearing the end of a house price boom. The subsequent collapse of the housing market and the phenomenon of negative equity in the early 1990s was undoubtedly a sobering experience for the banks and building societies, though one they, sadly, too soon forgot. They retreated from competing with the solicitors and licensed conveyancers. Indeed it may be posited that whenever the general economy and the housing market are booming, some large commercial organisations will always look to the possibility of extending their range of activities and services. They will be tempted in particular to cast covetous eyes in the direction of legal services, despite their lack of experience in the area and a mistaken belief that legal services can be commoditised and sold in unit form like packets of biscuits. Sager counsel in some big city boardrooms will discourage such avidity and will keep the company on the track of its own core business, but there will always be mavericks. However, once there is an economic downturn, and should that be associated with evidence that large financial and commercial concerns are not as economically competent as they might wish to appear, there will be a return to commonsense and solicitors can, for a while at least, breathe again. At the time of writing, Spring 2009, it is arguable that lesson is having to be learned again in the light of another catastrophic downturn in the housing market, which has had consequences for all those concerned with housing.

Careers Advice

In 1989 The Law Society launched SOLCAS (the Solicitors Careers Advisory Service) to coordinate the work of local law societies and individual firms with regard to promoting careers in the profession. Each local law society was asked to appoint a Local Careers Officer to provide links between the profession, locally and nationally, and colleges, universities and schools. It was also hoped that members of The Society would volunteer to attend careers events and local schools and universities. The Society had been trying to coordinate such activities for a while before the national initiative was launched and it was hoped that existing links and activities could be integrated into the new framework. Sadly by mid 1989 a very poor response to the SOLCAS initiative was recorded. In particular member firms were slow, as they had been previously with regard to local career placement initiatives, to inform The Society of the availability of placements. They also appeared unwilling to attend careers events in schools, etc.

It may be that attention was focussed on litigation issues affecting the locality. In May 1989 it was reported that the Leicester City Division had lost so many Court Clerks that, despite shifting some business to Hinckley and Loughborough, there would be an inevitable reduction in the number of sittings of the magistrates and consequent delays in all areas, including juvenile justice, road traffic and domestic violence. (Happily by the middle of the year appointments had been made to ease the crisis.) Members may also have been particularly concerned by the ban that was placed on the use of what were then called cell 'phones by the Governor of Leicester Prison: he was not prepared to allow such 'phones to be taken into visits to see inmate clients, nor was he able to offer secure facilities for such equipment to be left with prison staff. Indeed the restrictions at Welford Road increased throughout the year so that as from July 1989 Legal Advisers were only allowed to visit clients on official visit appointments on three days a week between 9.00 am and 11.00 am and 1.30 pm to 4.00 pm.

Legal Aid – Again

On 1st April 1989 responsibility for administering Legal Aid passed from The Law Society to the Legal Aid Board – a quango. The declared aim of the new board was 'to ensure ... that legal advice, assistance and representation is made available to those who need it, and that it is administered in ways that are effective and give the best possible value for money'. The link between the profession and the administration of Legal Aid was thus broken, and while The Law Society retained certain roles, in particular that of 'watchdog' to take up instances where the administration of legal aid had gone awry or where law or policy required clarification, nevertheless this was a further step in reducing the overall autonomy of the profession by subjecting an important source of income to external regulation.

Locally The Society held its 1989 AGM on 24th May and included amongst its committee members the Chairman of The Young Solicitors Group. The following sub Committees were also appointed, F&GP, Contentious Business, Non-Contentious Business, Public Relations, Education and Social. Salaries for articled clerks were also locally fixed at £7,300 (1989-90), £8,700 (1990-91) and £10,100 (1991-92).

The September 1989 issue of the Newsletter contained extensive coverage of developments at Leicester Polytechnic Law School, as described by its Head, Professor R Card. These included the creation of a Department of Professional Legal Studies (to sit alongside the academic Law Department) to offer the Common Professional Examination for non-law graduates wishing to enter the profession and the Law Society Finals Course, as it was then known, for those wishing to become solicitors.

Locally the social life of The Society was reinvigorated by the proposal to revive the Members' closed dinner, this time on 24th November 1989 at The Three Swans in Market Harborough at a price of £12.95 excluding drinks. Those who contemplated making 'a real evening of it' were able to obtain overnight accommodation and breakfast at a concessionary rate of £15.00. The Young Solicitors Group was also in good heart and reported concentrating on social events, especially encouraging the attendance of county members. There had been a Treasure Hunt in Leicester City Centre, a gourmet evening at Fernie Lodge (now another sadly lost feature of the County), a theatre trip, appropriately to see "The Merchant of Venice" and hear Portia's speech on the quality of mercy, a cricket match against the Bar, and Ten pin bowling against the CPS. One worrying comment was, however, 'it would be nice to see some new faces'. While the Young Solicitors appeared to be reviving some of the activities of the former Law Students Society, their fortunes were very much dependent on the willingness of members to become involved and attend. Indeed this has become an issue for the entire Society.

A very interesting feature of this issue of the Newsletter was the emergence of commercial sponsorship in the form of an advertisement for flats in the newly converted St John's Church in Albion Street. Was this one shape of things to come? A 'flyer' from a legal recruitment firm had been inserted in the July edition, and the same agency had an advertisement on the back cover of the November 1989 issue.

What characterises a most turbulent decade for The Society? Obviously the closure of The Library could have been a mortal blow because it was a most radical departure from what The Society had previously existed for. However, life did go on. In some ways The Society seems to have lost some of its special identity and to have become much more of a local reflection of The Law Society. This was perhaps inevitable given the pressures felt by the entire profession and the need to resist over mighty interference by government and regulatory bodies and untoward competition from powerful financial institutions. There was a need for solicitors to look to their moats both nationally and locally. The inception of the Newsletter was a major factor in maintaining the coherence and existence of The Society. From small beginnings it became a considerable organ of communication on a wide range of issues. The editors of the Newsletter achieved an enormous amount on behalf of their colleagues. The social life of The Society appears to have revived, as does that of the Young Solicitors Group, maybe because these were dedicated individuals prepared to make it so. Simple institutional structures were no longer enough in themselves to ensure a healthy continuation of The Society's life; there had to be very considerable effort on the part of individuals as officers and committee members. The institutional began to be replaced by the personal as a measure of the likely success of a venture. In other words the simple announcement of a new venture by The Society would not be enough to guarantee success, there had to be the right people 'on the bridge' driving the development forward.

To say this is not to belittle the achievements of past individual members of The Society, indeed there were occasions – the dark days of the Second World War and its aftermath in particular – when particular individuals undoubtedly breathed new life into an ailing institution. However, it has nowadays to be acknowledged that we live in a non-deferential society where respect is not automatically attached to rank or position but has to be earned by individuals. Individual long serving officers of the Society because of their obvious dedication to duty and tireless efforts inevitably influenced the way in which The Society developed, and their importance thus grew in comparison to the office of President which, being a yearly appointment, maybe suffered some diminution in importance, if not in prestige.

Chapter 9

Into the 1990s

The decade opened with the publication of The Courts & Legal Services Bill on which The Society joined with others in the East Midlands Region to exchange views, finding, to its surprise, that conveyancing charges in Leicestershire and Rutland were lower than those in surrounding areas. A programme of meetings with local estate agents was also inaugurated to deal with the issues of common concern such as explaining the legalities of conveyancing to estate agency staff. This may have been hastened by the proposed launch of a new national conveyancing protocol by The Law Society. As the year progressed there were further issues with regard to conveyancing such as relationships between practitioners and the Land Registry, issues of conflicts of interest with regard to anyone allowed to undertake conveyancing being able to act for both sides in a transaction, save in very limited circumstances, and fears for the future of the profession consequent on continuing proposals to open up conveyancing to financial institutions. This did not, however, stop The Society from enjoying a very successful annual dinner attended by some 320 people, slightly fewer than the record number for the previous year when the Kings Room at The Grand Hotel (now Ramada Jarvis) had been somewhat over full. Unfortunately The Lord Chancellor who had been due to speak at that dinner had been forced to pull out because of legislative commitments.

As far as litigation was concerned the March 1990 Newsletter was much concerned with disseminating information about the conduct of work in the various Courts in the area, principally to avoid the old enemy of delay. There was also an enclosure announcing the retirement of Mr Peter Smith after 10 years' service as Secretary during which time his tireless efforts had done much to ensure the continued health of The Society. A subscription was raised to present him with a suitable gift, which took the form of an antique writing desk and two bottles of champagne. A sign of the work pressure felt by the secretarial office was a notice in the May 1990 issue of the Newsletter enquiring whether any member had a 'word processor' for sale: 'ideally, amongst the other virtues of the word processor it should have a facility for producing labels'. In the 21st century we take such features of 'desk top publishing' for granted, but it is interesting to note how comparatively recent has been the adoption of such technology by The Society.

At the May 1990 AGM Peter Smith stood down as Secretary and was elected Vice President while Kennedy Leslie assumed the secretarial role. The Committee consisted of 17 other members, of whom 3 were female. A special general meeting after the AGM also altered the rules of The Society with regard to membership. This continued the power of the Committee to exclude members who had become bankrupt or who had made arrangements or compositions with creditors, but took away the power to exclude members practising in co-partnership each of whose partners or principals practising in the City or County of Leicester was neither a member of The Society nor a candidate for membership. Thus ended the rule requiring all members of a firm to be members of The Society if any sought membership.

The July issue of the Newsletter carried news of the continuing activities of the Young Solicitors Group who once again had been active in organising a skittles evening, a wine tasting, a gourmet meal, a hockey match and who planned a theatre trip, a barge party, cricket and tennis matches and an excursion to The Great Central Railway. There was also a Christmas Luncheon planned for Tuesday 18th December 1990. The Society also planned its Members Closed Dinner for 23rd November 1990 in Loughborough . There had also been yet another successful Lunchtime Meeting for The Society in June 1990 when the speaker was a barrister specialising in defamation – Mr Edward Garnier then the prospective Conservative Candidate for the Harborough Division. A further feature of note was a letter to members from Mr Hugh Staunton who had set up as a Practice Consultant offering advice on the problems facing practitioners in a rapidly changing world – yet further evidence of the rapidly evolving environment in which The Society was functioning.

The November 1990 Newsletter reflected the continued wide range of The Society's activities containing the usual considerable amount of information: on changes in the Law; information about court listings and problems affecting Industrial Tribunals; the continued involvement of members in The Citizens Advice Bureau and Business Advice Centre; the on-going development of the Solicitors Complaints Bureau, the creation of a Legal Ombudsman Service by The Lord Chancellor. The holder of this office was to become the Lay Observer on the SCB with extended powers which were to extend to barristers and licensed conveyancers. There was also a plea that members should support the work of the Solicitors' Benevolent

Association, an echo of previous years, notice of further continuing education courses, and the announcement of the creation of the MA (now LLM) in Environmental Law by Leicester Polytechnic (now De Montfort University). On a happy note, however, there was a news item indicating that solicitors were considered by consumers to be the best service providers with regard to property transactions, ahead of estate agents, surveyors and mortgage lenders – something to cheer the hearts of local professionals as Christmas 1990 approached. This may well have been reflected in the participation of members in the Law Society Law Aid '90 Appeal which locally raised £1120 for 'Shelter for the Homeless'. This raised the question of whether there should be a local charitable event each year for The Society or whether it was preferable for members to support national events on a private basis. The Society was not, however, able to reach consensus on whether there should be an annual local charitable activity at the 1991 AGM and the matter was remitted to The Committee.

1991 began with announcements for the usual round of lunch time meetings and CPD events, while the SCB had now extended its local conciliation scheme to encompass Leicestershire, Bedfordshire, Derbyshire and Nottinghamshire. March 1991 saw County Court Registrars becoming District Judges. Interestingly it was announced that they were still to be formally addressed as 'Sir' – evidently there were no female 'DJs'! Also with regard to litigation the Leicester Crown Court Users Committee had come into being in December 1990 and its first deliberations were reported in March 1991, while the same issue contained advance notification of the Annual Summer Ball which was to be held on 14th June 1991 at the Holiday Inn, price £16.80 including a carved buffet and dancing to the Graham Taylor Band. Other 'domestic issues' of the year included advice from The Society on the minimum salary to be paid to what were now 'Trainee Solicitors', some £10,100 from August 1991, and something on the new initiative from The Law Society concerning 'Client Care Letters'. The Society did not propose to issue any form of local letter but urged members to follow the terms of the centrally issued Client Care Guide.

In July 1991 came notice of the candidature of Mr K Byass of Messrs Moss Latham & Toone of Loughborough for the post of Constituency Member for the Council of The Law Society which continued the long, though occasionally intermittent, practice of a Member of The Society serving on the Council. The outgoing President, Mr R H Bloor, however, had to record his concern that The Lord Chancellor's Department was not adhering to undertakings given in respect of the provision of Legal

Services under the Courts & Legal Services Act and had written expressing concern to the LCD; he was not greatly hopeful of receiving a response, it appears! Another development of note was the proposed replacement of the old Law Society Finals by the new Legal Practice Course as from 1993, and information on this from the Department of Professional Legal Studies at Leicester Polytechnic was conveyed to members. While there was the usual plethora of notices in the July 1991 Newsletter, the overwhelming majority of which related to various aspects of contentious business, it is good to note that both younger and more senior members of The Society were able to enjoy summer recreation; the former in the shape of a 5-A-Side Tournament held at Melton College, the latter in the form of the annual golf match against the Leicester Medical Society. This was then in its 27ᵗʰ year and the Trophy was a Minton Chamber Pot presented by John Ervin for the Lawyers and Hugh Binnie[42] for the Doctors. There had been a trophy to be competed for by 'articled clerks', originally donated by E Morgan Barlow, but this appeared to have gone missing and Mr D M Charman appealed for its return. How many of today's trainee solicitors play golf to competitive standard – how many have the time?

Peter Smith (as President) continued Richard Bloor's pursuit of the Lord Chancellor's Department over the regulations to be issued under the Courts and Legal Services Act. He had enlisted the help of Nigel (now Lord) Lawson, then a local MP, and that prompted the LCD to make some response. The President had also enlisted the aid of Sir John Farr, Jim Marshall and Greville Janner, all well respected local MPs. This activity led to a response by The Society to the consultation on the Draft Authorised Practitioner Regulations which was drafted by the Non-Contentious Sub Committee.

Continuing with conveyancing issues, the September 1991 Newsletter contained a paper from Mr Robert Kemp, President of the Leicestershire Estate Agents Association, which sought to deal with complaints from Society members about the conduct of certain estate agents in respect of conveyancing transactions. In particular the practice of phoning up solicitors to chase after contracts and their progress. Does this still sound familiar to members?

With regard to social concerns, the Young Solicitors had once again participated in a 5-A-Side event, and played in the annual East Midlands Cricket Challenge, losing to Nottinghamshire, 134 runs to 112, while the Members Closed Dinner was advertised for 15ᵗʰ November 1991 to be held at the Victorian Gallery of the Leicester Museum.

---

[42] Society members who were students of the University of Leicester in the early 1970s may well remember the late Hugh Binnie as Head of The University Medical Service. He was a grand character who cheerfully proclaimed his own hypocrisy in smoking while advising others to shun the weed.

Continuing Professional Development and other happenings

The end of 1991 brought news of the extension of compulsory continuing education and professional development for all solicitors admitted after August 1985, a scheme subsequently extended to all practising solicitors. Compulsory Continuing Professional Development was extended to solicitors admitted on and after 1st November 1982 from 1st November 1994, and to *all* solicitors as from 1st November 1998. Any depression caused by this might have been exacerbated at the beginning of 1992 by the winter weather and no sign of an upturn in the conveyancing market. However, to begin the year on an upbeat note the January 1992 Newsletter announced the inauguration of what may be considered a 'stepchild' of The Society, namely The Leicester Medico-Legal Society whose first meeting was 'enlivened' by somewhat gruesome pathology slides. In the same issue The Highfields and Belgrave Law Centres appealed for help on either a paid or voluntary basis from local solicitors skilled in the areas of employment, immigration and nationality, housing and welfare rights. In view of this it was perhaps apt that The Society advertised a CPD lecture to be held at The City rooms in Leicester on 11th February 1992 on 'Residential Tenancies' which was to be given by the present author!

March 1992 brought the sad news of the death of Michael Farnworth formerly of Messrs Harvey Ingram who had been for many years the Newsletter Editor. It was largely due to his assiduity that the publication had become such a mainstay of The Society's existence. Mr M K Dunkley, also of Messrs Harvey Ingram, took over as a temporary editor. More happily The President, Peter Smith, was able to report a definite first, namely the birth of a son to Committee member Vera Stamenkovich. He was also happy to report another successful annual dinner on 7th February 1992 attended by 298 members and guests at the Grand Hotel.

By this time it was also becoming clear that financial institutions were unwilling to take on conveyancing work under The Courts & Legal Services Act, but the President urged continued vigilance and action both locally and nationally, and the lobbying of local MPs, to ensure that the Conveyancing Practitioners Regulations were not brought in by any manner likely to injure the profession *and* the consumer. 'The message must be that the consumer requires safeguards and the present regulations as drafted may undermine these safeguards.' At the same time as this, Legal Aid in Criminal Justice was also under threat and there were fears that many firms of solicitors would withdraw from criminal work on the basis they simply could not make it pay. In return the Lord Chancellor argued that Legal Aid expenditure had risen from £500m in 1987 to £1bn in 1992 and the only way to control this was by introducing standard fixed fees for the work. Following a conference on this issue at Westminster Central Hall on 12th February 1992, The President, Peter Smith, and the PR Officer, Robert Dews, were interviewed by BBC Radio 4 and then went to The House of Commons to lobby members on the issue. They received some support from MPs in the Labour Party, then in opposition, but less from Conservative members. However, correspondence between The Lord Chancellor and Mr Stephen Dorrell of 16th March 1992 indicated that there was insufficient interest to proceed with opening up the conveyancing market to financial institutions: campaigning had paid off!

In defence of members' interests the Committee reported a Market Harborough will writing firm who had utilised misleading language in publicity leaflets designed to promote their service. The complaint to the Advertising Standards Authority was upheld. It may be remembered that action to prevent 'muscling in' by outsiders had been a feature of Society activity in the early years of the 20th century; it was still needed as that century drew to its close.

By May 1992 Richard Adkinson of Messrs Crane & Walton had taken over as Newsletter Editor. He proposed to feature reports in each issue dealing with the work of the various sub committees, and this resulted in a lengthy item dealing with a wide range of contentious business arising from a meeting of the County Court User Committee in March 1992. It was further reported that Leicester was likely to have a Stipendiary Magistrate as from 1993. The Education and Training Sub Committee also announced an agreement with Leicester Polytechnic (Now De Montfort University), for the Department of Professional Legal Studies to offer an expanded programme of CPD courses for members. The initial subject matter included: VAT on Commercial Property, Criminal Justice, Domestic & Commercial Conveyancing Remedies, EC Law, Personal Injury Law, Wills, Trusts and Tax.

Social concerns were also in the news. Peter Smith marked the end of his year of office by handing over a cheque for £3,500 to the Lord Mayor of Leicester's appeal. This was the proceeds of a sponsored swim in which 45 members participated. The presentation ceremony received the honour of a picture in *The Mercury* – might that have been considered advertising in former days? Members' own pleasures were also not forgotten as The Summer Ball was again due to be held on 19th June 1992.

The Growing Importance of Women Solicitors

The inaugural meeting of The Leicester Association of Women Lawyers took place on 10th March 1992, perhaps somewhat incongruously at The Black Boy. An ad hoc committee was formed and an AGM fixed for June 1992. The object of the Association was to provide a network for the increasing numbers of women solicitors in Leicester Town and County. A Women's Representative was also appointed to the Committee of The Young Solicitors/ Trainee Solicitors Group who appeared to have merged their activities at this time. The formal beginning of the Leicester Association of Women Lawyers was announced in the Newsletter for September 1992. Membership was open to solicitors, female legal executives and trainees and barristers, and the annual subscription was set at £5.00. The 'next event' announced by the Association was to be a talk by District Judge Linda Eaton, who, of course, had some years previously been in practice in Leicester. Sadly this group did not last long, though at the time of writing, almost 20 years on, there are proposals to set up a branch of the Association of Women Solicitors.

One of Peter Smith's final acts in his year as President was to host a luncheon for surviving Past Presidents, and 19 out of 23 attended. It was agreed that the profession had changed beyond recognition. One problem The Society now faced was recruitment. In July 1992 Rupert Clarke, the new President, pointed out that many young solicitors could not afford to join, and while many firms automatically applied for membership for new solicitors and paid subscriptions, this was not universal. There was a danger The Society would lose touch with new blood.

Amongst new developments locally at this time was the opening of the new Magistrates Court Building in Pocklingtons Walk[43], while nationally there were still moves afoot to seek rights of audience for solicitors in Higher Courts. Some radical voices even advocated a fused profession. There continued to be controversy over Legal Aid. The Lord Chancellor backed down on one proposal that a defendant would have to produce 13 wage slips before qualifying for Legal Aid, but he pressed ahead with the notion of standard fees in Magistrates' Courts. The notion of franchising Legal Aid also became current, along with that of restricting certain kinds of work to specialist panel members only, while the well established fixed fee interview for £5.00 which enabled many to 'test the water' on a claim appeared to be doomed also. The first specialist panel was mentioned in the following issue of the Newsletter, that dealing with Personal Injury.

---

[43] The 'Official Opening' took place on 13th November 1992 when the ceremony was performed by the Lord Chancellor.

This was set up but not without some struggle for the terms of membership were very strict, for example, 60 personal injury instructions in the 5 years previous to application, or 36 in the 3 years prior to application. This and other restrictive rules had the effect of forcing many smaller firms out of the personal injury area of practice.

Change continued, and the pace of change also increased. Change affected legal education for it was announced that as from 1994, all Trainee Solicitors would have to undergo a further Professional Skills Course during their two years of training. This was likely to increase firms' costs, but it was hoped that the course could be offered at Leicester Polytechnic. In addition the minimum salary for trainees in the provinces was to be raised to £10,850. It was little wonder that many applicants for training contracts were finding it increasingly hard to obtain a place.

To protect members' business, all members were urged to participate in 'Make a Will Week' which was to run from 12th October to 18th October 1992. Amongst the resources to promote this initiative were theatrical costumes available for anyone willing to play the part of 'Will Power', including a turquoise suit in lycra with pants, cape and boots. This was reputed to be very stretchy and able to accommodate all shapes and sizes, and was said to be 'excellent for photocalls'.

On the social front the Members' Closed Dinner was fixed on 30th October 1992 to take place at The Three Swans in Market Harborough. This event took place and was well attended by 50 members, whereas a proposed similar event in 1991 had had to be abandoned for lack of support. In addition a joint skittles evening was arranged with the Legal Executives and the Young Solicitors Group for 28th October 1992. The Young Solicitors, in conjunction with groups from Derbyshire, Nottinghamshire, Cambridgeshire and Luton also planned a Christmas Ball to be held at The Grand Hotel in Leicester on 28th November 1992. Interestingly this was to be supported by sponsorship from the Wellman Smith Recruitment Agency. That was a token of things to come.

1992 closed with the President lamenting the disappearance of social get togethers: 'Surely it can only help our day to day dealings if we get to know our opponents and competitors in the profession on a social basis'. What a far cry that was from the situation in previous years when there was such a considerable degree of social cohesion within the local profession. Rupert Clarke also announced an initiative to write to all local solicitors who were not members asking them to join The Society and outlining the benefits of membership. Members were also urged to persuade solicitors in their offices who were not members to join up.

These developments were again an indication of the changes going on in The Society's environment – a less solidly cohesive profession and one in which a number of practitioners did not see the benefits of belonging to a local Law Society.

There was further gloom on the contentious business side with ever more initiatives from the Lord Chancellor to reduce the Legal Aid bill. Fixed fees for Criminal Legal Aid were to be extended into the Civil field, while eligibility for Legal Aid was to be tied to that for Income Support, making some 7m people ineligible for Legal Aid. The Law Society accepted that Legal Aid should only be offered by franchised firms and by early 1993 the initial standards for franchising were out for consultation. At the same time Legal Aid officials seemed ever more ready to reject applications on the basis of uncompleted technicalities. The Legal Aid system, whose inception had done so much to revive The Society at the end of the Second World War and to introduce a new era in legal practice was in danger as never before. A Campaign to Save Legal Aid was begun in 1992 and this continued into 1993. There was a mass lobby of MPs, at which The Society was well represented, on 3rd February 1993, and this also involved The Consumers Association, The National Consumer Council, The National Association of CABX, Age Concern, The Child Poverty Action Group, Relate and MIND. There were meetings on that day with some local MPs, but it became clear that a number of MPs were unaware of the likely consequences of cuts in Legal Aid and had not appreciated there could be a denial of justice to many.

1993 began locally with the F&GP forecasting a need for an increase in subscriptions consequent on rising expenditure and subsidies for the annual dinner and the setting up of an Advocacy Training Course, half of which was met by drawing on capital. Rupert Clarke, near the end of his year of office, was, however, able to report that his initiative in writing to all non member solicitors locally had produced some new recruits.

This was also the year when the new court complex for Leicester was proposed. The County Court was to move from Lower Hill Street and Leicester House and Epic House to a new building linked to the existing Crown Court in Wellington Street which had opened in 1982. The new building was predicted to cost £2.4m. Sadly it was reported that the officials responsible for planning the new building were unlikely to consult with The Society about its views on what provision should be made. The Chief Clerk at the County Court, Mr John Sansam, did, however, receive representations from local solicitors and forwarded these to central officials.

In 1993 Graham Moore took over the editorship of the Newsletter and had to produce what is something of an 'emergency issue' covering December 1993 and January 1994. This did, however, recount the sad experiences of The Society's Secretary, Mr Kennedy Leslie, at The Law Society's 1993 Brighton Conference. There was no booking for Mr Leslie, despite proof being given that a booking had been made, but there was one for Mr Leslie Kennedy! In the outcome the Hon. Secretary was allowed to stay.

The importance of The Newsletter

The format of the Newsletter changed under its new editor, but continuing concern appeared in the February/March 1994 issue about the state of the profession: 'It probably all boils down to pressure which has increased enormously on us all. We have to generate such a tremendous throughput of jobs these days to earn the money to pay the overheads which have increased out of all proportion to inflation, particularly in meeting Law Society Levies.' The editor could not have been alone in holding that opinion. In the following issue John Tillotson reinforced these comments by pointing out that: 'many good solicitors have retired early due to ... pressures'. Nationally the air of gloom was somewhat lightened by figures indicating that claims on the Compensation Fund had reduced by 33% in 1993, while The Law Society had been able to take action in respect of certain Building Societies who had removed sole practitioners from their conveyancing panels. In the meantime franchising with regard to both matrimonial and personal injury work loomed ever closer.

On a more light hearted note the President, Neil de Voil, announced that there would be a 'Jail and Bail' event to be held on May 14th 1994 consisting of a series of amusing mock trials to raise money for the NSPCC.

The June/July 1994 issue of the Newsletter allowed the incoming President, Arthur Price-Jones, to introduce himself to members. Though coming from a local government background, the new President acknowledged the existence of the pressures referred to above. He argued, however, that these were inevitable given the consumer driven market in which the profession had to operate. He added: 'Professionalism is often regarded these days as an outmoded concept; there is a growing tendency to regard the older professions, in particular, as technicians. The overwhelming emphasis upon price as opposed to value reinforces that trend'. He called for the profession locally to adopt high quality standards in the delivery of service in order to re-establish itself at 'the leading edge of personal and advisory services'.

At the national level The Law Society was at this time compiling a dossier of information in order to take action against unqualified will writers by seeking regulation of their activities. The Accident Line advice scheme was also due to be launched on June 30th 1994, while all firms wishing to register training contracts were reminded they needed Law Society authorisation as from 1st July 1994. This would cost £50 for a three year period.

On 18th May 1994 The Society received a visit from John Hayes, Secretary General of The Law Society. This coincided with the AGM and Mr Hayes addressed members prior to that meeting. He confirmed that certain issues were proceeding including the creation of further specialised panels, franchising of Legal Aid Services, while standard fees in litigation would come into force in 1995. There were two points of particular interest. The first was that, nationwide, conveyancing in 1994 only represented 8% of total fee income, while solicitors' fees had shrunk to, on average, half those of estate agents. The second issue was the degree standard required for entry into the profession. There had been an impression that an upper second class degree had become a prerequisite to entry, but John Hayes was clear that a lower second class graduate might have other personal qualities which made him/her attractive as a trainee, for example an ability to bring in work. The passing years may have eroded the force of that argument. There is nowadays an impression that 'if it isn't a 2:1, it isn't a degree'!

By the time the August/September 1994 Newsletter appeared the 3rd Edition of the National Conveyancing Protocol had come into effect. This marked yet another step in a long journey towards nationally standardised conveyancing practice. At the same time The Law Society was undertaking a further exercise 'Adapting to the future in Conveyancing'. The most contentious issue here was a requirement for separate representation of both parties. The Society's conclusion was that, overall, separate representation would be beneficial and would bring about a greater measure of order in conveyancing transactions.

At the end of 1994 the Newsletter contained notification of the setting up of the Leicester Branch of the Solicitors Family Law Association, now Resolution. The Law Society also announced that all local societies would henceforth be supplied with full details of any conditional practising certificates issued to solicitors in their areas. Also on the disciplinary front, The Society had organised a seminar on 27th July 1994 on the topic of money laundering, while The Law Society had issued guidance notes on this increasing problem to all firms via senior partners.

At the national level 1994 closed with no agreement between The Law Society and the Lord Chancellor with regard to franchising legal aid services, nor could the profession itself agree about the future of conveyancing, in particular the issue of separate representation of clients. Socially, however, things were looking up with a planned meal at the Barceloneta Tapas Bar on 19th October, a trip to Hoskins Brewery on 18th November, which included a meal and two pints of beer for £9.99 (what might it cost now?) and a Christmas Lunch at Leicester City Football Club (then in Filbert Street, of course) on 16th December. Members interested in attending were advised to book out the entire afternoon!

1995 commenced with the national 'Make a Will Week', and a stand was booked in 'The Shires' in connection with this event. Five local firms booked half day slots from Thursday lunchtime until Saturday evening. Hard on the heels of this event came the Annual Dinner at which The Society raised a collection of £580 for the Lord Mayor's Charitable Appeal. Advance notice was also given in the Newsletter of National Law Week which was to be held in May. The Society's contribution was to be a free legal clinic at The City Rooms on 24th May. It was also proposed to revive the Summer Ball which had fallen into abeyance, and a provisional date of 16th June 1995, again at The City Rooms, was announced, while on 22nd June senior members of The Law Society were to visit Leicester with the 'Roadshow'. This event was to be held at Leicester City Football Club from 4.30 to 7.30 pm. The 'Roadshow' consisted of a panel of members, to whom the views of local practitioners could be communicated. Members were urged to apply for tickets for this event. The Young Solicitors Group were also active organising, inter alia, a general knowledge charity quiz on 23rd February 1995 at The Globe public house, raising £151, and proposing a 'Quality of Life' Conference at The Stakis Hotel in Nottingham in May, to be run by the National Young Solicitors' Group and the Association of Women Solicitors.

On a practice level the April/May issue of the Newsletter contained an explanation of The Society's role in dealing with complaints from the public. Members were informed that some 41.3% of the annual practice fee went towards funding the Solicitors' Complaints Bureau and that handling complaints locally was a cost efficient way of ensuring that the cost of the annual practice certificate did not increase. Most complaints received locally related to delays in conducting matters, accounting for money due to clients and alleged overcharging. Some complaints could be handled by The Society without reference to the firms involved, but others had to be passed on and the Hon. Secretary explained that in such cases the role of The Society was to 'act as a bridge [where] communication between the client and [the solicitor] has broken down. It is not to act as the client's representative nor to act in a hostile manner'. It was further pointed out that prevention of complaints is better than cure and that many misunderstandings could be obviated by better client care letters setting out the basis of charging.

The changing role of women

An other important event of note was Leicester's first Solicitor Advocate. Rights of audience for solicitors in the Higher Courts were granted in 1994, and Leicester's first candidate, Olwen Davies, enrolled to take the qualification. This involved obtaining a certificate of eligibility, sitting an examination and going on a residential course which consisted of a number of weekend sessions, at the end of which Leicester had its first Solicitor Advocate, one of the first in the land and, indeed, one of, initially, only 20.

Most appropriately Olwen Davies's success was followed by the election of The Society's first female President, Vera Stamenkovich. The columns of the Newsletter indicated that there was quite a healthy yearly influx of new members, many of whom were women. On the other hand The Committee still had only 3 female members as opposed to 15 men. Vera Stamenkovich outlined her career in the Newsletter for September/ October 1995 admitting that her very first visit to Leicester had been when she attended an interview for articles at Messrs Headleys. She rapidly became involved in The Articled Clerks' Society and then the Young Solicitors Group, moving from Headleys to Messrs Marron Dodds on April 1st 1981; becoming a partner there in 1984. She was also notable in being elected to The Committee of The Society in a contested election after having previously been the representative for the Young Solicitors Group.

Nationally the profession was much concerned at this time with developments concerning accreditation of practice management standards, while further consultation was to take place concerning certification of conveyancing standards. The Law Society also made certain recommendations to local Law Societies concerning their role with regard to: consultation exercises; liaison with members of The Law Society Council; giving publicity to local conciliation services and complaints handling, and by encouraging regular meetings of senior partners of firms within their areas to liaise on the maintenance of good practice standards.

Socially it was proposed to close the year with the Members' Closed Dinner, once more to held at The Three Swans in Market Harborough on 1st December.

1996 commenced with a triumph for The Society. Its negotiations with Leicester County Court led to a substantial increase in hourly rates allowable on the taxation of contentious bills. The method of calculating the hourly rate was based on a questionnaire sent to all firms about their actual running costs. This information was fed into a computer to produce an average hourly figure. However, despite the information being collected on a confidential basis, many firms were unwilling to cooperate, indeed in 1995/96 almost 50% of those surveyed failed to respond. This was to be a continuing problem. Also in connection with litigation there had been a useful meeting between The Society and District Judges for Leicester in late 1995 which resulted in clarification of a number of issues of mutual concern, for example allowing trainee solicitors to gain experience by sitting in with District Judges on an individual basis. Elsewhere the news with regard to trainees was not so good as the future of The Professional Skills course in Leicester at De Montfort University was in question due to poor support by local firms, despite there being then more trainees in the County than ever before. Continuing lack of support led to the abandonment of the course as from 1997.

April 1996 found Vera Stamenkovich musing on her year in office. She was pleased to report that the standard of food and service at the Annual Dinner had improved following complaints by The Society, but floated the question of whether the Dinner could continue in its current location and format, pointing out that some organisations now only had bi-annual dinners, or no dinner at all. She also commented on the fact that while the number of female entrants to the solicitors' profession now exceeded males, she was still only 1 of 11 female local Law Society Presidents nationally. It was to be some years, however, before another woman became President of The Society. The President's concerns also extended to the internal wranglings then racking Chancery Lane – a topic which had been the subject of comments by Ken Byass in his Constituency Reports in issues of the Newsletter. The extraordinary contortions through which The Law Society went in the 1990s did nothing to enhance its public perception and harmed the profession considerably by dividing its principal representative body. Further gloom was cast by the increasing threat to Legal Aid and the march of franchising, though Leicestershire was still holding out against going down that route. To conclude her year in office Vera Stamenkovich launched a consultation exercise on The

Society's functions and aims. On a brighter note The Young Solicitors' Group announced details of its Annual Dinner and its AGM, to be held at The Black Boy on 15th May 1996; 6.30 for 7.00 pm – presumably to allow members to slake their thirst before debate began!

Mergers and Incomers

Issue No 72 of the Newsletter carried an item on the merged firm of Harvey Ingram Owston. David Mitchell, joint managing partner, explained, inter alia, that 'Each of the former firms were conscious that some leading work providers are under pressure to transfer work to larger regional firms which meant work leaving Leicester ... For Leicester to have its own city based major firm ought to ensure that top class work remains in the area and enhances the commercial activity within the area'. This was indeed a sign of the times. Leicester had, as has been commented on in previous chapters, been a 'land of small firms'. However, such enterprises were finding it hard to compete with major regional firms from Nottingham and Birmingham, and even some national firms operating on a regional basis. The presence of these 'outsiders' was to become increasingly a feature of Leicester's legal landscape, especially as a number of incoming firms took over old established local practices to acquire a share in the local market.

By August 1996 the next President of The Society was installed. He was Trevor Kirkman who brought yet another first to the President's office in becoming the only President later to be ordained into the priesthood of The Church of England. Trevor Kirkman was already a Reader in The Church, and was ordained Deacon in 1996 and Priest in 1997. He served in a non-stipendiary capacity in rural parishes in Nottinghamshire (Southwell Diocese) and was also able to bring his legal training to bear as Diocesan Registrar and Bishop's Legal Advisor for Leicester from 2002 onwards.

This issue of The Newsletter also contained items of further 'signs of the times' such as offers of advertising space in the national press for local solicitors, a national conference on 'Survival in the High Street', and, perhaps most importantly, advice on setting up a website and getting advice on how to use the internet to promote a firm. A further 'sign' came in the October 1996 Newsletter with the announcement of proposed separation of the representative and regulatory functions of The Law Society. This did not then come about but it was not ultimately to be avoided. If, however, The Law Society was wracked with divisions, The Society was in a happier mode. The results of the consultation exercise begun by Vera Stamenkovich indicated that members were generally happy with the way The Society represented them and the lines of communication between The Society and members. Members were also generally happy with the training and continuing education programmes. There was also support for the notion that The Society should offer a conciliation service between firms and clients, but no support for an idea from Chancery Lane that there should be regular meetings of senior partners of local firms to discuss matters of common interest. It was felt locally that the concept of 'senior partner' was too vague – how many firms had such a person who would guarantee to carry the support of all other partners? The Law Society had tried to push local societies in the direction of becoming more social organisations, but Leicestershire determined to maintain its independence here by having only its annual dinner and Members' Closed Dinner and one or two 'low key' events each year. This was because members did not regard social activities as an important aspect of membership.

1996 closed with two further portents for the future. Somewhat ominously The Legal Aid Board Area No 10 commented on the low level of franchising in Leicester, Loughborough, Melton Mowbray, Oakham and Market Harborough and 'encouraged' firms to apply for franchises asking 'what is so different about these areas?' The answer, of course, was the cohesive nature of the local profession in being suspicious of franchising and the perceived erosion of Legal Aid which, some half century before, The Society had embraced so enthusiastically. The second development was an announcement that The Society had decided to seek the services of a Part Time Administrator to assist in its running. Nottinghamshire had had an administrator for several years, and Derby had recently gone down the same route. The Administrator was to assist with course organisation, with marketing and The Society's financial requirements and to relieve the officers who were finding it increasingly difficult to devote the amount of time needed to run it and make contact with members and potential members. The first, part time, appointee was Alan Baum, an early-retired Banking Officer whose interests included walking, DIY and music, the latter involving him as an organist and choirmaster. Alan Baum took up his appointment in early 1997 and served on a part time basis until 2008. One of his first tasks was to address the issue of members' specialisms on the Society's database so as to target information more efficiently. At the same time Mark Dunkley of Messrs Harvey Ingram Owston was appointed by the Committee using its constitutional powers to fill the office of Vice President which had been vacant for some time. It is interesting in this connection to note that it has not always been easy for The Society to fill the offices leading to the Presidency, and that this is not a recent phenomenon. The Members' Register to which attention has been drawn in earlier chapters and which ran from the 1930s through to the late 1970s records a number of instances where Committee members declined the Presidency from the 1950s onwards. Sometimes the honour was declined on a number of occasions, though some decliners did accept in due course.

By April 1997 Trevor Kirkman was nearing the end of his year in office, but was able to announce that Tony Girling, The President of The Law Society, would be attending The Society's AGM, the first time a National President had attended such an event for many years.

Sponsorship

The next issues of the Newsletter were sponsored by The Royal Bank of Scotland, who, not unnaturally, took the opportunity to advertise their wares and services, for example about how to make the most of client cash balances and going about buying a share in a partnership. Advertising was to bulk increasingly large in the Newsletter as the decade wore on.

Internally following the May AGM Mark Dunkley became President, Kennedy Leslie stepped down as Secretary to become Vice President and his place was taken by Henry Doyle. At the same time as new faces were settling down in office The Society's accounting system was also overhauled and new software for this was acquired.

In June 1997 it was announced that in connection with litigious matters only 11 County Courts in England and Wales allowed a higher hourly rate than that in Leicester. This was largely due to the assiduity of The Society's Contentious Business Sub Committee in compiling statistics enabling the rate figure to be computed. However, if this situation was to be maintained even more firms needed to participate in the questionnaire – plus ça change!

Several regular features of The Society's year were also publicised in June 1997. These included the annual visit to the House of Commons to lobby local MPs on the concerns of members, once again organised by the untiring Peter Smith who continued on the Committee as Parliamentary Liaison Officer. Also announced were the 1997 Members' Closed Dinner and the Annual Dinner for 1998, yet again to be held at the Grand Hotel (Ramada Jarvis).

By the end of 1997 there were, however, some dark clouds on the horizon. Once again there was concern over the current administration and future direction of Legal Aid. Members were requested to coordinate action with regard to apparent shortcomings in the local administration of Legal Aid and to lobby Parliament with regard to proposals to once again reduce the ambit of the Legal Aid Scheme. In particular members were alerted to the need to counter the Government's 'spin' on the legal profession as 'fat cat legal aid lawyers', by arguing the need for access to justice for those entitled to it. The struggle was becoming one of those who espoused the notion of a state funded system of access to justice against those who favoured a 'modernised' approach combining a mixture of legal costs insurance (a form of self help), Conditional Fee Agreements and 'No Win, No Fee' arrangements. Another concern also affecting litigation was the proposed closure of Loughborough County Court. The Society wrote to The Lord Chancellor's Office protesting against the closure and putting forward its own proposals to retain some civil litigation ability in Loughborough.

1998 opened with news of the formation of a local Solicitor Advocates group, CalvusNet, able to serve the profession in the Higher Courts when sitting in Leicester, Derby or Nottingham. It also saw continuing debate over the rule forbidding solicitors from acting for both buyer and seller in the same conveyancing transactions. This rule was subject to a number of exceptions, however, and it was hoped that these might be widened. The Solicitors' Indemnity Fund also continued to be a major source of contention nationally, as did the uncertain future of Legal Aid, compounded locally by computer problems in the Legal Aid Area Office in Nottingham. There were also local concerns that Leicestershire's low number of Legal Aid Franchises (17 out of 94 firms undertaking legal aid work with 6 applications pending) would restrict the number of those able to submit bills in respect of block contracts. To the chagrin of the government, however, the Spring of 1998 saw publication of a report which indicated that while the UK's conveyancing system is slow, and could be getting slower, it was also one of the cheapest in the world – one cannot have it all ways! A local survey of conveyancing fees carried out for The Society indicated, however, that most firms felt they were carrying out conveyancing too cheaply, and that a 28% increase in costs would be required to make fees fairly reflect the work done. The report concluded: 'firms have charged fees on the sole criterion of whether they can get the job or not and irrespective of the amount of work or the risk that is involved. The fact that no firm who replied to the survey charges for acting for a lender is staggering. What other profession would act for an institutional client in a high risk area of business and charge no fee?' Indeed cost cutting and competition had carried the local profession way away from The Society's founders who so ardently opposed undercutting and touting.

Socially there were changes afoot at this time. The June 1998 Newsletter carried the news that the next Annual Dinner and the Members' Closed Dinner would be held at the Leicester City Football Club, then, of course, still situated at its historic site in Filbert Street. The May AGM also heard that The Society was acquiring new members but there was a degree of concern that those aged under 36 were not able to play as active a role in The Society as they might wish to do because of increasing pressures of work.

One of the last links with the earlier days of The Society was broken at this time by the death of Charles Edward Jesse Freer, aged 97. He had missed being born a Victorian by just 6 weeks and was a direct descendant of Edward Freer who had founded his practice over two centuries previously.

For the rest of 1998 and into 1999 The Society had a very full programme of events, including a social visit to the Galleries of Justice in Nottingham, a lunchtime gathering, a reception for new members, a reception for Loughborough members (though for these events there was a sad fate in store as we shall see), the Closed and Annual Dinners, a seminar with local accounts on 'The Internet in Practice', and a considerable number of courses, many organised in conjunction with De Montfort University, (including the present author lecturing on planning and environmental law!). Other issues affecting The Society were the computerisation of its accounts and consideration by the 'F&GP' of the Law Society's proposals on Professional Indemnity Insurance. The costs of providing indemnity cover were impacting on all firms and a particular issue was those firms reliant on domestic conveyancing who might not charge appropriately for their work and so be unable to bear the proper proportion of the cost of providing cover. There was also news in October 1998, of a new Law Society Code on Introduction and Referral Fees. The existing code was not working well, but the proposals were for draconian restrictions which would forbid any payment in cash or kind in relation to referral business. Solicitors would no longer be able to take Estate Agents out to lunch?

1998 closed with both bad and good news. The bad news was the failure to create a website for the Society which would have served to enhance the image of the profession locally. However, the idea was not entirely abandoned. The much better good news was the influx of still more new members.

Constitutional Change and the end of the decade

Socially 1999 began badly. During 1998 62 new members had been admitted to The Society and it was decided to hold a reception at The Grand Hotel to welcome them. Only 12 accepted the invitation and on the day only 4 actually turned up, including one from Ashby-de-la-Zouch and one from Loughborough. A proposed buffet reception for Loughborough members also had to be cancelled for lack of support. Was that to be an omen for the future signifying difficulty in getting members to attend events?

Nationally the structure of The Law Society was once more a matter for debate with Council Members becoming ever more concerned that effective decision taking was passing from them to permanent staff, but, in the light of hindsight, this was nothing compared to the disruption and litigation that was to affect the workings of Chancery Lane in just a few years. As the year continued a number of other issues of concern nationally occurred. The sore issue of restrictions on the ability of solicitors to act for both sides in a conveyancing transaction grumbled on, as did the saga of the indemnity fund if individual firms were allowed to seek their own insurance in the open market. There was also an ominous warning about the increasing prevalence of fraud, money laundering and scams. Members were advised to read the information on these issues available from The Law Society and to call on The Fraud Intelligence Office of the Office for the Supervision of Solicitors in cases of doubt and concern. Further warnings concerning frauds were given in the June 1999 Newsletter.

In May 1999, following revising work by the 'F&GP' The Society adopted its current Rules. These differed only in minor respects from those previously in force. The Society also looked forward to a number of events for the rest of the year, a number of courses planned with De Montfort University, and, of course, considerable attention was paid to the impact of the Woolf reforms in relation to civil procedure. The Closed Dinner was planned for November 19th 1999, and the Annual Dinner for 4th February 2000. This was to return to its traditional venue, The Grand Hotel, it being clear that the venue for the 1999 dinner had not been particularly appropriate, and that may have contributed to the less than happy atmosphere that had somewhat marred the event. The Society still, however, had to act in defence of its members' interests, and the October 1999 Newsletter contained a request for information about the activities of unqualified will writers to be sent to the Non-Contentious Business Sub-Committee for appropriate action to be taken.

The year closed with an important announcement, namely that The Society was to be sponsored by the Royal Bank of Scotland and Messrs MacIntyre Hudson Accountants. Sponsorship has of course become a considerable feature of The Society's life and its role will be touched on below.

Conclusions

The 1980s and 90s were undoubtedly a traumatic time for solicitors in general and The Society in particular. There were undoubtedly many – and not just those nearing the end of their careers – who regretted the direction in which solicitors were constrained to go, and who felt their heritage and their profession was being taken away from them. This, combined with the upheavals and internal conflicts which afflicted The Law Society nationally, led some to question the value of that organisation and The Society's links with it. On the other hand it has to be remembered that the UK went through a very considerable economic and social revolution during this time. No nation shed industrial capacity faster than the UK during the 1980s, and in Leicestershire that decline had set in even earlier with regard to 'boot and shoe', hosiery and textiles and their supporting engineering trades. In addition the nation veered from the 'young fogeyism' of Margaret Thatcher's days in power to the 'cool Britannia' period of Tony Blair. It is hardly surprising then that solicitors were swept along with all other sections of society into a post-industrial modernising phase of British history.

Locally, The Society mirrored these changes. Many new initiatives were essayed, some failed and passed quietly into history, but others succeeded. Amongst the latter was the undoubted success of The Newsletter which not only disseminated information to members, but also helped to give The Society a 'human face' by the inclusion of regular comments from The President, The Secretary, The Constituency Member and a number of other members keen to play a part in this important organ of communication. Regular Parliamentary liaison also continued very successfully and The Society's voice was heard both nationally and locally.

The Society survived the upheaval of disposing of its Library – a major break with the past. Increasing numbers of women and ethnic minority members also began to affect the way in which The Society thought about itself, though it was not always easy to involve these elements in the active life of the organisation. One thing, however, is clear. By the end of the 20th Century The Society was a very different body from what it had been some

25 to 30 years earlier, and was profoundly different from what its original founders had envisaged, even though many of their original aspirations remained embedded in The Society's constitution and operations.

Chapter 10

Into a New Millenium

Before considering the events of the first decade of the new millenium, it is instructive to pause and consider the changing face of the legal profession in Leicestershire. In 1971 Kelly's "Classified Directory of Leicester" listed 55 firms of solicitors in the City of Leicester. By 2003 there were 83 firms of solicitors ranging in size from sole practitioners (at least 23 in 2003) up to Harvey Ingram Owston which then had 21 partners, 10 associates and 27 assistants. By 2008/2009 'The Phone Book' listed 123 firms in Leicestershire. That same volume indicates the diversity of local practice. While some firms offer what may be considered traditional 'High Street' services, eg Family, Probate, Conveyancing, Employment, others are clearly highly specialised niche practices, eg Criminal Defence. There are other points of interest: the advertising of 'national helplines' operating '24/7', and specialising in 'no win – no fee' personal injury claims. Indeed there is one 'PI' advertisement from a firm in Manchester! Another striking feature is the sex of the person chosen to appear in the full colour advertisements; overwhelmingly the 'acceptable face' is female, and men feature hardly at all. This, of course, reflects the very considerable change in the composition of the profession. Carrie Morrison was admitted as the first woman solicitor in 1922, 85 years on in 2007/2008 62% of trainee solicitors were women, and 44% of those holding practising certificates were also female. This change has been reflected locally. By 2003 in Leicester there were 99 women solicitors holding assistant or associate posts, the majority of them having quite recently qualified, and 35 female partners.

A further major change in the organisation of the profession has been the ability to create 'LLPs'. The Limited Liability Partnership Act 2000 introduced the LLP which, while not a company with shareholders, is a body corporate with its own legal personality. LLPs may limit liability to clients by agreement, though this is subject to limits with regard to minimum levels of indemnity cover. Individual members of a LLP are not generally liable in contract or tort for acts of their fellow members or employees, nor, subject to limitations, for the debts and obligations of the LLP. This was a considerable change from the previous position of the Law of Partnership. Few firms in Leicestershire initially chose to take advantage of this new system of trading. On the evidence of websites and the 'Phone Book' in 2008 there were only a small number of LLPs in Leicestershire and a number of those were 'incoming' large firms operating on regional or even national scale.

This was the very different world from that of the 'founding fathers' into which The Society stepped with its 1999 revised rules. The objects of The Society for the new millenium are: the promotion of honourable practice and the protection and enhancement of the character, status and interests of solicitors practising in Leicester, Leicestershire and Rutland; the encouragement of legal education; the consideration of general questions affecting the interests of the profession and the alteration or administration of the law. Membership is open to solicitors practising or residing in Leicester, Leicestershire or Rutland, though provision is made for honorary membership, which can be extended to trainee solicitors. Provision is also made for the expulsion of members guilty of misconduct or who have become bankrupt. The day to day business of The Society is entrusted to its Committee and a number of Sub Committees which then numbered 8, Finance and General Purposes, Public Relations, Education and Training, Contentious Business, Non-Contentious Business, Social, Parliamentary Liaison and Newsletter, of which it is very arguable that the 'F&GP' is the most important and influential. Succession to the Presidency is achieved by the long standing rule that the Vice President is elected with a view to succeeding from among those who have served as President, Vice President, Secretary or Treasurer or as a Committee member for at least two years. The most recent change with regard to the Presidency has been the inauguration of the post of Deputy Vice President to allow for two 'training years' before a President takes up his/her duties.

How then has The Society fared during the past decade?

An ominous cloud over Chancery Lane

2000 opened badly for The Law Society with allegations against the Vice President of The Law Society of bullying of staff. This was to develop into the sadly notorious Kamlesh Bahl saga in which allegations and counter allegations and a round of litigation did much to weaken The Law Society and yet further reduce its reputation. Indeed it is arguable that the events of the 'early noughties' made it inevitable that a major root and branch reform of The Law Society, whereby the representative and regulatory functions became effectively separated, would take place. The concept of a totally autonomous professional body both acting for itself and providing its own internal regulation, for which so many had striven in the 19th Century, thus passed into history. In its place has come the notion that a solicitor's practice is an economic activity which, like the provision of utility services, has to be externally regulated in the interests of consumers. This change has, of course, been further promoted by ministerial mistrust of professional bodies dating from Margaret Thatcher's time in office and reinforced under Tony Blair by a characterisation of professional bodies as 'forces of conservatism' which must not be allowed to hold up 'modernisation' of British society and its economy.

A further ill omen was the imposition of Legal Aid Civil Contracting from January 2000. Some 5000 general civil legal aid contracts were awarded by November 1999 to solicitors' firms with 330 others going to not-for-profit bodies. There were concerns that a number of firms would 'miss out' during the contracting process, that the whole system would become a bureaucratic nightmare and that legal aid might disappear from some areas as there would be no firms willing to undergo the contracting process. At the same time all firms were being encouraged to adopt a more client friendly and constructive attitude towards dealing with complaints. A list of 'Dos' and 'Don'ts' was issued by the Office for the Supervision of Solicitors which was designed to secure early and local solutions to complaints. The advice drew on a considerable amount of academic research into the nature and functioning of complaints systems which had been sponsored by the Social and Economic Research Council in the 1990s.[44] It is thus interesting to note the recommendation to 'learn from the complaint, understand how it arose, introduce changes to prevent a recurrence'. All that reflected the findings of research exercises which concluded that proper complaint handling should enable an organisation to learn how to improve its service so that the opportunity for future complaints to arise is diminished.

More optimistically The Society had enjoyed a considerable influx of new members in 1999 and most of the new members renewed their subscriptions for 2000 so that membership stood at 385. There was, however, a problem in getting members to attend social events, and they were encouraged to support the 2001 Annual Dinner, the November 2000 Members' Closed Dinner and a 'Grand Charity Team Quiz' also planned for November 2000, though, sadly, this had disappeared from the social

---

[44] The present author, along with the late Professor V A Karn of the Universities of Salford and Manchester, was, for example, much involved in drawing up codes of practice to enable housing organisations to deal with complaints.

calendar by October 2000. Concern was also expressed during the course of the year that while bookings for courses and seminars organised by The Society were sometimes quite healthy, actual attendances could be quite poor.

The April 2000 Newsletter provided some light relief in the form of information from Mr Richard Bloor. It may be remembered from earlier chapters that at one time attempts had been made to gather together a collection of photographs of past presidents. Those attempts had never been particularly successful and when The Society closed its library premises the three or four photographs were sent to the firms from which their subjects had come, and Mr Bloor was certain 'they were glad to have them'. He also passed on the information that the De Montfort University Debating Cup which had been presented by The Society had previously been The Loughborough Canine Society's 'Top Dog in the Show' award. Mr Bloor commented: 'I wonder if the successful students realise what they are competing for!' Indeed we may all join in that.

Legal Aid was removed from Personal Injury cases on 1st April 2000 and so the somewhat doleful note which characterised the start of that year was continued in an open letter from Mike Jerman, The Society's outgoing President, in the June 2000 Newsletter lamenting the end of Legal Aid and forecasting a considerable restriction on access to justice for the average citizen. At the same time The Law Society announced that there was to be enhanced monitoring of those firms and organisations authorised to take trainees as from 1st July 2000. The doleful news continued, at least nationally, with the prospect of a divisive presidential election at Chancery Lane – which was fortunately avoided by the defeat of a candidate who was estranged from The Law Society Council – and public criticism by ministers of The Office for the Supervision of Solicitors for its alleged slowness in dealing with complaints.

Locally Society members were urged to take note of the imminent commencement of The Human Rights Act 1998 as from 2nd October and to consider any areas of practice which might be thereby affected, while The Society also planned the launch of its own website from August. The website was designed to advertise the services of the profession, to carry a 'situations vacant' service and to have a comprehensive members' area for which a password was required. This latter function was intended to provide members with event more updated information than the Newsletter could contain. Members were urged to browse it regularly.

In August 2000 came news of further developments with local implications. The Criminal Defence Service was to come into operation on

1st October and only those firms franchised for crime would be allowed to take on CDS funded cases. The justification for this development was, in part at least, to end the variety of forms whereby Criminal Legal Aid could be delivered, and to reassure the profession that the new CDS system was not to be a low-budget, fixed cost operation, certain undertakings were given, one being that contracts would not be awarded by the CDS to non-solicitor agencies. The CDS for Leicester was, however, to operate from Nottingham. As this new initiative was launched six East Midlands Community Legal Service Partnerships (CLSPs) had already been launched; one of these was to operate in Leicester. These organisations were designed to bring together funders, providers and consumers of legal and advice services to cooperate and plan the delivery of services, including improved referral channels between providers to ensure access to justice.

On 1st September 2000 the new indemnity insurance regime for solicitors finally came into force with firms being free to seek their own insurance on the open market as opposed to the former mutual system of The Solicitors' Indemnity Fund. As the President, Mr J M Crane, commented in the October 2000 Newsletter: 'The Profession is now in the open market and must learn to live with it.' Indeed the abandonment of the mutual SIF was yet another move away from the concept of the self regulating self protecting profession.

The year closed with more news of proposed reform of The Law Society. Yet more consultation documents were issued and there was a proposal that The President, Vice President and Deputy Vice President should be elected by The Council as opposed to the membership as a whole, only some 30% of whom bothered to vote in elections anyway. While that proposal may not have been welcome to activists, there was, apparently, general agreement amongst the profession that The Law Society should retain both its regulatory and representative functions. That was, long term, not to be.

2001 opened with The Society advertising for a Part Time Clerical Assistant to help the Administrator, while an 'old chestnut' reappeared in the form of yet further consultation over the application of the rules requiring separate representation in conveyancing transactions. Nottinghamshire Law Society also advertised the existence of its Library, with over 320 sets of reports and journals, and the services of a legal researcher, and indicated Leicester firms could utilise these services at a rate of £40 per hour plus VAT - did Leicester firms now regret disposing of The Society's Library? Another 'old friend' reappeared in the April 2001 Newsletter in relation to the cost of conveyancing. Once again the myth of 'easy conveyancing' was abroad and The President, Mr J M Crane, urged members' firms to inform clients of exactly what is involved in offering a quality conveyancing service. This was opportune in view of a report from the Office of Fair Trading that Banks and Building Societies should be able to offer conveyancing services. The President was confident that such organisations would not find it economical to offer conveyancing, but this was another example of the 'Tesco Law' mindset so often encountered on the part of ministers and governmental bodies which sees the provision of services by those who are qualified to provide them as somehow inimical to the interests of the public. This mindset is still, of course, prevalent.

The Law Society was still going through the toils and turmoils of constitutional reforms while also having to deal with a budget shortfall of £4.5m and proposals for multi-disciplinary partnerships, but members of The Society could look forward to the revived Charity Quiz Night on 2nd May 2001. This in the outcome proved to be a considerable success, but both Alan Baum as Administrator and Graham Moore as incoming President for 2001/2002 lamented the poor attendance of members at Society social events and other functions. Indeed at the 2001 AGM out of 390 members only 12 attended with 30 others sending apologies. Graham Moore particularly regretted the passing of the time when local solicitors used 'to strive like lions and eat and drink as friends', and lamented especially the former annual dinner dance. There were, however, a number of new initiatives to cheer members' spirits, in particular the creation of a new sub-committee to oversee The Society's website and coordinate its use of IT.

August 2001 brought news that the Privy Council had approved the restructuring of The Law Society with a new board structure and a new system of representation to include members representing particular areas of practice in addition to constituency members. One consequence of this was that the enlarged Council was too large to sit in the Council Chamber at Chancery Lane and had to look elsewhere for a home, including in December 2001 The Royal College of Surgeons in Lincolns Inn Fields. A further major change was ending the annual election for President,Vice President and Deputy Vice President. For the future The Council would elect the 'DVP' who would, in normal circumstances, proceed to the other chairs. It was hoped this would end the divisive electioneering that had so damaged The Law Society in the previous two decades. It was also announced that as from 1st November 2001 all solicitors would be subject to a new CPD regime of 16 hours of training during each complete year in practice. To assist local members in acquiring the required 'points' a series of courses had been arranged including conveyancing, alternative dispute resolution and a 'Land Charges Open Day'. To add the sweetness of refreshment to toil The Members' Closed Dinner was fixed for 9th November, once again at The Three Swans in Market Harborough (when some 50 members attended) and the Annual Dinner for 2nd February 2002. By October 2001 there had been a number of additions and substitutions to the list of courses organised by The Society. How were members to keep up with developments- by clicking on to the website, of course!

The October 2001 Newsletter carried the result of the Annual Expense of Time Survey which had resulted in a considerable increase in allowable expenses, but, once again, the response from members to the survey had been poor. More pleasingly the names of 33 new members were recorded, of whom almost a third were from ethnic minority communities – another sign of change and development.

Related Organisations

It will be remembered from earlier chapters that under the overall 'wing' of The Society there was room for specialist related organisations. By the beginning of the 'noughties' The Young Solicitors' Group and the Trainee Solicitors appeared to be going through a quiet time, and they had no representation as such on The Committee. Other bodies had, however, developed, including the local branch of The Solicitors' Family Law Association, now Resolution, which announced a successful 2001, a highlight of which was a workshop on domestic violence attended by Esther Rantzen. This group also looked forward to an active 2002.

It is interesting to note that as 2001 drew to a close there were 6 female members of The Committee, yet another sign of change and development in The Society's life.

2002 began with The Society welcoming a further 11 new members, but the very dark cloud which had gathered over Chancery Lane in consequence of the resignation of Kamlesh Bahl as Law Society Vice President and the subsequent allegations by her of racial and sexual discrimination cast a shadow as far as Leicestershire. The long standing Constituency Member covering the Leicestershire Area, Mr K P Byass, gave evidence to the Enquiry chaired by a retired Law Lord, Lord Griffiths, into the entire sorry saga. His comments on his experiences are worth repeating: 'Having spent the best part of the day being beaten up by Kamlesh Bahl's very able counsel with the express intention of proving me either a fool or a liar or both, I would not personally relish a further

Enquiry'. Rather more positively The Law Society adopted an Equality and Diversity Strategy in January 2002 to ensure that equal opportunities should extend throughout The Law Society irrespective of race, gender or sexuality. By implication this would clearly in due course apply to the entire profession in consequence of existing legislation and new Directives to be issued under the EU Amsterdam Treaty. The Chief Executive of The Law Society, Janet Paraskeva, had been invited to attend The Society's AGM to speak further on Law Society issues. A further feature of this event was to be the inauguration of a new custom of presenting a Past President's Jewel to the outgoing President. At the end of his year in office Mr Graham Moore hoped as many previous Presidents as possible would attend the AGM to receive their jewels as the presentation had been made retrospective. Before leaving office, however, Mr Moore also had a reception for 'in-house' solicitors planned in April and a little later in the same month a Charity Quiz Evening with a hot buffet and wine.

Further guidance was issued to solicitors on the issue of money laundering and this was featured in the April 2002 Newsletter. A 'Money Laundering Roadshow' was also to be hosted by the Nottinghamshire Law Society and the Law Society East Midlands Regional Office on 27th June 2002. Society members were reminded this would be their only opportunity to attend this presentation in the East Midlands. In Leicester, however, a money laundering event was proposed for 23rd October 2002 to be presented by Messrs McIntyre Hudson at the Spearing Waite Conference Centre on 'Money Laundering: lawyers as gatekeepers'. Clearly this had become a 'hot topic'. This event was part of a very busy schedule of events organised by The Society, including seminars, hosted road shows, demonstration of IT as well as The Members Closed Dinner to take place at Leicester Football Club on 15th November and the Annual Dinner once again at The Ramada Jarvis Grand Hotel on 7th February 2002. The mounting of courses and seminars, etc, had by this time become a major feature of The Society's functioning, the facilitation of which depended to a considerable extent on the services of The Society's Administrator.

The Committee was in mid 2002 also actively pursuing: the notion of creating student bursaries at each of Leicester's two University Law Schools; the provision of a Solicitors' robing room at court; the formation of an 'in-house' solicitors' group; the annual survey of court costs; taking steps against will writing firms who had once again resurfaced in Leicester and who were advertising in *The Mercury*; new developments proposed for 'E-conveyancing', and the work of The Legal Services Commission. Of course there was a cost implication in consequence of The Society's clearly increased activities. While The Society derived some income from education and training events, and while there was sponsorship from The Royal Bank of Scotland and Macintyre Hudson, Chartered Accountants, it was clear subscriptions had to be reviewed. This had last occurred in 1997. It was proposed that members could opt for 'ordinary membership' at a rate of £50 pa for partners and £20 pa for assistant solicitors, or 'corporate membership' whereby by if *all* partners in a firm joined The Society at a rate of £60 pa all their assistants would become members at no cost.

Continuing money laundering 'scams' were still plaguing the profession (further guidance on this issue was contained in the December 2002 Newsletter) as were the government's proposals to resurrect their predecessors' policies on opening up High Street practice to competition from non-solicitor owned organisations, but on a more optimistic note the East Midlands Regional Office of The Law Society was created in February 2002 with a view to supporting and representing the profession in the East Midlands and had set up a temporary base for its operations in Leicester while more permanent accommodation was sought.

The Regional Office (EMRO) was actively functioning by the beginning of 2003 and had been responsible for, inter alia, meetings of a Sole Practitioners Group with a view to supporting that particular part of the profession. EMRO was also keen to promote Pro Bono work, and The Leicester Law Centre (LLC) was keen on this also. LLC found itself limited in the range of advice it could offer and appealed to Society members in February 2003 for volunteers to offer initial advice in the areas of Family and Matrimonial, Small Claims, Personal Injury, Clinical Negligence and Civil Disputes. Were there echoes here of the former Poor Man's Lawyer Scheme for so many years a feature of The Society's life?

A Law Society Roadshow on the future of publicly funded legal services was due to visit Leicester on 8th April 2003 and in connection with this the Local Law Society Council member, now Linda Lee, indicated to members her impression that there was to be no 'new' money for such a service. Developments would have to take place within a cash limited budget. She also indicated that the new Independent Commissioner for complaints against solicitors at the OSS was not averse to the notion of local law societies being involved in grievance procedures.

The April 2003 Newsletter contained the news that the new Corporate membership scheme alluded to above had been successfully introduced and had let to a gratifying increase in membership to 460, indeed 40 new members were welcomed in that Newsletter. Interestingly 22 of them were female, a further indication of the changing nature of the profession.

Will Writers – Again

The present author remembers as a law student being told: 'Be thankful for the man who makes his own will, because he will be sure to make a mess of it, for where there's a will there's relatives, and where there is no will there'll be even more relatives!' The April 2003 Newsletter confirmed this with an article from Mr J Shaw, the Probate Manager of the Leicester Probate Sub-Registry, indicating the problems he encountered following the activities of unqualified will writers. One was the case of a will writer who supplied the client with only a photocopy of the will, retaining the original. The will writer then disappeared and on the client's death the issue had to be dealt with on a 'lost will' basis. A similar problem occurred when a will writer was appointed executor and then could not be traced. Some will writers referred to lists and memorandums in wills but then did not attach them, while others dealt only with property in only one part of the world and did not mention property elsewhere. Maybe such an article should have appeared in the local press to warn against the pitfalls of using unqualified assistance, for while Mr Shaw stated that 'the majority of wills drawn up by will writers pass through our system without difficulty', he added that his Registry was primarily concerned with issues of validity rather than the more contentious issues of ambiguity and poor drafting.

By mid 2003 a number of matters of continuing concern or interest were the subject of report. May 2003 had seen Henry Doyle take over as President and on this occasion Janet Paraskeva, Law Society Chief Executive, had been able to be present to talk about The Law Society. This may well have accounted for an increased attendance at the AGM of 42 members. EMRO was able to report that it had acquired a permanent home and had signed a lease with a view to taking up occupation in July/August. The President's Charity Quiz Night on 30th April had been successful in raising £200 for the Red Cross Special Toy Library. The Society also welcomed a further 25 new members, while also announcing a comprehensive programme of courses and seminars for the rest of the year; many of these events were in conjunction with De Montfort University School of Law. The Administrator, Alan Baum, reported that he received about 5 complaints a week about services offered by members. He was pleased to add that few of these had to be referred on to the OSS and that he was able to deal with most by referring the issue to the senior or complaints partner in the firm concerned. He pointed out that many complaints could be avoided if firms issued adequate client care letters.

New Premises

By October 2003 The Society finally had its own premises, being able to share in the EMRO accommodation at 12 York Road Leicester. The Members' Closed Dinner was also advertised for 21st November, this time at Devonshire Place in Leicester with guest speaker Lord Willie Bach, the government's Spokesman for Defence in the House of Lords and previously a well known Leicester barrister. The Annual Dinner was also announced for 20th February 2004 at The Walkers Stadium when the chief speaker was to be Digby Jones, Chief Executive of the CBI. The Charity event for Henry Doyle's year was to take the form of a Golf Day in association with Northamptonshire Law Society at Cold Ashby.

2003 closed, however, with further rumblings from The Law Society. Linda Lee had already predicted that The Law Society would probably be forced to give up handling complaints, but would retain its regulatory and representative functions. The Government proposed that the existing complaints function should be subsumed into the office of the Legal Services Ombudsman, officially The Office of the Legal Services Commissioner, but which would be funded by The Law Society. A further contentious issue was our old friend referral fees. The Office of Fair Trading had warned that competition laws required referral fees to be accepted and two schemes had been put forward to enable solicitors, in defined circumstances, to make payments to third parties in respect of the introduction of clients. However, both schemes had been rejected so debate was to rumble on! Fee sharing and referral fees were finally accepted by The Law Society almost at the last minute for 2003, on 18th December 2003. Otherwise there was gloom nationally over the funding of legal aid and criticism by the Legal Services Ombudsman that The Law Society was too slow in handling complaints against solicitors. The Clementi Review of legal services had also commenced and this was to dominate thinking within the profession for a number of years to come.

2004 saw The Society looking forward locally to a full programme of courses and other events. As premises were now available in central Leicester all courses an seminars were now held 'in house' at the EMRO office in York Road. A further sign of changing times was that there were now 8 female Committee members as opposed to 12 men.

In his valedictory Presidential column in the April 2004 Newsletter Henry Doyle drew attention to the annual changes affecting the profession and commented on the increasing number of firms who were withdrawing from legal aid work, while at the same time pointing out that a crossroads in the way the profession was to be organised and run would be reached with the report from the Clementi Review. In the same issue there was good news in the form of the election of 26 new members to The Society and an article from Michael Swift, a solicitor who was also a director of Intelligent Conveyancing Ltd, a company producing case management systems for conveyancers. This predicted that while some conveyancing work would be lost to 'conveyancing factories' acting for mortgage lenders who 'sold' such a service to borrowers, many local estate agents would still recommend their clients to use a local solicitor, but only where that solicitor was fully geared up with the necessary 'IT' and ready to move towards 'e-conveyancing'. This article was reinforced by a 'follow up' in the June 2004 Newsletter by Malcolm Price of BPE Solicitors and Chief Executive of BPE Homemove LLP.

National and Local Concerns

By mid 2004 there was considerable concern that the Clementi Review could recommend direct government regulation of the profession, and questions were raised about whether a non-independent legal profession was compatible with International Law. It was, however, becoming the accepted view at Chancery Lane that there would have to be a much greater degree of separation between the regulatory and representative functions of The Law Society. Locally Lindsay Brydson, the EMRO manager, reported on a number of local trends, first of all the increasing number of employed solicitors outside private practice. Almost one third of all holders of practising certificates in the EMRO area in 2004 were so employed, while nearly half of all practitioners were aged under 40. She concluded that the character of the profession was clearly changing. In addition survey evidence indicated that young employed solicitors 'did not feel engaged with the profession in the region, or with the national or local Law Societies'. In particular she commented on the lack of a Young Solicitors Group for Leicester, and her hopes for this to be rectified. History is, of course, replete with examples of the rise and fall of such a representative group in Leicestershire. Much has always depended on the willingness of a core body of individuals to promote the group.

In an attempt to make The Society's social events more popular it was decided that the Members' Closed Dinner, which had become increasingly poorly attended, should be replaced by a less formal event taking the form of a Curry Supper at The Guildhall on 12th November 2004 where entertainment would be provided by the Hiss and Boo Band in which a Society member,

Mr Mike Jerman, played. This innovation was a popular success, though a number of solicitors declined to attend on the basis they 'wouldn't know anybody there' – in itself a sad reflection on a degree of atomisation within the ranks of local solicitors. The Young Solicitors Group was up and running by October 2004 and planned to start monthly events with a Christmas Ball on 16th December 2004. Members were also urged to attend the Annual Dinner on 11th February 2005 which was to return to The Ramada Jarvis Grand Hotel in consequence of increased attendance in 2004. It was pointed out that as Society membership now stood at over 500 filling the Kings Room at The Grand should not be an insuperable problem.

By September 2004 it was clear that The Law Society would have to separate its regulatory and representational functions if it was to be able to co-exist with the Clementi Review proposals – the question was how to do this and what model to adopt. At the same time there was still dissatisfaction with complaints handling and the dreaded word 'target' appeared in communications from the Legal Services Complaints Commission. It appeared the LSCC wished to impose targets with regard to the handling of complaints. Events nationally were moving apace and on 16th November 2004 representatives of both The Law Society and The Bar met with The Prime Minister and The Lord Chancellor at No 10 Downing Street to consider future issues concerning the legal profession as a whole and the delivery legal services via a number of different models of provision as well as the issue of regulation and representation. This was considered to be an unprecedented meeting.

Locally 2004 closed with an ominous warning from the Leicester Law Centre that it would have to downsize its operation and move premises in consequence of a proposed reduction of 50% of its funding from Leicester City Council. It is, however, notable that 2004 saw the first member of the ethnic minority communities elected to The Society's committee. That was Mr Prakash M Suchak.

Clementi

The long awaited Clementi report dominated the opening of 2005. Following on from an OFT Report on Competition in the Professions of 2001 which had been followed by further studies in 2002/2003, the Clementi Review had been appointed by the Government to:

- Promote competition, innovation and a consumer led market in the provision of legal services;

- Create an efficient, effective and independent legal profession. The accepted framework was that regulation should be no more restrictive than was necessary and be consistent, flexible and transparent.

Clementi made the following recommendations:

- There should be a Legal Service Board (LSB) having all regulatory powers over solicitors currently held by The Master of The Rolls, Ministers, Judges and other bodies;
- The LSB would require 'front line bodies' having regulatory and representative functions to be separated;
- The LSB would have further powers to ensure an appropriate degree of separation;
- An Office for Legal Complaints would report to the LSB and take over issues concerning consumer redress, and would be an otherwise independent body based on the existing complaints service based at Leamington Spa;
- The 'front line body' having regulatory functions would have responsibility for disciplinary functions and the conduct of solicitors;
- New forms of practice would be allowed which permitted the involvement of non-legal partners, outside ownership (e.g. a financial institution) and investment. These 'Legal Disciplinary Practices' (LDPs) would be authorised by the LSB if the latter was satisfied as to competence and governance arrangements. The non-lawyers in such LDPs would be present to enhance the services of the practice. All members of a LDP would be subject to code of professional standards and outside ownership would only be permitted to those 'fit to own'.

Clementi made no recommendations about regulating claims farmers and will writers.

The Council of The Law Society accepted the inevitable separation of the regulatory and representative functions and began a process to propose a new Regulatory Body which would nevertheless have a degree of connection with The Law Society.

The other cloud on the national horizon was the proposal to introduce Home Information Packs which concerned Solicitors and Estate Agents alike. Locally The Society had once again organised a programme of courses (a programme developed as the year wore on) and seminars for the forthcoming year. Some of these were purely internally organised but the majority were effectively out-sourced so far as delivery and content was concerned by being held in conjunction with Central Law Training.

By June 2005 The Society had a new President, Christl Hughes. She was the second female President and, it is believed, the first Leicester University graduate to hold the post: certainly she was the first Leicester University Law graduate to do so. Mrs Hughes commented that her election enabled her to leave behind the Vice-Presidency and so she requested that she should no longer be addressed as 'Madam Vice!' Her first Presidential column also pointed out that while Society membership stood at over 500 that was only some 50% of the total number of practising solicitors in The Society's area. That was a real sign of the times and a far distant cry from the situation of The Society even thirty years previously when it would have been unthinkable for local solicitors *not* to be members.

Members of The Society were called on in the June 2005 Newsletter to support a resolution for The Law Society's AGM disapproving the Council's decision to 'hive off' regulation. There was clearly some feeling that the 'leaders' of the profession were too willing to listen to the arguments of the Government and had 'jumped the gun' by agreeing proposed new schemes of governance without knowing their details. There was particular concern over who would have the power to set the level of annual practice fees, and a general disenchantment with the lack of consultation and the erosion of the concept of self-regulation.

National events clearly dominated the thinking of Society members as well as the content of its Newsletter at this time. This continued with the August 2005 Newsletter where once again the vexed question of Referral Fees was a headline, on The Law Society considering a reinstatement of the ban on such fees. It is, however, worth recording that the Committee now composed 11 female members as against 10 men – a further indication of the long term changes occurring in relation to the profession.

Undermining the Profession

By October 2005 Birmingham Law Society had received a presentation from a local academic outlining how government policies were undermining the historic notion of a profession and to bring those bodies more under central control. There were many who viewed the entire Clementi Review process as an attack on the independence of the profession. It can, however, be argued that what was underway was a clash of two cultures. The older of these was the notion of the autonomous self regulating profession in which control over members and their activities is internalised and the relationship between the professional body and wider society depends on trust and reputation. The newer notion is concerned with the economic consequences of business activity (including the provision of legal services) in a consumer driven market. Here those who provide services are regulated by an external body, having an arm's length relationship with the Government, in order to protect the public interest which is measured very much in terms of value for money.

The Birmingham Law Society convened a meeting of Local Law Societies at which there was representation from The City of London, Westminster and Holborn, Blackpool, Northamptonshire, Staffordshire, Yorkshire, The North West, Worcestershire, Manchester, Surrey, Worthing, Hertfordshire and Leicestershire. This meeting was particularly concerned with the relationship between the national body and local societies. This meeting voiced concern over the role of Law Society Regional Offices which were seen to be encroaching on the role of Local Societies as well as being expensive to maintain. There was also general dismay at the way in which consultation over the Clementi proposals had taken place. In addition there was concern that there might be conflict over subscriptions should The Law Society become primarily a representative body. This would have to be paid for by a levy on solicitors, but would they then be prepared to pay an additional voluntary subscription to a local representative society as well? There was also concern felt that regional offices were arranging training courses for particular sectional interests amongst solicitors and that these might conflict with events organised by local societies on which many depended for their income.

The regional theme was continued in the October 2005 Newsletter by the announcement from the East Midlands Regional Office of the Legal Services Commission of the new Strategy for the Community Legal Service. There was much of the usual 'organisation speak' of piloting community legal advice centres and networks and expanding telephonic advice services, but the real core issue was a radical revision of legal aid services and the announcement of yet a further review, this time under Lord Carter of Coles into how the Government procures publicly funded services – this was a further augury of yet more change.

By the end of 2005 the Government had published its White Paper in response to the Clementi Review, with legislation, subject to consultation, expected by 2008. The White Paper 'The Future of Legal Services' appeared on 17th October 2005 and surprised many by going further than the Clementi recommendations, and angered others by indicating that the entire cost of the new framework should be borne by the profession. In anticipation of the outcome of the Clementi Review The Law Society Council had already set up two bodies having effectively total control over regulation and consumer complaints respectively while The Law Society remained as a representative body. For the future there had been a number of models for regulation, Model A having all regulatory powers along the lines of the Financial Services Authority and Model B under which The Law Society and The Bar Council would retain regulatory powers though under the supervision of The Legal Services Board. The White Paper, however, somewhat favoured Model A by proposing that the power of regulation should be with the Legal Services Board which would delegate those powers to the 'frontline professional bodies' and be able to revoke that delegation without further primary legislation if they were dissatisfied with governance arrangements, though then only as a last resort. There were concerns over the independence of the LSB and the lack of a requirement for that Board to consult with practitioners – only an obligation to consult with consumers was proposed. Furthermore there was concern that there was to be no judicial involvement in the appointment of the Chair of the LSB, and worry that the proposed role of the LSB in pursuing 'proportionate' regulation might lead to the LSB duplicating the roles of the frontline professional bodies (The Law Society and the Bar Council). There was also concern that the objectives of the LSB could be altered by secondary as opposed to primary legislation requiring Parliamentary debate and approval.

The White Paper also went beyond the Clementi Review in proposing that multi-disciplinary partnerships should be available as vehicles to deliver legal services. These would be known as Alternative Business Structures (ABS). Non-solicitors would be able to become partners in law firms, while 100% external ownership of firms would also be allowed. There would be no requirement for legally qualified persons to be in a majority in an ABS, while such bodies would be able to provide other services. If no frontline body wished to regulate the ABS they would fall under the wing of the LSB. There was some indication the Government might impose some form of regulation on claims managers, but not on will writers. The Government also wished to see increased liberalisation of the conveyancing and probate markets while all complaints should be referred to a new Office for Legal Complaints.

It was a gloomy end to 2005 nationally. A number of questions hung over the profession. Would it be possible to maintain the range of services offered by The Law Society given its likely reduced future role and the costs of paying for the new system of regulation which were to fall on the profession? How could local societies work in collaboration with Chancery Lane while at the same time retaining their independence? What should the role of local societies be?

Locally The Society urged all its members to become involved in the consultation exercise following the White Paper, for as the President wrote in the December 2005 Newsletter: 'Most of us "experienced" practitioners have seen marked changes already during our careers but this will eclipse them all'. The Society also continued its work of organisating local courses which members were again recommended to support. Socially there had been a successful Charity Quiz Night in aid of the Marie Curie Cancer Trust on 24th November 2005 while a little earlier The Society had enjoyed its first taste of being a Patron of the Arts by becoming involved in sponsorship for The Philharmonia Orchestra's Leicester Concert Series.

Scandals and threats

January 2006 brought news that steady progress was being made nationally towards the new regulatory and consumer complaints structures, though formal decision making powers still lay with The Law Society Council. There had also been no less than three consultation exercises in relation to proposed modifications of the Training Framework. It appeared that the LPC would remain as the general route to qualification, but with some exemptions in particular cases. There would also be a requirement for a training contract. Less welcome was the proposal that under the new complaints procedure firms should be required to pay for the handling of a complaint irrespective of the outcome and with no requirement for a complainant to pay. This was to prove a very contentious issue, especially as the estimated cost of handling a complaint was put at £800-£1600.

The January 2006 Newsletter also contained pleas for a volunteer to take over as Newsletter editor as Graham Moore wished to step down after 10 years meritorious service in which the print quality and quality of content of the publication improved greatly, contributing vastly to its importance as one of The Society's principal undertakings. The Leicester Law Centre also announced that it had moved home, but was struggling with a reduction in its resources and it asked for more volunteer support, especially in relation to family law. Finally, what had happened to the Leicestershire Young Solicitors' Group Chairman's Jewel of Office? This had not been seen for many years – perhaps a reflection of the mixed fortunes of the Group over time. No reward was offered for information as to its whereabouts!

April 2006 brought a valediction from Christl Hughes as outgoing President following a very successful annual dinner, while the Newsletter contained a very interesting list of firms that had been closed or merged over the previous few years. 63 firms were listed together with contact names as to the tracing of their files. Many of the firms had, of course, been merged into new concerns; some had been merged for years such as Harvey, Clarke & Adams and Ingrams. Unfortunately there were a number of names where the contact given indicated Law Society intervention. Over the years there have been a number of 'bad eggs' amongst local practitioners. This is no place to name them – their shame is already known to them, their families, their clients and their former associates – but it is somewhat unsettling to realise that there were at least 10 instances listed where questions as to conduct could be raised. In addition, of course, there have been other instances where individual solicitors within firms have been guilty of misconduct and have suffered appropriate penalties. On the whole the record of the local profession has not been poor with regard to professional misconduct, but it is a cause of concern that the number of interventions and disciplinary proceedings appears to have increased since the 1970s. Is this a reflection of the increased pressures under which solicitors labour? Have too many people been seduced by the lure of the short cut and the quick buck? Interestingly the same issue of the Newsletter contained information about 'Gatekeeper' the new Law Society money laundering newsletter, while the following issue detailed the existence of the 'Red Alert' telephone line enabling all members of the profession and their staff to report concerns about firms or colleagues. The August 2006 Newsletter contained information that in 2005 The Law Society had intervened in 60 firms, a slight increase on the previous year. As those are the national figures they cast some comforting light on local instances of default.

Community Legal Services

Leicester and Gateshead were chosen in 2006 to be the pilot centres for new Community Legal Advice Centres (CLAC) offering advice in the areas of family and social welfare law plus some more general categories. This would be funded by the Legal Services Commission and Leicester City Council on an initial three year basis, but the intention was that ultimately this new form of Legal Advice Centre would be put out to tender, and that the funding of existing Law Centres would expire in 2007. Those tendering for providing the service would be able to subvent their costs by offering other fee paying services, though not from the same premises as the CLAC.

By August 2006 a number of developments had occurred. Angela Titley-Vial had succeeded as Society President and, inter alia, urged members to support social functions including a Casino Night scheduled for 10th November, a Charity Quiz Night and the Annual Dinner which was to leave the Ramada Jarvis Grand and move to the new Marriott Hotel out at Grove Park. Interestingly this change of venue marked a move for The Society's principal social function outside the bounds of the City of Leicester for the first time in its history. There were further developments in the structure and functioning of The Law Society. Janet Paraskeva, for many years Chief Executive of The Law Society, was to step down and her place taken by three officers whose titles represented the separation of The Law Society's functions under the changing legal framework of supervision. There were now to be a Chief Executive of Consumer Complaints, whose Office of Legal Complaints would be located in the West Midlands, building on the work of the existing Consumer Complaints Service, a Chief Executive of Law Reform and Representation and a Chief Executive of Regulation, whose office was to be the largest of the three in terms of both staff and budget. The regulatory arm of The Law Society was to operate via the structure of a company, nicknamed 'Reg Co', to ensure an arm's length relationship with The Law Society.

The passage of The Legal Services Bill through Parliament gave solicitors a further chance to make their views known about will writers and Society members were urged to communicate their views to The Law Society so that it could lobby for regulatory protection for consumers.

Educationally The Society continued to promote both its own training courses, and those offered by Central Law Training, throughout 2006, while on the social front the earlier announced Casino Night was, in October, promoted as a 'James Bond Casino Royale Night' at the Belmont Hotel, Leicester, with a buffet and champagne reception costing £20.00, and prizes for the best dressed lady and gentleman. Numbers were limited to 100 so early applications for tickets were advised. The President's Charity Quiz Night was also advertised for 22nd February 2007 and a further Philharmonia Orchestra Concert on 11th February 2007, thus continuing The Society's charitable and arts sponsorship activities.

2006 ended with developments both nationally and locally. Nationally the name 'The Law Society' was reserved for the representative body of the profession while the regulatory body was to be known as The Solicitors Regulation Authority (SRA) and the Consumer Complaints organisation as The Legal Complaints Service. The Law Society determined to oppose the Government's proposals following the Carter Review for yet further changes to the Legal Aid System, while there was early news of an initiative from The SRA to approve a system of work based learning to complement the existing system of training contracts.

Locally Chris Smith of Messrs Wilson Browne assumed the office of Newsletter editor. 2006 was also the last year in office as Parliamentary Liaison Office of Peter Smith who had served The Society so well in many capacities over so many years, 25 years in fact. He was succeeded by Mark Dunckley of Messrs Harvey Ingram.

Concerns about the future of Legal Aid dominated the opening of 2007. A national survey indicated that most respondents believed that, at best, training, recruitment and fee income prospects for those involved in legal aid work would remain static or, more gloomily, would decrease. In particular there was concern that the proposed introduction of best value tendering with regard to criminal defence would interfere with the ability of clients to choose freely a solicitor to act in their defence, and this led to a special General Meeting being called on 17th January 2007 at Chancery Lane at which steps were taken to resist such developments.

Locally 2007 commenced with a round of social events. Because of proposed changes to the Annual Dinner a new venture was the Civic Dinner held at Devonshire Place, London Road, Leicester, on 2nd February, where The Society entertained two Lords Lieutenant, two High Sherriffs, The High Bailiff, The Lord Bishop, various parliamentarians and representatives of local authorities. Generous sponsorship from Messrs Hill-Osbourne enabled the event to be held at little expense to The Society. The Young Solicitors' Group was also active with a Quiz Night in aid of Shelter on 1st March, raising some £565, and their planned Annual Ball at The Marriott Hotel to be held jointly with the Trainee Solicitors' Group on 14th April. This event was attended by over 110 members and guests and over £700 was raised for charity. A 'Chinese Night' was then planned for 31st May. The Society also looked forward to its 'new style' Annual Dinner, to be sponsored once more by Allied Irish Bank and several new features, including musical entertainment (a revival of a very old idea from the turn of the 20th Century), after dinner dancing and the presentation of annual awards for Trainee Solicitor of the Year, Solicitor of the Year and Firm of the Year. These awards were to be sponsored by Bygott Biggs, the Nottingham based Legal Recruitment Agency. The dinner featured a charity auction at which £2000 was raised for LOROS. This dinner was attended by 220 members and guests. The President's Quiz Evening in February 2007 also raised £350 for Asthma UK.

Nationally the attention of the profession was focussed on the continually changing structure of regulation and practice. The Legal Services Bill was continuing its passage through Parliament and there were concerns about the Government's desire to press ahead with

Alternative Business Structures for the delivery of services and how these might lead providers to put the interests of investors over those of clients. There were also concerns that in some quarters outside the profession it appeared to be accepted that increasing the number of complaints made against solicitors would be in some way a healthy indication of an effective complaints service. The reality, as any student of complaints mechanisms should know, is that it is not the number of complaints received that is of prime importance, but how they are handled, what lessons are learned in consequence and how these are implemented as general good practice. On the other hand it is clearly only right that all those who may have a legitimate grievance should know how they may go about making a complaint and taking it forward should that be necessary. Figures supplied to the May 2007 meeting of The Law Society Council indicated that 40% of complaints received by the complaints service were regarded as 'unjustifiable', including those made by clients regarded as 'mad/bad'. 50% of complaints were dealt with by conciliation. Only 10% of complaints go to adjudication and of these only half are upheld. This is hardly a picture of a profession serving its clients badly. There were also continuing concerns about the increasing restrictions placed on Legal Aid by government insistence that the amount of money available for this service would be capped with means testing taking away support from numbers of people including some of the poor was well as the not so poor. There were particular concerns over the contractual arrangements for Legal Aid provision which many solicitors felt were being imposed on reluctant practitioners, and in March 2007 The Council of the Law Society passed a motion of no confidence in the Legal Services Commission's ability to provide a sustainable future for Legal Aid.

As Angela Titley-Vial's year of office drew to a close it is worth noting that The Society's Committee consisted of 10 male and 12 female members. Lesley Emery as the incoming President wrote in the August 2007 Newsletter of the vastly changed context in which solicitors were now operating, or were soon to do so, including the prospect of Alternative Business Structures, or 'Tesco Law' as it has been dubbed, further fixed fees and competitive tendering for legal aid work. She pointed out that The Society was providing monitoring and lobbying services for its members, together with local training events and some social functions, but she lamented the steady decrease of members' involvement in the life of The Society. She also pointed to a number of unfilled vacancies on the Committee, the posts of Chair of the Public Relations Committee, Dinner Secretary and Parliamentary Liaison Officer (and while by the end of

2007 the PR and Dinner posts had been filled, that of Parliamentary Liaison remained vacant, while other vacancies had occurred). In addition Alan Baum announced his retirement as administrator to take effect from September 2007, while there were other questions raised over The Society's premises as the Leicester EMRO office might not continue.

Closures and Appointments

By October 2007 The Society had taken the bold decision to appoint a new full time Manager for its services. Judith Sheen came to The Society with considerable expertise in IT and great experience in working from home – both invaluable attributes as The Society was shortly to lose its home in York Road, Leicester, with the closure of the EMRO office. In effect the soon-to-be-homeless Society – not an unprecedented condition – had now to operate in cyberspace, though a venue for its training events was found in Messrs Spearing Waite's conference centre in Friar Lane – a symbolic return to the ancestral grounds of The Society. The final move out of York Road occurred in March 2008 and as from 17th March the location of The Society became a PO Box number, combined with an e-mail address, a telephone line and a DX number. The Leicester Law Centre also closed its doors – a victim of a decision by Leicester City Council and the Legal Services Commission to award a Legal Advice Centre contract to A4E, a Sheffield based organisation. The Millstone Lane centre was due to close on 31st March 2008, while it was expected that A4E would operate from premises in Regent Road, Leicester. It was indeed, as Lesley Emery wrote in December 2007, then closed with continuing national uncertainty over the future of Legal Aid in general and Criminal Legal Aid Contracts in particular, while there was something of a back down on the complaints front when it was accepted that it would not be acceptable to publish complaints 'league tables'. 'Naming and shaming' it had been argued might well lead solicitors to be much less willing to take cases to conciliation and lead to a greater propensity to fight complaints cases through to adjudication. It was also argued that clients considered likely to be bad risks as potential complainers might find it hard to obtain legal services as firms would seek to protect their reputations from the stigma of being featured in a table of complaints.

The year closed with The Society Committee standing at 22 actual members with three vacancies. Of these 12 were female. There were also 3 members from ethnic minority backgrounds. The majority of committee members came from firms based in Leicester, while two represented the North and South of the County of Leicestershire. 3 members came from a 'public sector' background. What is perhaps of more significance is that, leaving aside the Constituency Member, Linda Lee, 6 members came from firms who were 'incomers' to the City of Leicester having been previously established elsewhere. The changing nature of The Committee certainly reflected the changing pattern of the profession locally and the considerable changes that had taken place in the nature and composition of The Society.

Nationally the end of 2007 saw a report from The Law Society that the number of practising solicitors had risen to some 107,000 – a figure shortly to be affected by a rapidly changing economic situation, while locally the December Newsletter contained a 'mini-profile' of local President Lesley Emery and a welcome to a new sponsor, Wesleyan for Lawyers who had undertaken to support both the Annual Dinner and the Charity Quiz Night. The former event was scheduled for 11th April 2008 and the latter took place on 21st February 2008 raising some £400 for AAAnorcap a charity working with adults affected by adoption – the trophy for the evening was won by a team from Messrs Harvey Ingram.

By April 2008 the changing pattern of responsibility for regulating the solicitors' profession was beginning to emerge with the 'arms length' regulator, The Solicitors Regulation Authority, becoming more distinct from The Law Society which nevertheless also continued its representation and membership services for solicitors, and which was due to run a major advertising and promotional campaign from April to June 2008 to focus on why using a solicitor would be a sensible choice for any consumer facing a legal issue. The Society was pledged to support this campaign.

February 2008 also witnessed the holding of the second Annual Civic Dinner at Devonshire Place, London Road, Leicester at which various attending councillors, MPs and local members of the House of Lords were entertained with both hospitality and music in the form of a vocal harmony quartet Harmon8.

The Annual Dinner and Awards Ceremony took place on 11th April 2008 and was held at the Marriott Hotel with a theme of 'A Night at the Oscars'.

The April 2008 Newsletter contained a 'mini-profile' of the Vice President, Mr Prakash Suchak who revealed that he had been greatly influenced by the life and example of Mahatma Ghandi who, of course, had been a barrister before becoming a political leader. Mr Suchak explained that he had been a victim of political forces in that he had been forced to leave Uganda by Idi Amin in 1972 at the age of 17, and had come to this country to find work with HM Customs and Excise. This brought him into contact with the law and he commenced a part time five year law degree at the then Leicester Polytechnic which was followed by a training contract with the erstwhile local firm of Geach Randall. Since then he had pursued his own career in civil and commercial litigation.

Mr Suchak became President of The Society on Tuesday 20th May 2008 at the AGM held at the premises of Messrs Weightmans. This was a notable event as Mr Suchak was the first solicitor from an ethnic minority background to become President and also the first from De Montfort University in its former guise as Leicester Polytechnic.

Various reports were made at that meeting on both local and national issues affecting The Society and its members. From a national point of view the most significant report was on the continuing implementation of the Legal Services Act 2007 whereunder the Legal Services Board would assume overall supervisory functions by the beginning of 2010 with a new Office for Legal Complaints to be in being by early 2009. In addition progress was being made with the implementation of Alternative Business Structures whereunder solicitors' firms might for example be wholly or partly owned by outside capital providers, and which would also enable solicitors to enter into multi disciplinary partnerships. This AGM also featured reports of two special meetings for the year 2007/2008, the first was concerned to amend the Rules of The Society with regard to the classes of membership and to formalise the introduction of the new post of Deputy Vice President as The Society accepted the need for a 'two year run up' to the Presidency. The second meeting was concerned with the issue of the post of manager to take over the day to day running of The Society from its officers who were experiencing increasing pressure of work in their firms. Earlier mention has been made of the implementation of this latter change, while the former was implemented by the election of Mr Stephen Woolfe, though, somewhat ominously, at the AGM the post of Vice President had no nomination and it was left to the Committee to fill the post. It was further somewhat gloomily noted that there was a deficit of some £5000 for the year which represented the cost of employing the new full time manager and having to hire premises for meetings in view of the loss of York Road. This would eat into reserves. On a happier note considerable progress had been made with developing and revamping The Society's website. Another happier note was subsequently struck when the services of Mr Noel Walsh of Messrs Weightmans were secured as Vice President.

Into the Credit Crunch

The June 2008 Newsletter featured a retrospect from retiring President Lesley Emery reflecting on the need to find a way forward for local law societies together with The Law Society as all sought to find their paths in the new world of regulation and oversight and the complexities of the Legal Services Act 2007. She argued that the launch of The Society's revamped website was an indication of a desire to give a better service to members and to promote and assist the profession locally. This issue also announced the launch of The Leicestershire Junior Lawyers Division, the result of the national merger between the Trainee Solicitors Group and the Young Solicitors Group. This new body declared its intention to hold promotional and social events, including an evening of advice for newly qualified solicitors to be addressed by the well known Nottingham based Legal Recruitment Agency, Bygott Biggs, and a Midsummer Masquerade Ball to be held on 27th June 2008 at the City Rooms in support of local charity Vista which supports the visually impaired. Sadly this event became an early victim of the 'credit crunch' as insufficient tickets were sold, though, nothing deterred, the JLD team determined to move the ball to October 2008.

On a more mundane, but just as important, level notice was also given of The Society's continuing programme of seminars in conjunction with Wesleyan for Lawyers and of a meeting members had arranged with Lord Hunt, Parliamentary Under Secretary of State at the Ministry of Justice to discuss, in particular, the concerns of criminal practitioners in the light of best value tendering for criminal legal aid.

The August 2008 edition of the Newsletter carried important information with regard to the future services to be offered by The Society to its members. 'Mail Blast' software enabled training events and seminars to be communicated to members by e-mail, and this was just the start of a move to 'E-communication' and away from 'hard copy' and its attendant costs and DX fees. Accordingly the August 2008 Newsletter was the last in traditional paper format, though arrangements were to be made for those requesting older 'snail mail' styles of communication.

That August 2008 Newsletter carried a statement from the President, Prakash Suchak, declaring his intent to increase The Society's membership, particularly among Asian solicitors in the area, especially as there were many Asian-led local firms who were not members of The Society. The issue also contained a list of the 2008 Committee Members (24), and this revealed that 15 members were either from 'traditional' locally based practices (12) or the local public sector (3), while the remainder came from 'incoming firms', predominantly Messrs Weightmans, once again a sign of the ever changing times through which The Society has had to navigate its course in recent years.

Those changing times were surely mirrored in The Society's Annual Dinner and Awards Ceremony on Friday 20th March 2009 which took place in the restored Art Deco splendour of 'Athena', formerly the Queen Street Odeon, in Leicester. The short speeches, the 'James Bond' film theme and on stage entertainment and the emphasis on the importance of rewarding achievement were evidence of the changing role not only of this annual event but also of that of The Society. The awards had been a feature of The Society's year since 2007, but this event made them much more central to its existence and indicated a discontinuity with the past. This change of emphasis was further evidence by the fact that there were many 'new faces' in attendance, particularly younger new faces and much of the dinner table discussion featured debate about how best to structure the provision of legal services in a new environment, especially in the light of Alternative Business Structures. There were not a few advocating that providers of services must see themselves not so much as 'traditional solicitors', but as business people providing an increasingly commoditised service in a highly competitive world. Maybe that could explain why some 'older faces' were conspicuous by their absence.

The Annual Dinner and Awards, as the event must now be called, were followed by the rather more staid Civic Dinner on 24th April 2009 at Devonshire Place, though a further sign of the times was the launch of a new Sub Committee for The Society, "Diversity and Equality" on 30th April 2009. This was the brainchild of Prakash Suchak as President and was an innovation very dear to his heart. Indeed he commented in his annual report at the end of his year of office: 'The profession has changed over the years and this trend continues. I believe that we should take heed of this change and embrace it so as to ensure that all members of the profession are attracted...' Mr Suchak also expressed the hope that more practitioners from small to medium sized firms would become involved with The Society, and that there should not be too many committee members from any one firm in the area. However, he also had to mention the economic situation which had 'deeply affected' firms of all sizes in the area. Indeed many, if not all firms, by 2009 had found it necessary to adopt a variety of survival packages ranging from salary reductions for employees, and 'takings' cuts for partners, through short time working for staff to redundancies and closures of uneconomic departments. In this, of course, Leicestershire and Rutland were no exception to the national situation which witnessed quite savage job cutting in some places, notably the City of London, and the closure of a number of smaller firms, or their amalgamation into larger units.

The 2008/2009 report nevertheless indicated that, despite the general economic situation, The Society was still robust. Work continued on developing and promoting the website and the 'e-communication' programme, and on the recruitment and retention of sponsors, while there had been a further successful Parliamentary Dinner in the House of Commons on 10th March. There had also been a successful continuing education programme with more than twenty courses, ten of which were arranged in conjunction with Central Law Training, while a further six were organised in conjunction with The Society's sponsors, Wesleyan for Lawyers. On a less happy note it was recorded that a number of course cancellations had been forced due to a lack of support by members and this had inevitably affected The Society's income from educational activities.

The Society's first 'E Newsletter' was despatched to members on 19th January 2009. Deliberately less formal in appearance than its printed predecessor, it was briefer in style and more 'newsy' in content. The longer articles and factual material previously appearing in printed form were now to be found on The Society's website.

Breaks with the past

Prakash Suchak's successor, Noel Walsh, represented an innovation for The Society in that he was a partner in Messrs Weightmans, an 'incoming firm'. As such he was the first person from a non-locally originating firm, other than those from a local government background, to become President.

A further break occurred, however, on 1st May 2009 when it was announced that Freer Bouskell was to be incorporated into Rich and Carr. The name of Leicester's oldest firm was retained but the premises where it had operated continuously for over 200 years were abandoned, leaving the ghost of William Napier Reeve to a very lonely vigil. Incidentally a manifestation was reported as the offices were being cleared and the old spirit was stated to have bowed very gravely and sadly to the employee who saw him.

On a happier note the second issue of the 'e Newsletter' reported that the 'JLD' had organised a successful quiz night on 24th March which had been for the benefit of Shelter, and some 90 people had attended. This issue also carried news of yet another 'first', a mention of the election of local constituency and Society committee member, Linda Lee, as President of

The Law Society from July 2010. A further 'first' should also be noted here, namely the election of Past President Christl Hughes on 18th March 2010 as National Chair of the Association of Women Solicitors

At the national level progress continued to be made with developing regulation of the solicitors' profession, but there was at least some recognition that the net of regulation should also encompass the services of will writers and those offering probate services as well as claims handling companies active in the area of personal injury. These concerns were addressed in a report commissioned by The Law Society from Lord Hunt of Wirral, a former Conservative MP and consultant with Beachcroft, a national law firm. These concerns were articulated at a time when an increasing number of 'High Street' firms found themselves without insurance cover for negligence claims and being forced into The Law Society's 'assigned risk pool', even if they had no history of being made subject to claims. In some cases firms were faced with increases of over 300% as insurers expressed fears that the economic situation would lead to an increase in claims. Such an increase only added to cash flow problems experienced by firms throughout the nation. While some of the 'big city' firms managed to ride out these storms, even in the golden 'Square Mile' of the City of London partners outside the 'Top 10' suffered a 28% fall in average profits, while at the same time being required to contribute more capital to their firms. Bill hours had fallen some 20% by the last quarter of 2009, while salaries for junior lawyers had fallen by an average of 8%. Maybe this contributed to The Law Society's decision, announced in The Law Society Gazette for 17th December, to step up its campaign to warn students of the risks and challenges faced in pursuing a legal career. Figures from the Solicitors Regulation Authority showed that 9,101 students started the LPC in 2009, a 25% decline on the previous year. But the number of training contracts fell by 32% from 6,321 in 2008 to 4,320 in 2009. The mismatch between LPC numbers and the number of training contracts had been known for some time, but now it was thrown into increasingly sharp focus. What was happening in London was mirrored in Leicester, so it is heartening to record that The Society could still find time to enjoy itself with a Quiz and Curry Night, 'Lawyers v Accountants', on 26th November. This was also a 'first' in that it was the first such event, and it was over subscribed. The prize winners were the 'Fun Lovin' Criminals' from Bray & Bray!

As 2009 drew to a close Noel Walsh writing in the e-Newsletter commented on what a 'challenging time' the last year had been, but he was happy to note that The Society had continued to serve its members, in particular by providing its courses at cost or for only a nominal charge. Relationships with the two Universities in Leicester had also developed and a number of work placements for students had been secured. A pro-bono legal clinic provided by Leicester University had also received the support of local firms and the JLD.

2010 dawned and with it the hope that the worst of the economic crisis might be over. Writing in *The Leicester Mercury* for 20th April, Society President Noel Walsh commented on the 'thin pickings' local firms had made over the previous twelve months, particularly in the commercial and property areas. While the spring of 2010 had witnessed some return of market confidence the volume of work was nowhere as great as it had been two years previously. The decline in volume house building, especially at the upper end of the scale, had had a particular impact on a number of local firms. This was also reflected in a depressed private conveyancing market for 'pre-owned' housing. Furthermore this market may face competition from alternative business providers as from October 2011 when the Legal Services Act 2007 comes fully into force. Mr Walsh argued that firms will need to review their business model in the face of fierce competition both 'inter se' and from new providers. Investment in the best technology will be essential if firms are to succeed: 'on line efficient and swift service will be key to the volume players'. He nevertheless concluded that: 'Leicestershire law firms can come out of the recession fitter and focussed on how they can offer the best cost effective service.' Time alone can demonstrate whether these words were prophetic, and to what extent.

Retrospect and Prospect

It is at this point that the author must give up the recording of fact and engage in an analysis of the The Society's history and speculate as to what may be to come and what its future role may be.

Had this history been written as intended to mark The Society's centenary, it would undoubtedly have been a very different document. It would have recorded a century of steady progress and meritorious service. It would have applauded the continuing work of the Library and the suppression of all forms of advertising and undercutting. It would have reflected a society entirely male bound together by common ties of values, family and affinity, geographical proximity, at least in Leicester, and a generally shared educational background. It would have pointed to some hard times, particularly during the Second World War, and it might have regretted the erosion of local autonomy and the rise in power of Chancery Lane. It might also have bemoaned the seeming eclipse of Leicester as a legal centre as the sun of Nottingham had arisen. Nevertheless it could have been justifiably proud of The Society's achievements and its near 100% of local solicitors as members.

It now has to be said that the 50 years since the centenary have seen some of the greatest and most challenging changes The Society has had to face. Some of these have been national in character, others local. Nationally the present author would argue that the first onslaught on the notion of the autonomous profession of solicitor came with the Wilson government's decision to refer solicitors' earnings to the Prices and Incomes Commission. This not only totally weakened the atmosphere of trust between solicitors and Government, but it led inevitably to the abandonment of scale fees which had been for so long the bedrock of the argument that solicitors were not in trade and had their remuneration fixed by law. One can argue that ever since the Wilson government the divide between profession and Ministers has been growing ever wider with the former ever more ready to seek legal redress against the latter by means of judicial review. This distancing increased under both Margaret Thatcher and Tony Blair as the former saw the legal profession as a barrier to entrepreneurial innovation and the latter saw it as a force of conservatism. Indeed the professions have often in the last forty years been cast as the enemy of government. The old notion of a profession as an autonomous self governing body fixing its own conditions of entry and providing for its own regulation now seems hopelessly outmoded, especially as we have witnessed the rise of a consumerist philosophy which demands that those who provide services should always be subject to external regulation. Indeed it may even be asked whether the concept of 'profession' is nowadays redundant, especially as so many callings and activities choose to style themselves as 'professions'.

Locally the greatest change in The Society's history was the loss of the Library. For 120 years this had been the core service offered to members. Once that had gone it became impossible to secure that all local solicitors should be members of The Society, and today many are not – indeed that is true of whole firms in some cases. At the same time the ranks of solicitors locally have materially increased in both size and diversity. Women increasingly make up much of the local membership and have become much more prominent in The Society's functioning. Racially and culturally The Society has had to adapt to local circumstances very different from those of fifty years ago. Another major theme of the last fifty years has been the gradual incursion, into Leicester in particular, of incoming firms, many of whom function on a national basis. For many Society members small scale partnership or sole practice has remained the norm, but it must be questioned how long this will continue.

And yet The Society has survived and has constantly reinvented itself. If the notion of 'a profession' is indeed outmoded, the concept of professionalism is not. There is still a need to encourage high standards of delivery and performance and to see these celebrated and rewarded. Moreover the notion of local voluntary association is still central to the functioning of wider British Society – and, yes, the present author would argue, pace Margaret Thatcher, that there *is* such a thing as 'society'. Moreover it is hard to see how local solicitors are to argue their various cases with both the general public and The Law Society unless they have an organisation that can articulate arguments and amass evidence. The Society may no longer have premises, but it has moved boldly into cyber space and is committed to the fullest use of new technology – though it is to be hoped that hard copies of all documents will be kept as without them how may the next edition of this work, which one supposes may be required in fifty years' time, be written?

Looking to the future local solicitors will certainly need the comfort and shelter of The Society as the implications of a new structure of governance are played out. How the relationships between the Legal Services Board, The Office for Legal Complaints, The Solicitors' Regulation Authority and The Law Society will develop remains to be seen. Even more obscurity hangs over the implementation of The Legal Services Act 2007 with regard to alternative business structures, multi disciplinary partnerships and ownership by external bodies. One may, however, argue that few citizens, in the light of the past few years, would be too ready to trust a legal services provider wholly owned by a bank! Equally there is little evidence that Tesco wishes to muscle in on the legal market though other organisations may be casting their eyes in that direction. Finally we may ask whether the current size of the Solicitors' Profession is sustainable, and we must be ever wary of those siren voices who argue that mere completion of the LPC without a training contract should entitle a person to become a solicitor.

One pointer to the continuing vigour of The Society was the invitation given to its current President, Mr Stephen Woolfe of Messrs Harvey Ingram, to address the National Presidents' and Secretaries' Conference of The Law Society in May 2010. This enabled him to make a presentation on how The Society interfaces with younger members, an area where it is considered to be a national leader and model for emulation.

The future pattern of the profession will thus be very different from what we currently view. Nevertheless The Society's success in adapting itself to changing circumstances gives cause for hope that it will continue to exist and, indeed to flourish. It could be that there will be an increasing need for The Society to involve itself in all stages of legal qualification, from going into schools and colleges to address those considering a career in the law, to working with Law students during the academic and professional stages of qualification, to supporting and mentoring the newly qualified. The young solicitors thus imbued with the wisdom and practice of those who are established will be the best guarantee that the Leicestershire Law Society will reach its second centenary.

Chapter 11

Change, Challenge and Opportunity: new developments for rapidly altering times

We left off this account of the Society's history in 2010, just as it was celebrating its 150th Anniversary. The first edition was launched by Stephen Woolfe during his Presidency 2010-2011 at a formal reception to mark the Anniversary. It might then have been thought that a further edition of this work might not have been needed for quite some time. The original print run was, however, somewhat limited and there have been numerous requests from those who did not obtain a copy of the original for a reprint. A simple reprint alone would not have done justice to the changing circumstances in which the Society has found itself and to which it has had to respond in imaginative and constructive ways: hence this new edition which takes the history of the Society forward to the year 2017.

The first sign of a desire for modernisation of the Society's structure was the adoption of its first business plan in 2011, under the Presidency of James Coningsby, and this led to the creation of a new constitution (more correctly "The Rules") in 2012.The first business plan ran from 2011 to 2014, and has now been replaced by the second plan which will take the Society into 2017, and which we shall consider later. The Objects of the Society were declared to be the promotion of Leicester as a centre of legal excellence, to give a voice to its members by means of local, regional and national lobbying, to be committed to the promotion of equal opportunities, diversity and human rights among the legal profession and those who employ legal professionals, to provide social and business networking opportunities within and amongst the local profession and business community, and by a relationship with local universities to encourage and support the study of law and to promote interaction and an exchange of opportunities. Membership of the Society was also widened to include the new classes of "Corporate Associate Member" for sets of Barristers' Chambers practising in Leicester, Leicestershire and Rutland, and "Individual Associate Member" for those conducting legal work within an appropriately regulated legal department or practice within the City or County, or a barrister not attached to chambers. This made way for members of the Bar with the necessary local connections and for legal executives to attain associate status. Social connections with the local Bar have strengthened as a result with barristers attending the Awards ceremony and solicitors present at judicial retirement events. These changes resulted not only from the diversification of the Society's membership over the previous twenty-five years or so, with, first, a greatly increased female membership, followed by the entry into local practice of members from an ethnic minority background, but also from what might still be considered radical in some quarters, namely a more liberal view of what the role of the Society should be in its modern civic context.

At the same time the Society took the opportunity to make a major revision of its governing structure. The former mode of governance still echoed the Society's Victorian origins when the Presidency had largely been honorific and was generally conferred on an elderly practitioner near the end of his active career to mark the respect in which he was held by his fellows. This resulted in the principal officer of the Society being the Secretary who might hold office for a number of years, and that was over time reinforced by the emergence of the Finance and General Purposes Committee as the forum in which the most important decisions were, to all intents and purposes, taken. This was clearly out of kilter with modern conditions where the President has to be the "public face" of the Society (for example with regard to the selection each year of a Charity the Society will support) and is expected to set the tone and agenda for his/her year of office and must therefore have a role clearly superior to that of the Secretary. The Society thus took the radical step of abolishing the "F and GP" along with the office of Secretary. Provision was made for the Society's Committee to consist of twelve members elected at the Annual General Meeting (AGM), plus up to nine coopted members together with the President, Immediate Past President, Vice-President and Deputy Vice-President, the Treasurer and the Executive Board Chair, along with any member of the Society who is for the time being a member of the Council of the national Law Society. The President, Vice-President and Deputy Vice-President are elected at the AGM the understanding being that they will hold successive office over a three year period to ensure that there is a degree of continuity in the succession. The Treasurer and Executive Board Chair are also elected at the AGM for a period of one year but they are eligible for re-election and once again this ensures a degree of continuity in the Society's affairs. The Committee then appoints the following sub-boards whose names indicate their functions: Executive, Education and Training, Litigation, Non-Contentious Business (which in practice has come to include regulatory matters), Media and Communications and Equality and Diversity. The President, Vice-President and Deputy Vice-President are ex officio members of each sub-board. Provision is also made for the employment of an administrator, an essential officer to ensure the execution of the Society's business.

Helen Johnson, President for 2012/2013, gave an interview to "Link," the magazine of the erstwhile Association of Women Solicitors, on the changes that had been made in the constitution and pointed out that during her year of office there would be a full CPD programme, a summer drinks party providing an informal occasion for Society members to network and meet new District Judges , a curry lunch with accountants, networking events with local Parliamentarians, liaison with the Junior Lawyers Division (JLD) as well as the now well established Awards Ceremony, and declared: "I intend to continue to modernise the Society making it relevant and accessible to its members and beyond." Clearly that marked a considerable move from the old 19th Century "Gentleman's Club" model to a new 21st Century concept of a vital network organisation.

The Second Business Plan covers the period May 2014 to April 2017. It began by reviewing the situation of the Society in 2014. At that point there were some 447 solicitors who work in firms which are corporate members of the Society, 53 individual members and some 503 barristers who were associate members. This made the Society the second largest in the East Midlands. The plan restated and re-affirmed the Objectives set out in the initial plan, and declared that the Society is an organisation primarily serving its members' interests as opposed to being a public interest body. In relation to the overhaul of the Society after 2010, it was noted that the Annual Dinner has ceased to be in decline having been replaced by the Annual Awards Ceremony, of which we shall see more later. There had been a much greater reliance on e-communication with members, including the provision of a revamped web-site with a more interactive facility. The Society enjoyed a well supported patronage scheme and its finances were in good order allowing it to employ the support services of two part time staff. Patrons are engaged fully, often for periods of years, while sponsors are recruited ad hoc for individual events and other items such as prizes.

The plan then set out a number of particular objectives to be pursued during its period. The first of these was to increase membership and also the involvement of members, though no changes to the structure of membership were envisaged. The second objective was to continue working together with local universities and other organisations within the legal profession, including bodies representing law students, legal executives and the JLD for example with regard to the promotion of joint events and the provision of work experience opportunities for those seeking a career in the Law.

A major objective of the plan was to improve the profile and perception of the Society in the eyes of the public, while at the same time to continue to lobby politicians and decision takers on issues affecting the membership, for example by continuing the tradition of holding a dinner at Westminster for local politicians. It may be stated at this point that the use of publicity material, particularly, by local firms, but also to an extent by the Society itself, has markedly increased in terms of quantity and quality and this issue will be examined in greater detail below. A further object was the continuing provision of training courses for local practitioners and the fruits of this initiative can be seen by visiting the Society's website where the syllabus of events can be seen. The next objective was the development of strategies for engaging with the rich and diverse membership base of the Society. It can be said here that a visit to the Society website will indicate pictorially how this has been achieved. Leicester as a community is blessed to have had for many years excellent and harmonious relations between its various ethnic groups and this is true of the Society also. Indeed it is from within the ethnic minority groups within the local profession that some of the most interesting and innovative business and professional developments have come, particularly with regard to the creation of niche practices. The next object was the continuing health of Society finances, and this may be said to have been achieved. Finally with regard to governance issues, the need to improve the operation and accountability of the sub boards was noted and to this end it was decided that each sub board should have its own terms of reference, that each should meet at least twice a year, that each sub board chair should either in person or through a nominee attend main Committee meetings in order to report on work, and that the chairs should attend the Executive Committee and present an account of work at least once a year.

It is possible to see an historical development in the current constitution from its predecessors, but it is undoubtedly a tidier and more efficient governing structure, and it serves the Society well at a time when the governance of voluntary organisations is increasingly under scrutiny.

"Change and decay in all around I see."

This somewhat ominous phrase, quoting from a 19th Century hymn writer, is intended to point towards the great degree of change in the composition of local Solicitors' firms, a change which some might see as the decay of old established organisations and practices, but which appears to be an inexorable development neatly summed up by the slogan:

"Get Big, Get Niche or Get Out!"

Just as the Society was renewing its constitutional structure one of the great pillars of the local profession was about to disappear. The names of Harvey, Ingram and Owston run like a thread throughout the Society's history as the foregoing chapters bear witness. Harvey Ingram following its inception in the 1960s grew larger by taking over other local firms (gradually expunging their names from its identity), and following its merger with Owstons (whose name also disappeared) seemed set fair to become the only large, predominantly commercial, "home-grown" firm in Leicester, and that at a time when there were a number of incoming large firms from other cities seeking a share in commercial and industrial work. Harvey Ingram itself set its sight on creating offices outside Leicestershire as part of its participation in the highly competitive commercial market and in 2011 it merged with Borneos a firm centred further south with offices in Northampton, Milton Keynes, Kettering, Bedford and Newport Pagnell. But within a year the news was announced that Harvey Ingram was to merge with Shakespeares, a Birmingham firm, and the effective take-over took place in 2012 with the name Harvey Ingram finally disappearing in 2013. Shakespeares had itself undertaken five mergers in as many years, and now in its current form as Shakespeare Martineau is the second largest law firm across the East and West Midlands. An historic identity thus quit the local legal stage, a casualty maybe of the "Get Big" impulse, but Shakespeare Martineau has declared its loyalty to Leicester by setting up its local office in the Colton Square development, where Freeth Cartwright, another "incomer" is also situated, while in addition having an office at Meridian Business Park, the former home of Marrons, another local name of many years standing which disappeared in the merger.

While "Get Big" has certainly been a force to reckon with, "Get Niche" has also been clearly a formative influence on the local profession. There are many comparatively young local firms who specialise only or predominantly in one form of legal work, for example Mental Health, Medical Negligence, Personal Injury, Family and Children, Mediation or

Immigration. The structure of such firms may often take the form of a sole director who is a solicitor assisted by a mix of solicitors, trainees, legal executives, LPC graduates and other para-legal staff, though this is not an exclusive business model. Prominent among such niche practices are those led by Solicitors whose racial background is Asian, a clear indication of the energy and vision which members of the Society from ethnic minority backgrounds have brought to the life of the local profession over a number of years. The establishment of Johar and Company in 1975 by the late Tilak Raj Johar may be cited as a seminal moment in this development. Since then the Society has enjoyed the Presidencies of Prakash Suchak, Ranjit Thaliwal, the first British born male President from an ethnic minority background, and Mehmooda Duke, the first female President from such a background. In this connection it should also be noted that the Society has strong links with the Midlands Asian Lawyers Association (MALA), many of whose members are prominent in Leicester's legal life.

"Get Out" has certainly shown itself to be an influence with a number of well established old firms either being subsumed under new entities or having to merge to maintain their existence. In this new world where traditional partnership is increasingly replaced by the LLP model or, in these times of "Alternative Business Structures," even that of a registered company, old names depart and are replaced with "snappy" new titles reflecting the changing pattern of legal professional provision. An example of this can be seen in the old Loughborough firm of Edward Hands and Lewis which now, from an organisational point of view, functions as EHL (Group) Limited and is a registered company with a board of directors and which adopts the operating structure of a network of local firms located currently in Beeston, Bulwell, Buxton, Carlton, Hinckley, Hucknall, Leicester, Lewisham, Loughborough, Lutterworth, Market Harborough, Melbourne, Oadby, Stockport, Syston and Woolwich.

On the other hand one might coin a slogan "Get In" to describe an organisation which has taken advantage of the ABS provisions to move into legal work. Qdos is based in the north eastern part of the City of Leicester in the midst of the Troon Way industrial complex. It is an Integrated Business Solutions Provider which began life in 1988 as a VAT Consultancy. It now provides a range of commercial services including accountancy, insurance, human resources, health and safety, recruitment, and legal advice for businesses, contractors, landlords and individuals in the areas of commercial law, contract, debt and property disputes, issues in employment, landlord and tenant matters, the provision of online legal documentation, and trade and membership organisation issues. Despite concerns that ABS entities such as Co-op Legal Services might decimate the traditional profession the impact so far has not been as strong as feared. That said however, the Qdos model shows that it is possible to combine cognate areas of activity all of which are relevant to commerce and industry and forge a successful enterprise.

Change and decay or change and innovation? Maybe the developments outlined above are the way in which matters must go in a market where law firms must increasingly operate as businesses actively seeking work and promoting themselves and are no longer able to rely on old professional models where work was guaranteed by client loyalty. Leicester was the traditional home of many small business enterprises and the old axiom was "small businesses prefer to do business with other small businesses." It cannot be assumed that such "old lore" will hold good, indeed it is probably well past its applicability. This is a theme to which we shall return in this chapter as we consider the ways in which local solicitors operate and how that in turn has had its effect on the functioning of the Society.

"Presenting the people to the people"

That sub-title takes us back well over sixty years to an old Radio Programme known as "Have a Go", but it is not out of place with regard to a quite recent development in the life of the Society, the birth of its own magazine. Despite claims that "e-communication" will sweep away all previous forms of publishing, "hard copy" remains resilient, and evidence from a wide variety of sources indicates that a "house journal" is important in fostering a sense of cohesion amongst the members of any society as well as indicating their ownership of the enterprise.

Issue 1 of the Magazine appeared in Spring 2015 and the journal has since settled down to appearing three times a year, while certain features have become regular in their inclusion, these being reports from the President for the year and from the Society's national Law Society Council Member, the former national Law Society President, Linda Lee. Otherwise a very wide range of subjects has been covered, some of practical interest to current solicitors while others have been of a more historical or social nature, including, of course, the Annual Awards Ceremony which will be considered in more detail below. The practical side of things has included articles on issues as diverse as cost budgets, the new Lexcel standard, issues in family justice, restrictive covenants, how to survive in partnership, criminal legal aid, acquiring another firm's practice, expert witnesses, probate management, drainage and water issues affecting property, gender reassignment, relief from forfeiture, the role of notaries, hearing loss claims, mental health, cyber protection and dealing with the problems of social media, paternity matters, the effects of Brexit, Pro Bono work, and outsourcing activities such as cashiering services. Every issue has contained at least one item of relevance to all practices, even though, as is probably inevitable, much of that relevance has stemmed from the need to ensure services are offered on a business like and profitable basis. On a more community based level items have been published on the Society's liaison with local schools as it encourages young people from the widest range of backgrounds to learn more about the law and to consider a legal career, and in addition there have been pieces on connecting with the wider local community and with both our local University Law Schools. The support of the Society and its members for local and national charities has also featured in the magazine, and here the well established practice for each year's President to nominate a charity of his/her choice should be noted as a continuing feature of the Society's annual round. For those with an interest in history there have magazine items, as one might predict, on Richard III, but also on the Society's first President, Joseph Harris, a notable son of Leicester. Naturally there has also been considerable coverage of the Society's own social events, the Civic Dinner, the Annual Awards Ceremony and a recent new event an afternoon tea for women solicitors which may well become another established feature of the Society's life. Lighter items include book reviews and news of recent happenings at local firms.

The Awards Ceremony was considered at some length in earlier chapters of this work, but it deserves further consideration here because it has continued to grow into a major themed event while at the same time reflecting the diversity and strengths of the local legal community. It is also a matter of major significance that the Awards are given in conjunction with the "Leicester Mercury", and that reflects the excellent relationship which the Society has created of late with Leicester's own newspaper. Long gone are the days when press coverage of a Society event would have sent shivers of fear that "advertising" might take place down the collective spine of members. The Society in its desire to be a fully integrated part of the local community recognises the need to interact with local media, and that interaction is not just one way as Society events provide more than useful items for press coverage.

Over the years the number of awards presented at the annual ceremony has increased, while the lead up to the ceremony has become an important part of the process with its own shortlisting event. Thus in 2015 there was a shortlisting event at which the entertainment was sponsored by Ropewalk Chambers and No 5 Chambers, 36, Bedford Row. There were just four categories at the shortlisting ceremony, Barrister of the Year, sponsored by Handelsbanken, Junior Lawyer of the Year, sponsored by the University of Leicester, Solicitor of the Year, sponsored by De Montfort University and Law Firm of the Year sponsored by Severn Trent Searches, though in each category there were multiple nominees. At the subsequent Awards Ceremony the Law Firm of the Year Award had to be divided because the judges felt there were two candidates of equal merit and that it would be invidious to distinguish between them. That led to a rethink of the nature of the ceremony because it did not well reflect the pattern of local professional activity. While the Ceremony has always had themed entertainment, for 2016 the event was moved to a new venue, The Platinum Suite, while members provided their own special form of themed entertainment by putting on a mixture of a masked ball picking up ideas from "The Phantom of the Opera" coupled with their very own version of "Strictly Come Dancing!" This glittering occasion was the brainchild of President Mehmooda Duke who began planning it more than 18 months before it took place. It involved "persuading" ten Society members to team up with professional dancers and dance teachers, to learn the necessary "numbers" and that demanded assiduous attendance at classes over the rehearsal period. Never have so many local solicitors tripped the fantastic so lightly or to such better effect.

With regard to the Awards themselves, the categories were increased in number the better to reflect the local profession with its increasing division into large commercial firms and smaller niche practices. Thus there were awards for the Junior Lawyer of the Year (sponsored by the University of Leicester), the Barrister of the Year (sponsored by MDS, Moosa Duke Solicitors), Large Law Firm of the Year (sponsored by De Montfort University), Small Law Firm of the Year (sponsored by Severn Trent Searches), Solicitor of the Year (sponsored by 36 Bedford Row), Chambers of the Year (sponsored by Finance Lab) and Trainee/ Paralegal of the Year (sponsored by Weightmans LLP). The judging panel comprised David Simms, Publisher and Managing Director of the "Leicester Mercury", David Monk of New Walk Chambers, Steve Evans, the University of Leicster, Sheree Peaple, De Montfort University, and District Judge Vera Stamenkovich.

One question must have been on the minds of members after this spectacular event, namely how would incoming President Imogen Cox mark her year? As will be revealed below there was an idea which had been the subject of much hard work and which would reach its own theatrical climax in the Autumn of 2016.

But other important social events in the Society's year must be chronicled in addition to the Awards Ceremony. The Annual Civic Dinner has continued to be an important yearly event as it enables the Society to engage with the leaders of other community groups in City and County. On 30th January 2015 the dinner was held at the City Rooms in Leicester when some 80 guests were entertained representing civic, parliamentary, professional, educational and business sectors locally. The guest speaker was the Rt Hon Nicky Morgan, MP for Loughborough and at the time Secretary of State for Education. Getting a Cabinet Minister to speak, especially in the run up to a General Election was clearly a defining moment for Steve Swanton in his year as President. The 2016 Civic Dinner moved to a new venue, College Court in Knighton and took the theme "Historic Leicester" with each of the tables being named in honour of a woman famed in history, the arts or the media and connected with either the City or the County. The 2017 dinner will celebrate the links of the Society with local business, educational and arts communities and will be held at the Grand Mercure Hotel. The Society holds a regular Garden Party and on June 25th 2015 this was held in the grounds of the Trinity House, De Montfort University, while a new event took place on 18th August 2015, a Women in Law Afternoon Tea at the Belmont House Hotel. This was followed in 2016 by a tea at Marco's Restaurant at the Grand Mercure Hotel. On this occasion President Imogen Cox secured the services of Jenny Cross of "Niche Magazine" and Cleo Lacey an image consultant and personal shopper—surely one of the newest professions. The Awards Shortlisting Event will be at the Grand Mercure in March 2017, and the Awards Ceremony itself will return to Athena in May.

From time to time there are other events in which the Society plays a prominent role as the representative of Solicitors locally. One such was the special service to mark the 800th anniversary of the signing of Magna Carta, generally regarded still as, at least symbolically, the foundation stone of our liberties. The High Sheriff of Leicestershire held a Magna Carta Justice Service taking the form of Choral Evensong at Leicester Cathedral where the Judiciary, Bar and Solicitors were all much in evidence. This was a contribution to the wider celebration of the Great Charter by the community of the City and County.

The Society continues to support local charities as it has been for many years the practice for each President to nominate a given charity for his/her year of office. On 26th September 2015 members of the Society joined with Fosse Business Breakfast Club to walk in the Peak District in aid of the Rik Basra Leukaemia Campaign, raising £12,000 for their efforts. Leicester's own "Charity Link" which supports local people in poverty, hardship or crisis, a task it has undertaken for nearly 140 years, received the Society's support in 2014 to 2015, while in 2016 the chosen charity was the Leicestershire Organisation for the Relief of Suffering (LOROS). A further charitable initiative has been the inception of the Leicester Legal Walk, which derives its inspiration from a similar event organised by Judges, Barristers and Solicitors in London. The 2016 walk on 20th June had 100 participants including the local Police and Crime Commissioner, Lord Willy Bach, well known to the legal profession in the City and County from his days in practice at the Bar. He was supported by the current President of the Society Imogen Cox plus four past Presidents Christl Hughes, Angela Titley-Vial, Helen Johnson and Ranjit Thaliwal. The walk raised £1500 for the Midland Legal Support Trust. A second nominated charity was supported by the Society in 2016 in the form of Spark Arts for Children which promotes the best in theatre, dance and music for children and families, often working with children in deprived areas and circumstances.

It should further be noted that members of the Society have during the period under survey gone on to achieve national achievements. Past President Helen Johnson was on 22nd October 2015 honoured as Solicitor Advocate of the Year at the Law Society's Legal Excellence Awards. She was recorded as having sound judgment and breadth of experience, which no doubt stemmed from her bold initiative in founding, along with her then partner Past President Lesley Emery, her own firm, Emery Johnson (now Emery Johnson Astills) at the youthful age of 29. The firm was a niche practice in family, child care and criminal law, and was the first female owned firm in Leicester at the time of formation. The firm won the Society's award for Alternative Dispute Resolution in 2012. Helen achieved rights of audience in 2007, and has since demonstrated considerable advocacy skills and a commitment to fostering those skills in the next generation of Solicitor Advocates. Past President Christl Hughes achieved distinction in another area by becoming the first woman to hold the Chair of the Solicitors' Charity, the SBA, for more than one year, being re-elected to the position in 2016. In that year she was present at the joyful, if rather damp, celebration of the Queen's 90th Birthday known as the Patron's Party when all the charities of which Her Majesty is the Patron celebrated in style in the Mall in London. Since then Christl has also gone on to become a full liveryman of the City Of London Solicitors' Company. Ranjit Thaliwal, Mental Health specialist, founder member of MALA and President 2013- 2014 was shortlisted for national Solicitor of the Year in 2014.

The Society, firms and the media, marketing and promotion.

Advertising and touting were traditionally absolute anathema to Solicitors nationwide and the earlier chapters of this work indicate how the Society was quite often called upon to discourage this type of activity. All that has long since changed and "it pays to advertise" has become an accepted axiom for many, if not all, practices. It is hard now to open an edition of the "Leicester Mercury" without encountering an advertisement for a local firm, sometimes full page or more, and it is clear that some firms have an extensive advertising budget. Advertisements may promote a particular form of service, for example personal injury or conveyancing, or they may promote a firm across a wide range of work. A more subtle use of the media by firms is the use of press releases which may detail the opening of new premises, mergers and acquisitions, the appointment of new members of staff, or perhaps detail the success a firm has enjoyed with regard to work undertaken or achievements in local and national awards ceremonies. Some firms may promote themselves by issuing advice on issues which may concern the local business community, and a particular favourite issue in the latter part of 2016 has been the impact of Brexit. Naturally the advice given is that businesses need expert legal advice, and, unsurprisingly, the firm will at this point promote its own expertise in the area. Sponsoring a local charity event for example is also popular.

More general coverage of the work of solicitors locally was included in a "Leicester Mercury" supplement of 16th April 2016 headed "Law Review." The began by detailing the results of a survey by the Law Society which had found that the strong legal sector in Leicestershire is contributing greatly to the local economy and creating many jobs. The Law Society figures showed that every time the legal sector grows by one percent some 8,000 jobs are created in legal services, while the sector had itself grown by 8 percent from 2014 to 2015. Local firms, Douglas Wemyss (now DWS Legal), Edward Hands and Lewis (now EHL as detailed earlier), Nelsons, Qdos (based in Thurmaston), Howes Percival, and Spearing Waite were specifically mentioned as experiencing a growth in their work.

One event, however, attracted considerable media attention, and that was the Society's first venture into Court Room Drama.

The Society and King Richard III

The discovery in 2012 of a male human skeleton in a car park off New Street in Leicester, and its subsequent identification in 2013 as that of the last Plantagenet monarch, Richard III, was a momentous event in Leicester's history, maybe even more momentous than the sad King's previous visit to Leicester in 1485 just before his defeat and death at what history now records as the Battle of Bosworth. Suddenly Leicester became a focus of media attention: academic reputations were enhanced; news conferences were held; reburial plans were made, and were then interrupted by a Judicial Review action; reburial plans were then recommenced; a visitor centre was planned; religious services were devised; members of the Royal Family and the peerage who had historic connections with the participants at Bosworth were invited to attend; a grand procession took place: the "King in the Car Park" left the University of Leicester where he had been examined and identified, and was taken to the likely place of his death to return once more to Leicester, this time in style and observed all over the world. Finally, with all the glare Channel 4 could muster, the most controversial of all English Kings was reinterred in Leicester Cathedral by the Archbishop of Canterbury and the Bishop of Leicester. The City has never been quite the same since those memorable events having gained more of a sense of its own historic importance in the years 2012 to 2015 than it ever previously had. Leicester became a tourist centre and the implications for the local economy were, and still are, vast. If one adds to that the utterly unforeseeable winning of the Football League Championship by Leicester City FC in 2016 and all that has flowed from that, it's not hard to understand why "a place on the way to other places" as Leicester has unkindly been called should feel an enormous sense of civic pride and hope for its future prosperity.

The question of how Imogen Cox would crown her Presidential year has already been raised, and the answer was that the Society would make its own very particular contribution to the continuing debate about the life and doings of Richard III by staging a trial of the monarch concerning his implication in the disappearance and presumed death of his nephews, Edward V, rightful King of England, and Richard, Duke of York. Imogen Cox immersed herself in the history of the period, created a script and assembled a team to carry the drama into effect. Accordingly on 3rd November 2016 in the Council Chamber of the City, masquerading for the event as "The Great Hall" the players assembled. Presiding as Judge was His Honour Judge Simon Hammond, well known in the local Crown Court for many years as a fair but firm dispenser of justice. The Prosecution was led by David Herbert QC of the 36 Group, chambers with a long association with the Society, assisted by President Imogen Cox, while the defence was in the hands of William Harbage QC, also of the 36 group assisted by Past President Helen Johnson. Narration was provided by David Lee a barrister of over 40 years standing and a "serious" amateur actor, and Past President Christl Hughes. Other historical characters were Sir Thomas More (Society member Adam Markillie), the Bishop of Lincoln, (Society member Mark Benton), Dominic Mancini (Ben Trott Marketing Manager at Cartwright King), while The Duchess of Burgundy was played by Jane Durant of Society Sponsors Berkeley Burke. A very special mention must be made of James Collins of the 36 Group whose glacial impassivity as Richard III made a deep impression on all present. There was a capacity audience as there had been quite a competition to get seats for the occasion, and "the crowd in Court" also formed the Jury with The Lord Mayor of Leicester acting as Foreman.

The trial took place according to modern court room standards with the "Prisoner" being arraigned and refusing to plead, so a "not guilty" plea was, of course, entered. The various witnesses were called and were examined and cross examined, and then came to time for the King to give evidence. According to the Law of his time Richard denied the jurisdiction of the Court to try him and maintained resolutely that "Kings are only answerable to God." That was, of course, absolutely correct legal doctrine until the English made a revolutionary change by trying, convicting and executing Charles I on the basis of tyranny - and how many know that the Solicitor General who led the prosecution at that trial was a Leicestershire man, John Cook?

But "our King" stood his ground and did so in a most impressive fashion. Closing speeches were made, the summing up was given and then all retired for tea! While refreshment was taken the "verdict" was reached by the casting of votes and the result when all returned to the Court Room was "Not Guilty" by a very substantial majority.

The event was covered on three days by the Leicester Mercury, on the day itself, on the following day by a two page "spread" and a week later with picture coverage. It also made the pages of the national legal press featuring in the Law Society's Gazette for 14th November. It was truly memorable and must give rise to the question whether a future President will seek to re-enact another memorable legal episode from Leicester's past.

Looking to the future

2017 will see the need for a third Business Plan for the Society, while a new website is also proposed. The well established events such as the Awards Ceremony and the other educational, social, and networking opportunities will also continue, indeed they are already planned. It is also apparent that the Society has an energetic membership reflecting the dynamism that runs through the local legal community in consequence of the influx of firms with a national or major regional focus alongside the emergence of vigorous niche practices. That has to be set against what will probably be the continued decline of entities unable or unwilling to embrace the need for advertising and marketing or the imperative of "Get Big, Get Niche or Get Out." Older firms in this category will almost certainly either have to merge to give themselves the income they need to compete in marketing, or they will be swept up into new conglomerates. The Society will have to live within that context of brand promotion by individual firms where aggressive advertising will be the norm, and where the large concerns will operate alongside the niche practices. It is not, nor can it be, the role of the Society to favour one type of practice over another, but it will remain essential for it to provide the services its members need, to provide a platform on which members can meet to discuss issues of common concern and to formulate appropriate responses, and to remain flexible and adaptable, for that is how it has survived and thrived for over one hundred and fifty years to become and remain one of the strongest and most respected of local law societies.

Two issues may, however, come to be of major concern to the Society.

"Fast Trains to London—again!"

The first issue relates to the City and County's position as a major centre for commerce and industry. It is surely no coincidence that the "Leicester Mercury" special business report for 22nd November 2016 featured no less than five Solicitors as commentators on the issue of railways serving Leicestershire. The issue of "fast trains to London" was a matter of concern to the Society in 1890, and it remains so currently in view of, first, the proposed route of the northern extension of HS2 which will come no nearer to Leicester than Toton which is in Nottinghamshire, and, secondly, the future electrification of the Midland Main line to and beyond Leicester. The matter is of concern because commerce and industry could relocate away from Leicester to take advantage of HS2 while without a guarantee that electrification will reach Leicester shortly, with appropriate rolling stock, the City and County could suffer a "double whammy" with regard to transport by rail. There is no doubt that fast connectivity to London and beyond by rail for both passengers and freight traffic is a major issue affecting local industrial and commercial life. "In the hour, on the hour, every hour" was a slogan used by the old Southern Railway for its London services in the inter-war period to promote the prosperity of Brighton, and may be Leicester and Leicestershire need something similar. It could well be that the Society will become involved in campaigning on this issue as Solicitors are certainly a key component in the local business community.

The second issue concerns once again the protection of the "brand" of Solicitor. When the "junior" branch of the Legal Profession emerged as a distinct entity in the second half of the 19th Century it was able to claim that its members were distinguished by being both clearly regulated and demonstrably qualified by examination. The forms of regulation and qualification have varied over the Society's lifetime, but there is no doubt that they are key to the quality of legal provision and essential to the identity of the calling of "Solicitor." In the name of promoting both competition and open entry into the profession there is now a great debate about, first, the need to have a properly qualified person leading any organisation which purports to provide legal services as "Solicitors", and secondly the level of knowledge, expertise and training a person needs before he/she can be recognised as a Solicitor. Is it acceptable for organisations where there may only be one legally qualified person present to provide legal services? Given the current diversity of means available to gain entry into the profession-—law degree followed by LPC and a training contract, degree in a non-law discipline followed by a conversion course, LPC and training contract, legal executive plus appropriate conversion course and period of work-- is it desirable to have yet further means of entry such as the ability to practice immediately after LPC without a training contract and also the possibility of qualification after some form of apprenticeship? Furthermore what of the proposed requirement for all those wishing to qualify as Solicitors to pass the Solicitors Qualifying Examination (SQE)? What will be the required standard for this test, will it examine practical as well as academic skills, will it be, effectively, post graduate in level as well as in time, who will administer it, who will teach and examine it?

These are issues with which the Society will surely have to grapple and formulate its collective response.

Leicestershire Solicitors will continue to need their own local Law Society in these "interesting times", and that may be the most appropriate point at which to close this work.

Officers since 2010/2011

	President	Vice President	Deputy Vice President
2010/2011	Stephen Woolfe	James Coningsby	Helen Johnson
2011/2012	James Coningsby	Helen Johnson	Ranjit Thaliwal
2012/2013	Helen Johnson	Ranjit Thaliwal	Steve Swanton
2013/2014	Ranjit Thaliwal	Steve Swanton	Mehmooda Duke
2014/2015	Steve Swanton	Mehmooda Duke	Imogen Cox
2015/2016	Mehmooda Duke	Imogen Cox	Jonathan Foster
2016/2017	Imogen Cox	Jonathan Foster	Bushra Ali

	Secretary
2010/2013	Wayne Hollingsworth (post abolished in 2013)

	Chairman of the Executive Board under the new Constitution
2013/2017	Noel Walsh

	Treasurer
2010/2016	Duncan Jefferson
2016/2017	Glynis Wright

	Editor of Leicestershire Law Society Magazine
2015/2016	Manbir Thandi
2016 to date	Adam Markillie

Patrons of the Leicestershire Law Society 2017

AON

Burcher Jennings

De Montfort University

Finance Lab

Finch Consulting

Jonstar

Severn Trent

University of Leicester

Addendum and Corrigendum

Thomas Ingram President 1868- 69

At page 49 of the first edition of this work it was stated that Thomas Ingram`s house in Wigston stood in the area between Albion Street, Glengate and Blaby Road, South Wigston, and that the dwelling had not survived. This was incorrect, and further information has since come to hand about Thomas Ingram which should be incorporated in this revision if only because it reveals much about the style of life which a successful Leicester Solicitor might expect to enjoy at the height of the 19th Century.

Ingram was born in 1811 and by 1841 the Census records him as living in High Street "Bowden Magna" (now Great Bowden) Market Harborough, where he is stated to be a married man employing six servants. In the 1851 Census he was recorded as a Solicitor employing two clerks and four other servants living on the Welford Road, Leicester. By 1856 he was living at No.3, Welford Place, Leicester, while in 1862 and 1864 his business premises were Nos. 34 and 36, Pocklingtons Walk, Leicester. By the end of the 1850`s Ingram was already a prominent local figure. He was by then a member of the Conservative Party being recorded as present at one of their meetings in 1859, while in the same year he was a member of the Leicester Volunteer Rifles. He became County Court Registrar in 1860, and was present at the laying of the first stones for the new tower of St Martin`s Church (now Leicester Cathedral) in 1861. His increasing prosperity is evidenced by his move to a new house in Wigston which he had built in 1862. This was for a while known as "Hawthorn Field" but it soon was called "Abington House" which name it still has, and which it gave for many years to one of Wigston`s secondary schools, now part of Wigston Academy, which was built within the extensive grounds of Ingram`s former home. He was registered as a voter in respect of the house in 1865, which was in the 1871 and 1881 Censuses said to be an unnumbered property in "Blaby Lane, Wigston", its historic identification. By the time of the 1891 Census the modern name of "Station Road" was in place indicating the importance of the coming of the Midland Railway line to London in the development of Wigston. A "Short History of Abington House" in Bulletin 22 of the Wigston Historical Society published in 1988 records that Ingram built the dwelling with stables for his own use in 1862, but he appears to have owned other land in the area because he was a member of the Royal Agricultural Society of England according to the "Farmers' Magazine" Volume XXXI (3rd Series) January to June 1867. That land may well have been situated in the Albion Street, Glengate and Blaby Road area of South Wigston, and that is the explanation for the error in the earlier edition.

But what of Ingram the man (and "local character" let it be added)? He had an interest in ancient artefacts which is evidenced by his acquisition of the old conduit which originally supplied water to the Borough of Leicester, and which gave its name to the current Conduit Street by London Road Station. This old structure Ingram had erected in the garden of his then new house in Wigston. He was also a founder of the Leicester Architectural and Historical Society in 1855 and was for many years its Honorary Secretary. His support for the Established Church has already been recorded in the earlier edition with regard to his donation of the organ to St Thomas's Church, South Wigston, but it should be noted that he gave the considerable sum, for the time, of £1000 towards the building of the current red brick structure which replaced an earlier "tin mission" which had been erected to serve the spiritual needs of the area. He also donated the pulpit and eight bells for the church, while not forgetting the historic Parish Church of All Saints, Wigston to which he gave two stained glass windows, also paying for the rebuilding of the churchyard wall to mark Queen Victoria`s Diamond Jubilee in 1897. Modestly, however, the commemorative plaque on the wall simply says that the restoration was paid for by "a parishioner." He allowed the grounds of his home to be used for village events and gave warm soup and clothing to the needy at Christmas. On the other hand he was mindful of the need to maintain the earnings of his practice and is said once to have charged a client seven shillings and six pence simply for "passing the time of day!" During the winter months he would go early into his office and would leave at mid-morning to go hunting, returning at dusk to work late into the evening. At the age of 90 he drove all the way from Leicester to Bognor Regis in an open carriage to visit his sister, and died on 23rd March 1909 seven days short of his one hundredth birthday. His was a way of life and of legal practice (76 years!) which has today completely disappeared. It is worth while noting that in the "Leicester Mercury Rich List" published with the newspaper on 15th November, 2016 that there was not one solicitor included amongst the most wealthy of the County. In Thomas Ingram`s time had there been such a list he (and not just him) would most assuredly have featured in it, and this should be borne in mind when the economic situation of solicitors today is under consideration.

APPENDIX

Presidents of the Leicestershire Law Society

Joseph Harris	1861
Samuel Stone	1862
William Freer	1863
Samuel Berridge	1864
Richard Toller	1865
William Latham	1866
Alfred Paget	1867
Thomas Ingram	1868
William Napier Reeve	1869
George Toller	1870
Charles Morris	1871
J B Haxby	1872
George Stevenson	1873
Thomas Miles	1874
Stephen Pilgrim	1875
Christopher Gates	1876
Joseph Harvey	1877
Clement Stretton	1878
G C Bellairs	1879
W Billson	1880
W H Macaulay	1881
R B Berridge	1882
H A Owston	1883
J Bouskell	1884
C S Burnaby	1885
W Billings	1886
J Arnall	1887
S F Stone	1888
S Harris	1889
T H Watson	1890
H Deane	1891
J B Fowler	1892

C S Preston	1893
T Watts	1894
B H C Fox	1895
S S Partridge	1896
A H Burgess	1897
G H Blunt	1898
R S Toller	1899
G Rowlatt	1900
W J Freer	1901
Sir Thomas Wright	1902
W L Salusbury	1903
J S Dickinson	1904
S Willcox	1905
Robert Harvey	1906
Joseph Hands	1907
Edmund Dutton	1908
G F Stevenson	1909
W F Beardsley	1910
B A Shires	1911
W Simpson	1912
W J New	1913
E J Holyoak	1914
John Storey	1915
S F M Stone	1916
George Bouskell	1917
John Parsons	1918
Stephen H Pilgrim	1919
Thomas H Wright	1920
Wilfrid Moss	1921
A E Brown	1922
W E Richardson	1923
F Davis	1924
J L Douglas	1925
K McAlpin	1926
W Harding	1927
W A Clarke	1928
V M Woodhouse	1929
W Cecil Harris	1930
E G B Fowler	1931

F Bouskell	1932
H M D Barnett	1933
O J Taylor	1934
H J Deane	1935
C F Bailey	1936
F H Toone	1937
R A Loseby	1938
W F Bent Beardsley	1939
A A Ironside	1940
C S Bigg	1941
A B Plummer	1942
E P Smyth	1943-1946
C E Crane	1947/48
C E Crane	1948/49
C F Bray	1949/50
G Day Adams	1950/51
T E Toller	1951/52
W B Frearson	1952/53
M H Moss	1953/54
H A Day	1954/55
S H Partridge	1955/56
C E J Freer	1956/57
H G Weston	1957/58
A P Marsh	1958/59
J Tempest Bouskell	1959/60
A H Headley	1960/61
M R Simpson	1961/62
R J Moore	1962/63
K P Webster	1963/64
B E Toland	1964/65
F E Stafford	1965/66
J Smyth	1966/67
A Denham Foxon	1967/68
J F P Evans	1968/69
G O Joyce	1969/70
D S Hunt	1970/71
R G Frisby	1971/72
E A Crane	1972/73
R D G Williams	1973/74

J B Ervin	1974/75
J F Tillotson	1975/76
M A Rich	1976/77
J H de la Rue	1977/78
J B C Blood	1978/79
R D Foxon	1979/80
J K McLauchlan	1980/81
D W Godfrey	1981/82
K P Byass	1982/83
J C Small	1983/84
M D Hubbard	1984/85
J E Adams	1985/86
R J Dews	1986/87
C L Mitchell	1987/88
T Harrison	1988/89
J A Threlfall	1989/90
R H Bloor	1990/91
A P Smith	1991/92
R A Clarke	1992/93
N M de Voil	1993/94
A P Price Jones	1994/95
Vera Stamenkovich	1995/96
T H Kirkman	1996/97
M K Dunkley	1997/98
K U Leslie	1998/99
J M Jerman	1999/2000
J M Crane	2000/2001
G K J Moore	2001/2002
P M Kilty	2002/2003
H T Doyle	2003/2004
D R Lindsey	2004/2005
Christl Hughes	2005/2006
Angela Titley-Vial	2006/2007
Lesley Emery	2007/2008
Prakash Suchak	2008/2009
Noel Walsh	2009/2010
Stephen Woolfe	2010/2011

Hon Treasurers

T Ingram	1861-1892
R Toller	1892-1901
S Willcox	1902-1921
S F M Stone	1921-1928
C S Bigg	1928-1935
S H Partridge	1935-1954
J T Bouskell	1954-1965
J H W Newman	1965-1971
N M de Voil	1971-1992
M Elisabeth Bass	1992-1998
M R Neal	1998-2000
D P Jefferson	2001-2016

Hon Secretaries

J Bouskell	1861-1864
H A Owston	1864-1872
T Berridge	1872-1875
G H Blunt	1875-1884
W Simpson	1884-1904
T H Wright	1904-1921
W B Freason	1921-1924
J S Parsons	1924-1935
N Beare	1935-1950
B E Toland	1950-1956
R Herbert	1956-1966
J A Holland	1966-1969
J K McLauchlan	1969-1974
D M B Hubbard	1974-1979
B J Chapman	1979-1981
A P Smith	1981-1990
K U Leslie	1990-1997
H Doyle	1997-2002
W K Hollingsworth	2002-2013

(post abolished)

Hon Librarians

A Halkyard	1924-1928
S H Partridge	1928-1935
H W Skillington	1935-1949
B E Toland	1949-1950
R Herbert	1950-1955
R D G Williams	1955-1961
D S Hunt	1961-1969
R Eadon	1969-1973
R P Harris	1973-1978
R H Bloor	1978-1982
J Hunt	1982-1985
T Harrison	1985-1986

(post abolished)